Sean Fallon

Celtic's Iron Man

Sean Fallon

Celtic's Iron Man

Stephen Sullivan

BackPage Press
World-class sports books

BackPage Press
Copyright © Stephen Sullivan, 2013
All rights reserved

The moral right of the author has been asserted
First published in the United Kingdom in 2013
by BackPage Press.
ISBN 978-1909430013

A catalogue record for this book is available from the British
Library

Design and typeset by Freight Design.
Printed and bound in Poland by Oz Graf

www.backpagepress.co.uk
@BackPagePress
@SeanFallonCelt

CONTENTS

Cambuslang. A red ash park. A boys' match. He knows it's a long shot. But this is Sean Fallon the scout. There is no-one better at sniffing out talent. No-one more diligent. No-one more devoted. "The worst mistake is not to make the effort," he reminds himself. Plenty of these trips are fruitless. But not this one. He likes what he sees. The boy can play.

Ibrox. A flat overlooking Rangers' training ground. The boy is not keen. Nor is his father. But this is Sean Fallon the charmer. Nobody sells Celtic better. Even with his wife and children waiting in the car outside, he bides his time. There will be no forcing of the issue. It takes hours. But he leaves with the father convinced and the boy converted.

Parkhead. A dressing room. The boy is troubled. Even in the reserves, the goals are not coming. But this is Sean Fallon the coach. Players trust him, are soothed and reassured by him. He hands the boy a bag of balls, watches as shot after shot hits the net. He smiles. The goals, he knows, are on the way.

Barrowfield. A training pitch. "He's too slow, Sean," the manager tells him. But this is Sean Fallon the trusted assistant. He advises his old friend to have patience. The boy has something special. He sees it, even if others don't. "Give him time, Jock," he says. "Trust me on this one."

Celtic Park. The manager's office. The boy is now a man. He is Celtic's star player. England and greater glories beckon. But this is Sean Fallon the strategist. He offers the captaincy, promises a better contract. "Leave the directors to me," he vows. The player's resolve weakens.
Kenneth Mathieson Dalglish agrees to stay. "I owe Sean that much," he reasons. He is not wrong. And he is not alone.

Prologue

"I was wracked with nerves. I've never been so nervous. I was thinking, 'How do I get through this?' But I realised that all you can do is tell the truth about the man and share some stories that give people an idea of all his talents and virtues. Because he really was such a great and honourable man. Someone you would trust with your life. In the end, it was a great honour."

The words are Sir Alex Ferguson's, the sentiments my own. In describing his fears about delivering the eulogy at Sean Fallon's funeral in January 2013, the then Manchester United manager crystallised my concerns about producing a book worthy of the man. But he was, of course, right about the simplicity of the solution. Sean and his life, his achievements, his values – his story – should be allowed to speak for themselves. Spreading the word should be a privilege, and it has been.

My debt to Sir Alex pre-dated this quote, and his foregoing of a rare day off to be interviewed about his friend and mentor. He, I learned, had been the man responsible for finally wearing Sean down, convincing him that a book was a must; that his story was simply too good not to be told. Again, I couldn't have put it better myself.

I had long considered Sean Fallon's to be one of his sport's great untold stories. The closeness of his relationship with Jock Stein and his unique perspective on a golden age, not only for Celtic but for Scottish football and the game in general, convinced me of it. But this focus on Stein, and on what Fallon saw and experienced, has resulted in a tendency to view him merely as a witness to history, rather than a key participant.

A consequence of this is the popular, accepted portrayal of Sean in newspapers, magazines and the vast bulk of Celtic literature. It entails the same recurring adjectives – devoted, loyal, trustworthy – and leaves the reader with the impression of a sturdy player, a faithful servant and a steadfast right-hand man. And it is true; he was all of these things. But he was a great deal more. The depiction of someone reliable but unremarkable, admirable but ordinary, is in need of major revision. For there was nothing ordinary about Sean Fallon.

Take just one aspect of the Irishman's story – his signings – and it could be argued that he was the greatest talent-spotter in the history of British football. This, after all, is a man who recruited most of the Lisbon Lions, then assembled another crop of players considered superior even by the Lions themselves. Fallon's Quality Street Gang should have conquered Europe, but the Celtic board of the time not only squandered that opportunity, but rewarded their assistant manager's efforts with demotion to the role of chief scout. Yet even in this lesser position, the Irishman bequeathed to the club Pat Bonner, one of its greatest goalkeepers, and Paul McStay, who was among Scottish football's foremost talents of the 1980s and early '90s.

When Celtic's fans were asked to vote for the club's greatest ever team in 2002, over half the players selected were Fallon signings. More recently, when BBC Radio 5 Live picked a post-war British XI, the Irishman could boast of having spotted and recruited the only two Scots to make the cut: Kenny Dalglish and Danny McGrain. His Midas touch was even applied at Dumbarton, where he snapped up two unknown teenagers and future internationals in Graeme Sharp and Owen Coyle.

But Fallon didn't just sign players. He also played an invaluable role in keeping them happy. Stein was a hard and, at times, cruel taskmaster at Celtic, and it required all of his assistant's psychological nous and natural charm to maintain a contented camp. Sean was also one of precious few brave enough to tell Stein when he was in the wrong, and one of fewer still whose opinion was heeded. Crucially, though, disagreements took place in private, and dressing-room diplomacy was carried out while remaining loyal to, and united with, the man in charge. "Jock couldn't have wished for anyone better," said Davie Hay, a Fallon signing and a former Celtic manager himself. "You hesitate to use the word perfect but Sean was the perfect assistant manager. I've never come across anyone who played that role as well."

Yet to focus solely on these backroom responsibilities, as so many do, is to do a disservice to Fallon the footballer. He did, after all, make over 250 appearances for Celtic, and earned his legendary 'Iron Man' nickname by playing on with a variety of cracked and broken bones. He also performed a heroic and largely unheralded role in the securing of the club's first double in four decades and played in the most famous Old Firm derby of all, the 7-1 League Cup final win of 1957. Fallon's presence on the bench in Lisbon 10 years later, therefore, gave him the distinction of direct involvement in Celtic's two greatest triumphs. Not even Stein could claim that.

So why, given all these feats and more, is he not better known throughout Scottish football and beyond? There are several reasons, but chief among them is that Sean himself allowed it to be so. Comparisons might be odious, but I continually found Peter Taylor, Brian Clough's celebrated deputy, a useful reference point. In some respects, the similarities between the two assistants were uncanny; in others, the disparities enormous.

In his excellent book on Clough, *Provided You Don't Kiss Me*, Duncan Hamilton wrote of Taylor: "I believe history hasn't given Peter the credit he deserves; and not just for his genius in regard to talent-spotting… He could also say 'no' to Brian, and often acted as a conduit between him and the players. If Brian had gone off in a rage, Peter could always chip in, 'What he really meant was…' and give a calmly rational explanation." Supplant 'Peter' with 'Sean' and 'Brian' with 'Jock', and every word would still ring true. It is for good reason that Clough and Stein rank among the greatest managers of all time, but both were indebted to their assistants' intuition, intelligence and eye for a player.

The major difference between these right-hand men lay in the level of their fame. 'Clough and Taylor' is common football currency, synonymous with great managerial partnerships, and both halves of this duo have been immortalised in bronze. Taylor is fully deserving of his statue too. He also merits every word of praise penned in his honour, and arguably many more besides. But no-one will ever convince me that his influence was more important to Clough and Nottingham Forest than Fallon's to Stein and Celtic. Nor will anyone have me believe that Taylor's signings – John McGovern, Archie Gemmill, Peter Shilton et al – were more inspired than the likes of Kenny Dalglish, Ronnie Simpson, Tommy Gemmell, Danny McGrain and Paul McStay. There had to be another reason, therefore, why Taylor was lauded and Fallon diminished; cast almost as an onlooker at Stein's one-man miracle.

Martin O'Neill managed Celtic and worked with Taylor at

Forest. During his time at Parkhead, he got to know and admire Fallon. "The fact is some men court the limelight, whereas some are quite happy to remain in the background, quietly doing their job," he said. "Peter Taylor wasn't the kind of man who was comfortable staying in the background. He was a very important figure and did a great amount for Forest, but he also made sure people knew about it." Sean, by contrast, purposely shunned, downplayed and deflected praise. Ask him, for example, about his legendary discoveries, and he would tell you: "Ah, they were Celtic's signings, not Sean Fallon's."

Clough wasn't so prone to humility, of course, but he did make one famous attempt at self-deprecation by referring to himself as "the shop front" and Taylor as "the goods in the back". Hamilton and O'Neill agreed that Clough never truly believed this, and nor should it ever be implied that Fallon was in some way 'the brains' behind Stein's success. Sean would have been the first to insist otherwise. He yielded to no-one in his admiration for Celtic's greatest manager, and was among the very first to spot the qualities that ultimately made Stein a football immortal. He also had enough humility and self-awareness to realise that he lacked several of the traits that marked out his friend for managerial greatness. But where we gain a true appreciation of Fallon is not by judging him against Stein, but in recognising what he brought to their partnership. By that measure, Stein and Fallon should be every bit as revered a double-act as Clough and Taylor.

To the Celtic players of that era, they are. The Lisbon Lions and the Quality Street Gang saw what the outside world did not: that their manager, while undoubtedly a genius, was not without his flaws. Had Stein's weaknesses not been his assistant's strengths, the club's glory days might not have been quite so glorious. "Jock needed Sean," is the view of goalkeeper John Fallon. "I honestly believe he wouldn't have had the success he did without Sean there." Among several to agree with this notion of indispensability is Billy McNeill, who speaks of Fallon "supplying all the things the big man wasn't particularly good at". No-one, to Stein's immense credit, was more aware of this than the manager himself. He was astute enough to appreciate his assistant's brilliance in scouting and psychology, and afforded him the trust and freedom to maximise those abilities. Celtic reaped the rewards.

Sadly though, Stein is not around to highlight Fallon's immense contribution, and the Irishman himself was always too modest to do so. The very reason it took until his 90th year for his story to be told is that he considered a book to be an essentially self-centred indulgence, and shunned it accordingly. "Sean wasn't the kind of man to push himself forward and boast about what he'd done," said Ferguson. "He was always happy just to get on with his life. Being appreciated by the people who worked with him was enough."

Laudable though this attitude was, it convinced me that an autobiography would sell him short. The motivation for telling his story, Sean told me, had been to "put something down for the grandkids". My job was therefore to provide those grandchildren – all 20 of them – with a full and accurate portrayal of their beloved 'Papa'. Making it impossible to do that solely through his own words were two factors: memory and modesty.

The former issue was to be expected in a man of 90 but was, in fact, the more surmountable of the two, and frustrated Sean a great deal more than it did me. "I'm hard work for you, son," he would say, patting me on the shoulder. "Too many kicks in the head, and heading that big bloody brown ball." A university study did find that the impact of those old water-soaked leather balls had been equivalent to "having 10 bags of coal dropped on your skull". And here was a man who had won his fair share of headers. But while specific matches occasionally proved difficult to recall, our interviews were – for me at least – an unremitting joy.

If there was a stumbling block, it was Fallon's adherence to the old adage that self-praise is no honour. It left only one option. If humility was to prevent him from setting out the full extent of his achievements, others would need to do it for him. Fortunately, I found a long list of enthusiastic and esteemed volunteers.

And so it is that you will read not only Sean Fallon's recollections of an amazing life, but the thoughts of former colleagues, protégés and friends on an extraordinary man. Sean would never have dreamed of describing himself in the way that these men and women do, or of highlighting the achievements they bring to light. He would also have let out that booming, throaty laugh of his if I told him that, in allowing me to write his book, he had given me the thrill of my professional life. Indeed, when this unfailing gentleman and his wonderful wife, Myra, weren't plying me with tea and sandwiches, he spent most of his time apologising. "I feel I'm giving you nothing here, son," was a favourite lament. In imparting his story, as in his life as a whole, Sean Fallon had nothing to apologise for. Far from "giving me nothing", he granted me more than I could ever have dared expect. Sir Alex called it right: "In the end, it was a great honour". The greatest.

Stephen Sullivan
August 2013

Chapter 1
Fallon of the Rangers

The story of a legendary Celt must begin with the tale of a Ranger.

John Fallon, Sean's father, fought with the Connaught Rangers for the British and Allies during the First World War. He was one of over 200,000 Irishmen drawn to this colossal conflict, many with the simple but compelling motivation of earning a wage in a time of great poverty and uncertainty. Yet this was not Corporal Fallon's motivation. In enlisting, he surrendered a privileged position among the ranks of the employed, leaving his job at McArthur's Bakery in Sligo to sign up with three friends in the nearby town of Boyle. He was engaged to a local girl, Margaret Forde, and still just 17, necessitating a white lie to the recruiting officer.

With no mercenary incentive for volunteering, and plenty of reason to stay out of the fighting, this was a young man motivated – as he was throughout his life – by principle. Like many in Ireland, he empathised with the plight of the besieged Belgian people, and had been told by nationalist leaders that going to war would help bring about home rule. As Aidan Mannion, a Sligo historian, explained: "Fighting for the British in that war was actually seen as the republican thing to do, strange as that might seem now. So many Sligo men went off to fight, and a lot of John Fallon's group would have been politically minded. I'm sure they felt very let down afterwards."

Of Fallon's circle of friends, only he lived to feel any sense of grievance. The others with whom he enlisted that day, Pete Burnside, John Henry and Edward Kelly, perished along with 130,000 others on the barren and blood-stained slopes of Gallipoli. Sean's father would himself likely have numbered among the slaughtered masses but for the intervention of fate in a distinctly unpleasant form. His destiny was essentially determined when the Connaught Rangers, upon landing in August 1915, began work with the gruesome task of gathering and burying Australian bodies. The heat, the sand flies – and the fact that over 48 hours had passed since the brutal exchange that necessitated the clear-up – meant that sickness among the Irish newcomers was both inevitable and rife. Fallon remained healthy long enough to play his part in a successful attack on the Turkish positions on August 21. But by the time the next major offensive took place a week later, he and several others had succumbed to dysentery and been evacuated to Egypt.

"When you have dysentery you simply can't fight – it's physically impossible. John Fallon would have died had it not been for receiving treatment." This is the verdict of Oliver Fallon, secretary of the Connaught Rangers Association, who studied closely the army history of Sean's father. His research found that John Fallon never returned to Gallipoli. Nor, sadly, did he ever see his friends again. The three men with whom he made that fateful train journey to Boyle either perished or suffered mortal wounds in the battle that took place while Fallon was en route to Alexandria. Not that there was any time for him to mourn either them or the Allies' infamous defeat on the peninsula. The young corporal was soon on the move again, this time to Serbia – and the Salonica front.

"By that time, John Fallon had qualified as a bomber," said Oliver Fallon, "which essentially involved carrying two big bags of grenades and – when the infantry were held up – going forward and lobbing the grenades into enemy territory. The job would have made him an even more obvious target. And during one battle in Serbia, there's a very specific reference to the bombers being sent forward, one being killed and a couple more being wounded."

Fallon found himself in the latter category, but only just. He had been hit in the right shoulder by a dum-dum bullet, the kind specifically engineered to expand on impact and cause maximum internal damage. Slipping in and out of consciousness, he was left for dead in a trench with men who had either been killed or mortally wounded. Whether through fate, luck or divine intervention, his life was again saved when he was recognised amid the bodies by an old acquaintance from Sligo, who carried the bloodied teenager to a nearby medical station. Not for the first time, Fallon lived where many others died. A permanent loss of functionality in his right arm seemed a small price to pay.

> It was a bad wound. I used to be able to put my hand right into the hole that dum-dum had left behind. But my dad knew he'd been lucky. It always stayed with him – all those young lives wasted by stupidity from the people in charge. The call from the officers was, 'Up and at 'em! Charge!' But these poor lads were charging into bullets. That was just the way in that war. So many lives were needlessly wasted. My dad's brigade were famous for always being out there, fighting at the front, and they were cut to ribbons. He was very fortunate to get out alive.

John Fallon was discharged from the army in November 1917 with the war badge and a character reference as a "good, sober and honest man". Those words would be as close as this battle-scarred young veteran would come to acclaim. The political ground had shifted while he was abroad, with the 1916 Easter Rising and Britain's failure to implement home rule leaving Ireland's Great War volunteers cast not as heroes, but as bystanders or, worse still, colluders. As a popular Irish ballad of the time, 'Shores of Gallipoli', put it: "You fought for the wrong country, you died for the wrong cause... while the greatest war was at home." Harsh judgment had been passed on a man who, like so many others, had endured unimaginable horrors for the most honourable of motives.

Dwelling on such injustice was not, however, a luxury Fallon could afford. By the time he was discharged, he had a wife and two young daughters to support, not to mention a new city in which to find work. It was, after all, in Glasgow – where Margaret Forde, his young fiancée, had moved during the war to find work in a munitions factory – that he settled after leaving hospital. The inter-war years in Scotland's largest city were to become synonymous with rising sectarian tensions and fierce anti-Irish feeling, but Fallon's ability to read at least enabled him to gain employment as a postman. And, crucially for Sean's story, it wasn't all work and no play.

> My dad was always a great football man. It's funny to think it now, but he actually lived and worked just a stone's throw away from Ibrox when he and my mum were in Glasgow. Not that there was much chance of him supporting his local team. Right from the start, he fell in love with Celtic. He'd heard about this great club, founded by a Sligo man, and once he went along to a game that was him hooked. As soon as I was old enough, he was always telling me stories about Celtic. My love for the club definitely began through him. In fact, I always felt that my connection to Celtic, even though I wasn't born at the time, began when he went over to Glasgow and became such a big supporter.

It might have been tales of Brother Walfrid, the Irish Marist Brother who founded the club, that lured John Fallon to Celtic Park, but he left enchanted by another Irishman. At that time, Patsy Gallacher, the Mighty Atom, the player described as "the greatest who ever kicked a ball" by Rangers stalwart Tommy Cairns, was in his peerless pomp. And what a sight he was to behold. "Gallacher was always advancing; there was no doubling back and playing across the field. Everything he did was positive," is how team-mate Jimmy McGrory remembered him five decades later. "There is no present day player in this country that I would put anywhere near his class. Even Jimmy Johnstone, with all his talents, never reached the Gallacher heights."

John Fallon was among many thousands smitten. His time in Scotland was transitory, and it wasn't long before he returned to Sligo, family in tow, to resume his job at McArthur's bakery. But Celtic left a lasting impression. Indeed, the earliest known image of Sean is of a restless looking toddler in 1924 at the front of a local football club's team photograph. The outfit had been founded by his father after his return from Glasgow. Its name? Sligo Celtic. Nor was it an accident that Sligo Rovers, a club John Fallon helped establish in 1928, should visit and lay a wreath at the grave of John Thomson – the young Celtic goalkeeper who died after an accidental collision during an Old Firm match in 1931 – on its first visit to Scottish shores.

Stories of Celtic became Sean's fairy tales. It was only inevitable that he should inherit his father's passion and begin forming a seemingly fantastic dream. And yet, ironically, there was another unintended and potentially negative consequence of the esteem in which John Fallon held all things Celtic.

My dad had thought the world of the players he had seen and would always tell me about the incredible skill that these men had. Scotland was seen by many people as the home of skilful football in those days and my dad was very much of that view. Having heard all these grand stories, and not being blessed with great natural skill myself, I was actually very worried when I came over to Celtic that I wouldn't measure up. And I'm sure my dad, for all he was proud of me, had his reservations too. But Lord rest him, there's no doubt he realised a dream when he saw me in the green-and-white jersey.

It was him who had instilled in me not only my love of Celtic, but my love of football. He was such a great football man. I heard from a few people that he could have been a fine player himself but for the shoulder injury he sustained during the war. But he kept going even with that injury, and I remember watching him play for Sligo Celtic when I was just a boy. He was a tough defender, didn't take any prisoners, and anyone who watched me during my career might recognise that description.

Whereas I played all sorts of sports, football was my dad's one big passion. Anything to do with the game in Sligo, whether it was Sligo Rovers or any local tournaments, you could guarantee he would be involved in some way. He was chairman of Rovers for a while and even finished up refereeing just to be involved in whatever way he could. When I was growing up, we'd go down to the beach at Rosses Point together and the one thing he would always bring would be a ball. But there was no thought at that stage of training me to become a footballer; he was just a father enjoying a kick-about with his boy.

Even later, he encouraged me in the game, but left it down to me to decide how far to take it. All the big decisions were mine to make. He was proud of my football successes, but what was more important to him was that I grow up to become a good man. 'Never let yourself down, son,' he'd tell me. 'The kind of man you are will be remembered more than all the football you play'. That always stayed with me. It was values, principles, that kind of thing, he influenced me on more than anything. And Celtic of course!

John Fallon had no worries on that front. His ardour had proved infectious. But Sean also suspected later that there had been another unseen force at work, nudging him towards Celtic Park, making sure that nothing was left to chance. It was that force, he believed, which brought a stranger to stoke the fire his father had kindled. Even if it was merely coincidence, Joe McMenemy succeeded in adding a layer of romance to an already enchanting love story, and would have been an important figure to Sean regardless of his identity. He had, after all, averted a family tragedy by diving in to Lough Gill, a popular Sligo swimming spot, to save Sean's sister, Lilly, from drowning. But it was when the young Scot was persuaded to join the Fallons for dinner, to thank him for his courageous intervention, that he took on even greater significance.

It turned out that he was the son of the great Celtic player Jimmy McMenemy, who'd been known as 'Napoleon' when my dad went to watch the team. We couldn't believe it. No doubt my dad and I plied the poor lad with questions for the entire night. But it didn't stop Joe and I becoming friends and, after he returned to Glasgow, he was kind enough to send me a Celtic shirt and a copy of Willie Maley's book, *The Story of the Celtic*, both of which I treasured more than you can imagine. I read that book from front to back countless times and the shirt was hardly off my back. I knew then that there was only one thing I wanted to do in life, and one club I wanted to play for. And something I've never lost sight of is how fortunate I was to be able to realise my dream. So many people have grand ambitions in their lives, especially when it comes to football, but so few realise them. I was one of the lucky ones. Everything fell into place.

Yet Celtic, despite this multitude of unlikely connections, was not always seen as Sean's destiny. His sister, Marie, remembers it being considered unlikely that he would ever become a footballer, far less join the club of his dreams. In the days before sport became an all-encompassing focus in Sean's life, there was little in this obedient and well-mannered boy to suggest that a fearsome full-back – an Iron Man – was waiting to emerge. "Sean was the apple of my mother's eye and definitely a mammy's boy in his early years," Marie said. "As time went by, he became closer to my father, especially through the football. But I don't think anyone envisaged Sean becoming a footballer when he was young.

"What I do remember about Sean growing up is that he was very religious. He'd been an altar boy and it really stirred something in him. We used to talk about it; we were all convinced that he was going to be a priest. I always felt Sean was very lucky because it was clear his faith was so strong. Every night, no matter who was in the house, he would kneel down beside the fire and say his prayers. We only had a small living-room but he would follow that routine every night, quietly, and then say goodnight and go off to his bed."

Religion remained a cornerstone of Fallon's life. Even at 90, and with knees that bore all the painful reminders of a long life and punishing career, he maintained that nightly routine of kneeling to pray, and credited his longevity to the strength and serenity his faith provided. He also admitted that his siblings weren't the only ones who envisaged him being called to the priesthood.

I thought the same myself; it was in my head for a long time. It was assumed by pretty much everyone that that's where I was heading and I was quite set on it at one stage. My mum would have loved it too. Every Irish mother dreams of having one of her sons become a priest and I was the likeliest candidate in our house. But as time went on, other things were becoming more and more important to me. I wasn't as certain anymore – and you can't afford not to be certain with something like becoming a priest.

Those "other things" were not, as one might suspect, girls. Sean remained, in his sister's words, "very choosy". His weakness was sport. And if temperament had marked him out as a candidate for the priesthood, his robust physique, love of competition and constant quest for self-improvement established him as a born athlete. Nor was he as selective with his pastimes as he was with potential girlfriends. It would be many years before football would take precedence for a young sportsman who was as inexhaustible as he was accomplished. Finding enough hours in the day would have been the only problem as he excelled at badminton, billiards, football, boxing, rowing and Gaelic football. He also captained the Sligo swimming team, and won trophies in another, unexpected pursuit. "He was a lovely ballroom dancer," revealed Marie. "All the girls loved the chance to go up to have a dance with Sean."

If his achievements identified him as someone out of the ordinary, so too did his attitude. While team-mates years later would marvel at his transformation from a charming, easy-going character into the most uncompromising of players, the effects of this competitive streak were raising eyebrows from an early stage. John Gilmartin, a childhood friend who went on to play football in England, recalled a telling incident from Fallon's youth that hinted at the man and footballer he would become.

"We were all in a field, having a bit of our own athletics. Paddy Barry, a former Sligo Rovers player, was good at putting the weight (throwing a rock). Paddy came in first place; Sean didn't figure at all. Afterwards, we all went home, except Sean. In the evening we came down to the Abbey Street corner, where we always met before going to the Savoy Picture House. But when Sean arrived, he asked Paddy to go back to the field to throw the rock, which was around 12lb in weight, once again. Only this time Sean beat him by four feet! He had practised throwing this rock for three hours so that he could beat Paddy. That was how determined he was at anything. Sean was only 16 years of age and Paddy was a grown man. We all admired him for that incident."

Such single-mindedness would have served Fallon well in several vocations. But there was one job he had no hesitation in ruling out. Living through turbulent times – having been born in 1922, a momentous year in which the Irish Free State came into being and partition was enshrined – had not aroused in him a passion for politics. This was fairly unusual in young Irishmen and particularly surprising in Sean's case as his father, a man he so evidently admired, joined Sligo's Corporation and County Council in 1934 and devoted the remaining 46 years of his life to political service.

And yet, while there was never any prospect of Sean following in his footsteps, John Fallon's decades as a councillor, alderman and, latterly, mayor taught his son a great deal. "More than anything," he reflected, "I learned the importance of honesty, integrity and principles." These were to be the hallmarks of his father's career, and it was only such admirable traits that enabled him to overcome a background that was becoming increasingly problematic.

> Growing up, I remember people being proud of the Connaught Rangers. But as time went on, they forgot the reasons why these men had gone to war, forgot what they had been trying to achieve for Ireland, and only remembered one thing: that they had fought with the British. There was a lot of anti-British sentiment back then, and anyone with any British connections – especially British army connections – came in for a hard time.

What left an indelible impression on Sean was his father's response to the sneers and whispers. As a politician, he might have been expected to downplay or distance himself from a connection that could prove toxic at the ballot box. John Fallon did exactly the opposite. Embracing his past, he not only became secretary and treasurer of the British Legion, but was steadfast in organising Remembrance Day parades – rare in Ireland and hugely contentious – to honour his friends and others like them.

> There's no doubt it cost him positions in politics but values were more important to my dad. He always made sure those men he fought with were remembered, and that people who couldn't look after themselves were taken care of. My father had taught himself to write with his left hand due to the damage to his right arm and he would send letters away to make sure these men got their pensions and were able to feed their families. He knew he was doing the right thing and that meant more to him than getting people's approval.

Less palatable to John Fallon than courting criticism and controversy was the impact it had on his family. Marie, Sean's younger sister, recalled helping her father sell poppies around Sligo in the run-up to Remembrance Day and being "chased from the door" by some angry residents. It is a memory that stayed with Sean too. He would, however, temper such recollections by reflecting with evident pride on his father's consistent topping of the popular vote.

> People could see that he was in it for them. That was more important than the army connection. My dad had more honesty and integrity than anyone I've ever known, and someone like that is always going to be popular. I was on holiday in Sligo when he was finally made mayor, and I can't tell you how proud I felt.

Whether it was in raising funds to build a care home, Nazareth House, or rattling tins to save Sligo Rovers during a financial crisis, no job was too big or small for this devoted public servant. A fellow councillor, Sean McManus, spoke of John Fallon "working endlessly for the poor, the disabled, the handicapped and the elderly", while Tony McLaughlin, a former mayor, suggested that "no-one in Sligo will ever know the true extent of his work on their behalf".

However, as Sean alluded, the legacy of his father's army history, allied to petty political jealousies, did prevent him from rising to the rank of mayor until much later than his record merited. In 1959, the *Sligo Champion* reported on a perceived "vendetta" against him. It would be another nine years before John Fallon was finally elected to serve the first of two mayoral terms, and so popular was the appointment that a large crowd gathered outside the town hall and, in the words of the *Champion*, "gave vent to their delight with proud and long applause".

By the time of his death in 1980, he was known as the 'grand old gentleman of Sligo' and the streets were packed for his funeral. Indeed, while Sean was voted Sligo's 'most outstanding living person' during the 1970s, it would not have been easy to establish which of these two Fallons was better known – or more highly respected.

"Sligo was pretty nationalist and, in certain areas of Ireland, former soldiers weren't only shunned – they were shot," said Oliver Fallon. "For John Fallon to manage to get past all that and rise to the position of mayor really was some achievement."

It was a remarkable feat from a remarkable man. For the young Sean Fallon, emerging from his father's substantial shadow would be no easy task. Yet that was the challenge. The question was how to go about it.

Chapter 2
Foreign Games

"I was just an ordinary player with a big heart and a fighting spirit to recommend me."

This is almost certainly the most famous of Sean Fallon's quotes and exemplifies his humility. It also contains more than a grain of truth.

Fallon was a fine defender: powerful and aggressive, and intelligent in his positioning, reading of the game and use of the ball. He made more than 250 appearances for Celtic and represented his country on eight occasions. But he was not a natural-born footballer. He was, in fact, almost entirely self-made, with attributes that emanated from training harder than his contemporaries, and from analysing the game and his own shortcomings.

The older he got, the better he became. But during Fallon's youth and early adulthood, "ordinary" would have been a reasonable description. Football, it seems, wasn't even his strongest sport.

I was a better swimmer than I was a footballer. I did a lot of long-distance swimming in my younger years, and it was something I felt I was a natural at. Most of the other sports I played, football included, needed more work. But I loved the swimming and always felt confident in my ability and technique.

It was this natural aptitude that earned Fallon the first significant trophy of his adult life. The Henry Cup was a notoriously punishing race from the Atlantic at his beloved Rosses Point along five miles of the Garavogue River and into Sligo itself. Fallon took the trophy twice, and his recollection of the second of those wins – on August 24, 1947 – indicates the developing of a strategic mind to match his physical prowess.

> I worked out that the best way was to take a different route from the rest, swim out, catch the tide before it hit the channel, and be swept in. There were about 14 in the race that year, but knowing the currents as well as I did gave me an advantage. I was delighted that my strategy had worked as well as it did, and it was good to get a taste for winning trophies.

While there was undoubtedly glory to be had, swimming was a passion that came accompanied by a sense of responsibility. Fallon felt compelled to train as a lifeguard, then as a lifesaving instructor, and his training took place in the temperamental, bitterly cold north Atlantic. The reward for enduring such conditions and patrolling the dangerous west-coast beaches was a small lifeguard's salary from the council, which he donated to help fund a local swimming pool.

This post came with the understanding that the Gardai could call on him whenever required, and on one occasion he was woken during the night for a particularly grisly task. A young woman had drowned in the Garavogue, seemingly having committed suicide, and it fell to Fallon to locate and retrieve her body. The concerns of friends and onlookers were shrugged off – "I'm fine, I'm fine," they were assured – but delayed shock caused him to collapse without warning the following day.

The incident did not affect his love for swimming though, and nor did he ever lose his lifeguard's instincts. In 1962, relaxing by a Valencia swimming pool ahead of Celtic's first-ever European tie, he was alerted by frantic shouts that a Swiss tourist's 10-year-old son had been swept off a raft and out to sea. The boy was 300 yards from shore when Fallon and then club secretary Desmond White plunged into the Mediterranean and swam out to pull him to safety.

Their gallantry did not go unnoticed. 'Celtic coach and director heroes of sea rescue drama' was the headline in the following day's *Evening Citizen*. Yet it was the strapline – 'Nothing to it' says Iron Man' – that Fallon stuck by, even decades later. As White pointed out to the *Citizen*: "It was almost routine stuff for Sean."

> I heard stories later that the boy was disappearing beyond the horizon and that I had to swim for miles. People don't half exaggerate sometimes. But he was certainly too far out. It caused a bit of drama at the time but I honestly didn't see the fuss in it at all. Those kinds of incidents were common on some of the more dangerous Sligo beaches. The boy's family didn't see it that way though. His father was so delighted he made me pose for pictures with his sons. And the lad himself worshipped me for it. He followed me around for the rest of the day – even out on the golf course.

This Swiss youngster was not unique in finding himself indebted to Sean in such circumstances. Journalist Rodger Baillie recalled with a smile how he found himself in need of the former lifeguard's assistance during an otherwise idyllic 1966 pre-season tour. "Tommy Gemmell had asked for a look at my new cine camera and then began filming as Bertie Auld pushed me into the hotel swimming pool. It was only high jinks and should have been harmless but, much to my shame, I hadn't yet learned to swim. I was gurgling down for the third or fourth time when Sean leapt in and yanked me to the side."

Bobby Collins, a team-mate of Fallon's at Celtic, told a near-identical story, his emergency having arisen after being shoved off a raft and into Lake Lucerne during the squad's sojourn to the 1954 World Cup. The prankster on that occasion? A certain Jock Stein. Typically, Stein made a mental note of his future assistant's speedy intervention, and hatched a plan for later in the same trip. On that occasion, Fallon's swimming was to earn both men a tidy sum.

> We'd all gone out on a boat trip and were a fair distance from land. Jock gave me a little nudge and offered to bet everyone there that I could swim all the way back to shore. We were far out and it was a glacier lake – something I only realised once I

was in the water – so there were more than a few takers. Jock was cute and spent a while trying to reel more of them in to put their money down. By the end, there was a lot riding on it, and he was telling me, 'Don't let me down now'. I told him, 'You know bloody well I won't let you down, otherwise you'd never have put your money on the table!' Sure enough, I made it back. All that swimming in my younger years, all those races, had prepared me well. I might not have been the best footballer in that Celtic team, but I was the best swimmer!

As someone so accustomed to excelling in sport, Fallon had found school to be an anti-climax. He candidly described his academic abilities as "mediocre", and admitted to having had his eye on the exit long before leaving at the age of 14. He told an endearing story of his pet dog at the time, Slater, who would follow him to morning lessons, disappear to roam countryside and, hours later – right in time for the bell ringing – trot back to the school gate. Fallon's amazement at the dog's uncanny sense of timing soon turned to envy at its hours of freedom.

I couldn't wait to get out of school in the end. My mum and dad, Lord rest them, would sit and watch me do my homework, make sure I was giving it everything. They also used to send me to violin lessons to try to get me interested in something other than sport. I must confess, though, that I started skipping the lessons and saved the money to buy a pair of football boots. I suppose it ended up being a good decision – I don't think you'd ever have heard of Sean Fallon the violinist – but I can see now that my parents were only trying to steer me in the right direction. These days, I'm so proud at how my own kids and grandkids have stuck in at school and university; they're all much smarter than I ever was. But back then, I was just determined to get out and actually do something.

Restless though he was, Sean did learn one lesson at school for which he would remain forever grateful. It was not, however, imparted in the classroom.

I went to the Sisters of Mercy school and one of the nuns – I forget her name – would come out to kick the ball around with us during our break in her big tackety boots. And she was good!

If she'd been born a man, she'd have been straight in the Sligo Rovers team. She did a lot to encourage me. But more important than anything was that she made a point of telling me I would never make it as a footballer unless I improved my weaker foot.

The gauntlet had been thrown down and Fallon responded in a manner that was fast becoming his trademark. For months thereafter, he would turn up for his usual kick-abouts with a football boot on his left foot and a sandshoe or sock on his right. This was a far-sighted approach, impairing his performance in the short term with the hope of improving his prospects over time. It worked. A left foot that had once been a weakness steadily became a strength, affording him a versatility that would see him play as Celtic's left-back almost as often as he lined up on the right.

If coaching courses from the convent were unexpected, Fallon's next source of football inspiration was positively astounding. Dixie Dean had long been a hero of his, with fantastic tales of the Everton icon's goalscoring feats often the talk of the playground. Described by Sir Matt Busby as "a perfect specimen of an athlete, beautifully proportioned, with immense strength, adept on the ground but with extraordinary skill in the air", Dean was widely considered the greatest footballer of his generation. Decades before Roy of the Rovers made his first, fictional appearance, Everton's striker supreme was every schoolboy's mythical hero. The great Dixie seemed too good to be true.

Then, in January 1939, the unthinkable happened: he signed for Sligo Rovers. The club had been looking for an experienced striker, a star name, to spearhead its FAI Cup campaign. But when Dean was suggested by a contact in England, laughter ensued. Though past his brilliant best, he was still a few weeks short of his 32nd birthday and remained big box office throughout English football. However, after an unsuccessful initial proposal, Rovers received a telegram with the fateful words: 'Offer accepted'.

To this day, I still don't know how they pulled it off. To a lot of people in those days, Dixie Dean was the greatest striker there had ever been, and it was one of my biggest thrills as a young man to see him play for my hometown team. I remember the train station being absolutely packed when he arrived to sign;

the fuss it created was unbelievable. Although his best years were behind him, he was still an outstanding player. His time in Sligo didn't last long but it was still a great success, and I remember him scoring five times in one match against Waterford. I also got to meet him because of my dad's involvement at the club and, like Jimmy McGrory – whom he'd been vying with for all the goalscoring records – he was a true gentleman.

He was also an invaluable source of inspiration. After all, before making his name and earning his legendary moniker, William Ralph Dean had left school at 14 and joined his father on the railways as an apprentice fitter. For Fallon, who had abandoned education at an identical age and was now working under his dad, the parallels were sufficient to stir his imagination. It showed him that his own dreams need not, as he had feared, become submerged in daily drudgery.

A few months before Dixie arrived, my dad arranged for me to begin work as an apprentice confectioner in McArthur's bakery. I had already been working for a couple of years at the Avery weighing scale company by that stage and hadn't been enjoying it. I knew I had to help pay my way and wouldn't have shirked my responsibilities, but I wasn't enthusiastic about going out to work. All I wanted to do was be in the outdoors, swimming and playing sport.

I already knew that I wanted to become a footballer or some kind of sportsman, and I knew, too, that I needed to train as hard as I possibly could to have a chance of making that happen. But my dad, quite rightly, pointed out how few people manage to make a living through sport, and wanted me to have a trade. Years later, when I was signing young players for Celtic, I would tell them exactly the same thing: that only a few make it, and that they should have something to fall back on.

Fortunately, I seemed to have an aptitude for decorating cakes and although my dad trained me up, he'd have told you himself that I was soon better than he was. The wingers who played against me might not believe it but it was the artistic stuff I specialised in – wedding cakes and the like. I took a real pride in them and, before long, I realised I was actually enjoying my work.

Working at McArthur's had another benefit: it brought Fallon into contact with a new mentor. James 'Jumbo' McCarrick was the bakery's master confectioner, but his fame in Sligo owed to another speciality: boxing. He had been a champion middleweight, represented Ireland in international bouts and, like Fallon, he was an outstanding swimmer and an accomplished, enthusiastic all-round athlete. In McArthur's young apprentice, he saw a kindred spirit who could, given the right encouragement, surpass his own achievements. A lifelong friendship was duly formed.

> I couldn't have had a better teacher. We stayed great pals even long after I'd left Sligo, and I made Jumbo godfather to my daughter, Louise Anne. Football wasn't his speciality but he trained me in just about everything else. He was a great rower and swimmer, and we'd also go for long walks around the hills of Sligo, camping out. In the morning before breakfast he would put me through an exercise routine, and then it would be on to some more swimming, walking or running.
>
> He also trained me as a boxer and, for a while, I loved it. The great Jack Dempsey was a big hero of mine when I was a boy, and I stayed a boxing fan all my life. Jock and myself would go to all the big fights in Glasgow together, and I can still remember the time that Muhammad Ali paid us a visit at Celtic Park. I met a lot of supposed big names who seemed only to have time for themselves, but Ali wasn't like that at all. He was a lovely man with tremendous charisma and, believe it or not, he was very humble when we met him.
>
> Not that there was ever much chance of me becoming another Ali. I was decent enough and fought competitively for a time, but I began filling out and by the age of 18 was too heavy for my height and reach. I'd gone past middleweight and was up against six-footers, good boxers, so it was hard to get near them. Their reach meant they kept on landing punches on me and although I kept on coming back, my nose started to get a bit flat. In the end, I looked in the mirror one day and thought, 'You're too handsome to be getting that face bashed in!' And though I'm not so sure that Jumbo went along with that opinion of my good looks, he did agree that I wasn't going to make it as a boxer.
>
> I had always loved my sport, but at McArthur's – thanks to Jumbo – I became a fitness fanatic. Although I started work early, I would get up while it was still dark to go running for miles up to the Holy Well, along the side of Lough Gill, say my morning

prayers and then run back to clock on. Now these were the days long before people started jogging the way they do today, and I remember folk saying: 'Look at that Fallon, he's off his head!' But I didn't bother. I knew all that running would be good for building my stamina.

Decades later, driving past hordes of joggers pounding the pavements, it would be Fallon who would chuckle, thinking back to his trailblazing days. He would recall too that, far from stifling his sporting prospects, his apprenticeship at McArthur's had enhanced them. McCarrick had been tailor-made to take this impressionable teenager and strengthen not only his athletic endurance, but the principles passed on by his father.

Jumbo drummed in to me habits and values that helped me become successful and stayed with me for the rest of my life. He didn't drink or smoke, for example, and taught me that if you look after the body, the body will look after you. Sure enough, even when I picked up injuries, I always tended to get over them quicker than most. I always stayed away from the drink too, although I have to admit that I didn't follow his advice on the smoking. That became a habit when I was in the dugout at Celtic, just to relieve the tension, and has been my one vice ever since.

I see that Alex Ferguson goes in for the chewing gum instead during matches, which is definitely a healthier habit. I'm just glad he hasn't taken after Jock. He would fret more than any of us during matches but he didn't smoke, so what he used to do was throw stones from the trackside into his mouth and chew on them. I'd tell him, 'I'm glad I'm not your dentist'. The smoking might actually have been better for him!

If there had been one flaw in McCarrick's mentoring, it was that it was too thorough; too wide-ranging. Fallon was coached in all of his many sports and encouraged to take up others when, for the sake of his stated ambition, focusing on football would have been more beneficial. The consequences were worrying. By his mid-20s, the boy who'd dreamed of starring for Celtic had become a man mired in the ranks of amateur football. Longford Town in the Leinster Senior League represented the extent of his progression, and further advancement was by no means certain.

An objective ranking of Fallon's sporting performances at this stage would have graded football a clear and distant third. Only in the fast, physical, 15-a-side Gaelic version was he coming close to emulating his swimming successes.

> I didn't see a problem at the time. I was enjoying myself in three sports and enjoying a bit of success, so I saw no motivation for giving any of them up. Gaelic football in particular seemed to be going well at that stage. I was being selected for Sligo County and I was enjoying the game thoroughly. It was tough and non-stop; you always went home knowing you'd been in a game. I was probably seen as one of the hardest players for Celtic and the other soccer teams I played for, but in Gaelic everyone was hard. And once they hit you, there was no lifting you up and making sure you were ok.
>
> Fortunately, I was always able to take a clout without it bothering me. I just came back for more. In fact, I enjoyed that whole aspect of the game. Gaelic was *the* sport in Ireland and always the biggest news on the back pages. If all I had cared about was being a bit of a celebrity in Sligo, that would have been the game to stick with.

There would have been another key justification prioritising Gaelic over soccer. Put simply, he was better at it. While out of sight and out of mind at his lower-league football club, Fallon had become something of a star in his national game, establishing himself as one of the county's outstanding players.

It was brilliant form for his club teams, Craobh Rua and Coolera, that earned him his first senior call-up by the Sligo selectors in 1946, and from that moment there was no looking back. In one game alone against Mayo, he contributed four goals and 14 points overall. His bravery and commitment to the team were also underlined when he ended the Connaught final against Rosscommon with two fewer teeth than he'd kicked off with. But Fallon's greatest Gaelic match had yet to come. It would also be his last.

> This was in April 1948, and Sligo were going up against Kerry, who were the dominant team and the main attraction in the sport at that time. Their biggest star was the goalkeeper, Dan

O'Keeffe, who's still considered the best there has ever been in Gaelic football. It was a huge game for the town, so we ended up playing it in The Showgrounds, Sligo Rovers' stadium. It was absolutely packed, a record crowd from what I can remember, and no-one expected us to do anything. But after a couple of minutes, we'd already put two goals past the great O'Keeffe. And I'd scored both of them.

Kerry fought back to claim a hard-fought win, but Sligo was abuzz with tales of Fallon's feat. The following week's *Sligo Champion* featured a two-page spread dominated by a picture of the town's new hero, broad-shouldered and beaming. Fallon didn't realise it at the time, but the local newspaper had inadvertently ended his Gaelic career.

The photograph might have looked innocent enough, but the devil was in the detail. With no shot of his Kerry heroics available, an image of Fallon in the colours of Longford Town had been deemed acceptable. What neither the *Champion* nor indeed Fallon himself had considered was the GAA's notorious Rule 27, better known as 'The Ban'. This rule, which had been in place since 1901, forbade Gaelic players from playing or even watching what the governing body classed as 'foreign games'. Anyone caught flouting the ban faced immediate suspension.

It was a ridiculous rule. The GAA folk were paranoid about losing players to soccer and wanted to make sure the Gaelic kept going, as did I. But the way they went about it was bloody stupid. They tried to make it a political issue too by linking soccer to the British army and describing it as a 'garrison game'. That kind of talk just annoyed me. The ban had been going for a while by the time I was caught out and I had kept playing soccer regardless. I couldn't accept someone dictating to me what sports I could and couldn't play.

I told the GAA folk exactly that when I was called to a disciplinary meeting a few days after the Kerry match. But they maintained that it wasn't acceptable and insisted I choose one sport or the other, no doubt thinking I'd back down and stick with the Gaelic. That attitude helped me make up my mind, and not the way they expected. From then on, it would be soccer for me, and soccer alone.

It was a choice I resented having to make because I loved playing Gaelic, and it was frustrating to have to stop just as I was reaching a good level. I'm convinced, though, that my experiences in the sport helped me become the footballer I was. It definitely hardened me up and showed me how to take physical contact without getting annoyed. I can honestly say that I never lost my temper during a match, and that was because Gaelic had taught me to give and take without complaining. I was sorry to have to give it up.

Fallon had taken a brave and principled stand. But those close to him must have feared that his decision had been reckless. He was, after all, leaving behind adulation and growing renown for a sport in which he was seemingly standing still. His 26th birthday was looming and Fallon appeared no closer to making it at the top level in Ireland, never mind earning a move across the channel. If this ordinary footballer was to achieve the extraordinary, he needed to get a move on.

Chapter 3
A Fading Dream

Throughout Sean Fallon's childhood, Sligo and Glasgow were linked by a direct steamer service. It was this boat that had taken his mother and father to Scotland, and undertaking the same voyage had become his great ambition. Then, in the 1930s, Sligo's harbour became clogged with silt and the route was closed. For Fallon, it must have seemed like a cruel metaphor.

By the summer of 1948, fears were growing that his grand dreams had been no more than childish fantasies. And he was right to be worried. Not many players reach their 26th birthday without a senior club and go on to enjoy a stellar career. Of Celtic's other Irish stars of the 1950s, Bertie Peacock made the move to Glasgow when he was still 20. Charlie Tully was 23, but had already been starring in professional football for half-a-decade. Fallon, by contrast, was wasting his mid-20s in a regional Irish league, playing in front of a handful of hardy enthusiasts. He did not cut the figure of a legend-in-the-making.

So, how had he found himself in this predicament? The raw talent, the athleticism and the competitive spirit were all there and he had also managed to steer clear of major injuries. It was difficult to understand, therefore, why his quest to join Celtic had fallen so spectacularly behind schedule. The problem, I learned, was that there was no schedule. A man for whom the glass was always half-full, Fallon had been savouring all that Sligo offered – friends, family and sporting excellence – without devising an exit strategy. In fact, he was drifting contentedly towards becoming another Jumbo McCarrick: a local celebrity, a fine man and an impressive athlete, but a perennial amateur.

It is true that he was also a victim of circumstance. In 1940, just as he was turning 18, financial difficulties forced Sligo Rovers to dissolve temporarily and withdraw from the League of Ireland. A potential avenue directly into senior football with his hometown team had closed and would not reopen for another eight years. By then, Fallon had spent close to a decade in near-anonymity with St Mary's Juniors, Distillery and Longford Town.

However, he hadn't gone completely unnoticed. Indeed, one of the most revelatory discoveries in researching Fallon's story came in stumbling across this *Sligo Champion* article of September 6, 1947. What it confirmed was that his sluggish progress through the ranks had been a problem largely of his own making.

"Sean Fallon has been asked to sign for Shelbourne, Dublin. Sean declined this offer, however, as he prefers to remain an amateur. This very sturdy player will again don the Longford colours during 1947-48, operating in the Leinster Senior League."

Here was a chance to sign for a team that, just a few months before, had been crowned champions of Ireland. Better still, it would have taken him away from the west coast, where talent scouts rarely ventured, and east to the capital, within easy reach of Britain's football hubs – Glasgow included. Only Fallon himself could explain the seemingly inexplicable.

> Looking back at it now, it seems a strange decision even to me. Why would you turn down the Irish champions to stay an amateur? But at that time, I just wasn't sure about leaving Sligo. I had a trade, I was doing well in the soccer and the Gaelic, and I was a home-bird at heart. A lot of people were leaving the town in those days, many of them going to America – my brother Padraig included – but I never felt the urge to get out. I loved Sligo and had a great life there, so going to Dublin didn't appeal to me. It was tempting, of course, because I had this aim of furthering myself. But maybe I just lacked a bit of ambition and confidence at that stage. The idea of playing for Celtic probably seemed like one of those dreams that so many people

have, which always stay unfulfilled. It was only when I started playing for Sligo Rovers and realised that I could cope in League of Ireland without any problems that I convinced myself I had to give it a go.

Fallon, of course, succeeded in making up for lost time, and snubbing Shelbourne did not prove costly. But this episode led me to reassess the GAA's role in his story. Suddenly, it became clear that the Gaelic authorities were not villains, but heroes – however unwitting.

Few memories irked the star of Sligo's full-forward line more than his experience of this absurd ban on 'foreign games'. Yet the GAA was owed a substantial debt of gratitude. Before the suspension, and by his own admission, Fallon had been no closer to dedicating his energies to football. Though his ability in, and enthusiasm for, such a variety of sports was laudable, he was spreading himself too thin. The Gaelic hierarchy forced him into a decision he would never have arrived at unaided.

By Sunday, May 16, 1948, a month on from the fateful Kerry encounter, the benefits of his suspension were already becoming apparent. Sligo GAA were once again in action, although Fallon was naturally conspicuous by his absence as they were beaten by Donegal. Fortunately, he was otherwise occupied. That same afternoon, he found himself back in front of another big crowd at The Showgrounds, only this time as part of a Sligo soccer select drawing 2-2 with Dublin outfit Transport. The *Sligo Champion* singled him out for praise, remarking that he had been "a splendid partner for D. Rogers (previously of Shamrock Rovers)" and "played a great game". This was encouraging. The mere fact that he was now featuring in the sports pages for his soccer exploits represented a significant development. Yet had this fixture clash arisen before his suspension, one wonders in what sport he would have represented his county. Would he have voluntarily walked away from Gaelic after his heroics against Kerry and the adulation that followed? Even Fallon had to admit it was as well that his hand had been forced.

The suspension will always annoy me, just because it was so stupid. But I can see it probably was a good thing because it played a big part in the way everything worked out over the next couple of years. It was after finishing with the Gaelic that I really started to focus on the soccer and it was then that things started to take off for me. I was a late starter in senior football, so it can only have helped that I was able to focus completely on making the most of the time I had.

Nor could the streamlining of Fallon's options have come at a more opportune time. Sligo Rovers were within weeks of returning to the League of Ireland for the coming season and a recruitment drive would soon be under way for this historic campaign. Fallon might have been better known in the town for his exploits in Gaelic football, but he had nonetheless been Longford Town's captain and star player for the past two seasons. He had also been called up to play for a Leinster Senior League select against an equivalent team from the Scottish Intermediate League. And his father was on the Sligo Rovers board. If ever a transfer was inevitable, surely this was it.

Yet it spoke volumes that, less than two years before he joined Celtic, Fallon's status was such that he did not feature among the reformed Rovers' first batch of recruits. It was only on August 14, a fortnight after his 26th birthday, that he was belatedly signed up, albeit on amateur terms. A season of huge importance lay in wait.

But while excitement in Sligo was high ahead of Rovers' return, the same could not be said of expectations for their cobbled-together team, nor for the local lad from 34 St Anne's Terrace. Even in this small, tight-knit town, there was precious little known about Sean Fallon the footballer, and nothing to set pulses racing.

Not many Rovers supporters would have made the 60-mile journey to watch him at Longford, and few would have remembered him from his earlier days with St Mary's and Sligo Distillery. But one man who witnessed Fallon's formative steps in football, former team-mate, Georgie Finan, has vivid memories of the town's greatest sporting export.

"Sean was some man; a great guy," said Finan. "He even used to keep bread aside for me in the bakery when things were tight, and I never forgot that. But my favourite memory of him is when we played together for a local select team against the Sligo foundry. At the time, the foundry were the best team in the county because they'd such a big staff to pick from. But they didn't know about Fallon. He just took charge. Jesus, he was hard. Like spring steel, he was.

"Everyone got a pep talk from Sean beforehand. He took me aside and said, 'Georgie, all I want you to do is keep an eye on the young fella from Strandhill. He's a grand player, so just do your best to keep him away from the goal'. Sean scored a hat-trick that day, he grabbed hold of the midfield, and I always remember he made a point of coming over to me after we'd won, shaking me by the hand and saying: 'Thanks very much, Georgie. You did exactly what I asked'. I was never a great footballer but that's a great memory for me."

Finan might have been a fan, and his story is early evidence of the on-field characteristics that would become Fallon's hallmarks. But even in those early days, this aspiring footballer was not without his detractors, as his sister Marie recalled.

She said: "I remember watching Sean play for the local junior team, Distillery. He must have been around 18 then and, naturally, my mother was always there, looking out for him, making sure he was ok. But there was another lady, Nancy Callaghan, who was involved with one of the other teams in the area. She used to always get on to Sean and would be shouting all sorts at him from the side of park. I think it was because he was seen as the hard man of the team and Nancy didn't like him tackling her boys. Sean would take no heed of it, of course. But I remember my mother not being happy. Sean was my mammy's favourite – he could never lift a finger in the house – and here was this woman calling him for everything."

The fearsome Ms Callaghan was herself a Sligo legend. Known as the 'Queen of the Hill', she was steadfast in her refusal to adhere to the role expected of her in 1940s Ireland, and ran a football club known as The Stars. Her fame was so enduring that, as recently as 2010, she was the subject of a wall-side mural in her beloved area of Holborn Hill.

"She was an old witch!" is Finan's candid recollection. "Nancy Callaghan didn't like anyone unless they were playing for The Stars. Sean didn't let it bother him but it got too much for some of the others. I remember one game when Nancy had been shouting non-stop. Sean normally took the free-kicks, but that afternoon his pal Jack Monaghan said: 'Let me have this one, Sean. I've had enough.' He took the kick and hit it straight at Nancy! I tell you, Jack was lucky to wake up the next morning."

It was with a chuckle, rather than a grimace, that Fallon recalled his old tormentor.

How could I ever forget Nancy Callaghan? She was famous in Sligo. She came from Holborn Hill, which was supposed to be a hard area, and she was stronger than most of the men in the town. She was also football daft. Everyone was afraid of her and she didn't like me because I didn't mess about when I played against her boys. The Stars were meant to be the toughest team around, but I always made it clear that I wouldn't be standing back when we played against them. Distillery were my club back then and I used to play across the midfield. I'd be all over the park, scoring goals, dominating the game where I could. Those were the days. It took quite a while before I moved back to defence – that happened at Longford, where I was mainly centre-half – although every team I played for also tried me in attack at some stage. Even Ireland gave me a go at centre-forward.

I look back with a lot of happy memories on those times with Distillery. We were playing just for the enjoyment of the game and I was in the same team as a lot of the boys I'd grown up with. Even when I moved on to Longford in 1946, a couple of my pals from Sligo and my cousin, Kevin Fallon – who everyone knew as 'Neighbour' – signed with me. It was a bit of a drive to get there but it was a step up and I enjoyed it. It showed me that I wasn't as good a player as I'd thought I was in those early days. When you come up against a good player, it shows you where you need to improve. Back then, I had a lot of room for improvement. By the time I left, though, I was the team captain and doing well. I know they didn't want me to leave. But the chance to play for Sligo Rovers was something I couldn't say no to.

It might have been enjoyable, but Fallon's time with Longford Town was fairly unremarkable. The closest he came to even moderate success with the Midlands outfit was as a losing semi-finalist in the FAI Intermediate Cup. This might be why, until his death, he merited not a single mention on the club's website, and why most fans on Longford's message board were amazed to learn of this famous former player.

There is, though, one man who still remembers Fallon's time at the club. Mickey Sweeney played alongside him in that forgettable Longford side and remembers that their shared journey from Sligo wasn't always made in comfort. "There was a petrol shortage in 1947, so there ended up being nine of us – including Sean and myself – travelling to games in the same car, all jammed in together," explained Sweeney, who would also line up alongside Fallon for Sligo Rovers. "I liked Sean – he was a real gentleman – and naturally I followed his career when he went to Celtic. I remember the radio commentator saying in one match, 'To get past Sean Fallon is to get around the mountains of Ore'. And he was right. That's how I remember Sean from playing beside him."

It was in central defence that Longford utilised Fallon's apparent defensive attributes, and the little evidence that exists suggests he acquitted himself well. The report of that FAI Intermediate Cup semi-final in the local newspaper, the *Longford Leader*, included a quote from an elderly fan describing Sean as "the best centre-half he had seen in years". Yet the kind words of supporters, and of team-mates such as Sweeney, were insignificant in comparison to the parting gift Longford bequeathed. The Football Association of Ireland had asked that each club in the Leinster Senior League nominate one player to travel to Dublin for a coaching course by the England captain of the time, George Hardwick. Longford selected Fallon, and it was during the summer of 1948 – a period which arguably shaped his career – that he made the journey to the capital.

> That was a great experience. George Hardwick was a huge figure in football at that time and it was obvious that he knew the game inside-out. Working with him in Dublin was the first proper football coaching I received, and it opened my eyes. I saw the game in a completely different light after that. He was a very nice man and one thing I noticed about him was that he didn't over-complicate things. What he did stress was the importance of learning the basics and passing them on to any youngsters you come into contact with. I know you'd think that by that stage, almost 26, I would have known all the basics. But I went back home having learned a great deal that I would later be grateful for.

As well as opening his eyes, the trip to Dublin broadened Fallon's horizons. He returned with a fresh appreciation of the opportunities that lay beyond Sligo's boundaries, and a determination to pursue them. Equally momentous was the sparking of an interest in coaching, with the 26-year-old greatly impressed by the way in which Hardwick – who would go on to manage Sunderland, PSV and the Netherlands – imparted his message with patience and passion.

That seed, sown by the England captain, was to be cultivated the following summer by another of the era's footballing giants. Johnny Carey would one day be an international team-mate of Fallon's, but he arrived in Sligo in 1949 from a seemingly different world, as Ireland and Manchester United's biggest star and England's newly-crowned player of the year. His visit to coach the town's youngsters had been arranged by John Fallon, then chairman of the Connaught Football Association, and Sean – increasingly hungry for knowledge – immediately volunteered to assist. His reward was yet more sage advice, and Carey left having convinced his not-so-young apprentice of the need to get out of Sligo, and fast.

First, though, Fallon had to earn the opportunity to leave and, at the start of the 1948/49 season, he and Sligo Rovers found themselves in a near-identical position. Both were essentially beginning life in the League of Ireland from a standing start, and each was hoping that the process of acclimatisation would be swift and painless.

Playing for his hometown team was an undoubted thrill, and Fallon followed their fortunes for the remainder of his life, delighting in the 2012 title win – Rovers' first in 35 years. But the club in 1948 was not an ideal fit for a player looking to hone his craft. There were no long-serving stalwarts to offer advice and no established team structure in which he could find his niche. Everyone in this squad of strangers was a newcomer, and each of them – including Sam Waters, the player-manager and captain – was starting from square one. Inconsistency was inevitable, and applied as much to team selection as to results. No fewer than 41 players were used over the course of a turbulent campaign and, while Fallon was one of the few constants, his position on the field was anything but.

I was all over the place. After five months at Sligo Rovers, I'd played in six different positions. By the end of the season, I'd played every role bar goalkeeper and wing-forward. That wasn't good for my development because, by that stage, I was looking to nail down a position and perfect it as much as I could. But that was the nature of things that season. I just got on with it and, although I wasn't there long, I felt I did a decent job.

That assessment is borne out by the reports. Though his early progress at The Showgrounds was hampered by an ankle injury that would haunt him for years, he was quickly earning plaudits from the local press. By late September, playing in defence, he was described by the *Sligo Champion* as having "complete control of the inside-forwards" in a win at Limerick. A week later, he was patrolling the midfield and gaining positive reviews for his "well manoeuvred passes".

Results had improved with Fallon's return to the side and, despite his frequent positional changes, the *Champion* quickly arrived at a conclusion that many – including the player himself – would wholeheartedly echo in years to come. "Fallon is much better as a defender than an attacker," stated its report of a 2-2 draw at Shamrock Rovers in which he had played both positions.

The management took heed of this advice, for a while at least, and Fallon was lauded as "a grand back", "gallant" and "a glutton for work" in the weeks that followed. He was steadily emerging as one of the team's star players, and acknowledgement of this came midway through the season when he was appointed captain in Waters' absence. By this stage, and perhaps more surprisingly, he had also established himself as a dead ball expert. Barely a week went by without a goal or near miss from free-kicks that, by the turn of the year, were being labelled "Fallon specials" by the *Champion*.

That was a speciality of mine back then. I was pretty good and scored quite a few goals from set pieces. If it was far out, I'd go for power. Further in and I'd look to be a bit more precise. But I never got a look-in with the free-kicks at Celtic. That was left to the technicians, so Charlie Tully and the others kept me away from them. I was told to keep myself at the back – 'back where I belonged', they told me.

Rovers' results worsened as the season reached its conclusion but, despite his manager's seeming inability to decide whether he was a full-back, centre-half or centre-forward, Fallon was becoming a footballer of repute. Even the national authorities began taking note. Three times he was the sole Sligo representative in a League of Ireland select although, on each occasion, he remained inactive and frustrated in the role of first reserve.

Back in Sligo, Rovers ultimately ended the season second from bottom, although their campaign was regarded as a promising first step – and Fallon as one of its most striking success stories. A tireless and versatile player, he had made 34 appearances and scored five goals, leading the *Champion* to declare him "a certain for next season". Fallon, though, had his own, more ambitious plans.

Sligo Rovers were my hometown team and I was always proud to have played for them. But the club was just starting up again and still finding its feet. I was getting on in years so I couldn't really afford to waste too much time. I knew I had to get away from Sligo if I wanted to make something out of myself as a footballer. I felt if I didn't make a move quickly, I would never get out.

An escape route presented itself following a 4-2 friendly win over Glenavon. Such was the impression Fallon made on Rovers' visitors that that he was approached immediately after the match about a transfer. The offer entailed professional football, a significantly increased wage and, most enticing of all, a move to a region frequented far more often by British scouts. Yet, still, the home-bird wasn't quite ready to fly the nest. Concerned that joining the Lurgan outfit might represent a move sideways, the 27-year-old advised Rovers that he would be prepared to spurn the northerners' advances. There was only one condition: he wanted a pay rise. The princely sum of 10 shillings was all it would have taken to keep him at The Showgrounds.

They knocked me back. Can you believe that? Instead of giving me those extra shillings, they went looking for a transfer fee of £200 from Glenavon, which they had a cheek doing since I was an amateur. At least I can laugh about it now. But you do wonder what might have been had they given me the rise I was looking for. I might not be talking to you now. I might never have left Sligo.

Like the GAA before them, Rovers ultimately found themselves in the role of accidental heroes. But while their parsimony prevented Fallon from staying, it was an act of great generosity that finally convinced him to leave.

> I was worried about giving up my job in the bakery. Work wasn't easy to come by in those days and if things at Glenavon didn't work out, where would that have left me? But Mr McArthur, Alec, God rest him, took me aside and told me not to let anything hold me back. He said he had faith in me, that I would make it, but that if for whatever reason I didn't, my job would be waiting for me when I came back. That was a tremendous gesture and it put to rest the last few doubts I had.
>
> So I went back to Glenavon and told them, 'Ok, I'll sign – as long as you can get me a job in my own trade'. They agreed and were good to their word, fixing me up with a job as a foreman confectioner in Lurgan. By the time it was all agreed, I was actually looking forward to leaving Sligo. I would always miss it, and I was very homesick in those first couple of years away. But I wanted to test and improve myself and I felt it would help me to finally stand on my own two feet.

Mature and motivated, Fallon had made a decisive move in leaving behind all that he held dear. It was to prove a step in the right direction and a giant leap towards fulfilling his dream. Sligo's old steamer service to Glasgow never did resume, but another route to Scotland was about to be forged.

Chapter 4
A Visit From Mr McGrory

B efore Glenavon, Fallon's football career had been a story of slow, steady progress. More of the same would no longer suffice. The pace had to be upped and that meant making an immediate and eye-catching impact in Lurgan, where he arrived shortly after his 27th birthday. Scoring five times on his Glenavon debut made for a booming statement of intent.

The fact that the goals arrived in a mere friendly mattered little. Fallon's seven months and 10 days at Mourneview Park would be time well spent, and this match set the tone. It also served some notable early purposes, not least settling the newcomer's nerves. The move to Glenavon had been a calculated gamble, but a gamble nonetheless. It was not a club at which a warm welcome was assured.

"Sean going to Glenavon would have been a big deal back then because there were very few, if any, southern players playing in the north," explained historian Aiden Mannion. "He'd have been a very rare animal and it wouldn't have been easy for him. He would have had to win over a few people."

Sceptics were to be found in the dressing room as well as on the terraces. Lurgan may be best known to Celtic fans as the birthplace of Neil Lennon, but the town in which Fallon arrived was a unionist stronghold at the heart of an increasingly troubled province. The Ireland Act, which severed the south's remaining links with the Commonwealth, had been given royal assent just a couple of months earlier, and passions were running high.

> There were one or two who were a bit funny with me to begin with just because of the politics of it all. It wasn't an easy time in Ireland and I'd half expected that kind of reaction, although it was still annoying because you always hope you'll be treated the same way you treat others. But once I started playing and they saw I was a good player who'd give the club everything I had, I made a lot of friends there. That's the good thing about football – you can earn people's respect quite quickly by what you do on the field.
>
> Away from the club, the people in Lurgan were tremendous. The fact I was a Catholic from the south didn't stop them from making me feel very welcome. The lady who put me up in my digs was a Protestant herself, but she couldn't have been more accommodating. She would say on Sunday: 'I know you'll be going to Mass, so I understand you won't want your breakfast yet. I'll save that for you later.' It was a small gesture, but it meant a lot that she had such an accepting attitude.
>
> I always made sure to be the same way myself. The whole Catholic-Protestant thing was never an issue for me. I took people as I found them. As it happened, my closest friend in that Glenavon team was a guy called Wilbur Cush, a great little wing-half who played for Northern Ireland, and he was as blue as they come. It was the same at Celtic, where my best pals were Bertie Peacock and then Jock, both Protestants. It never mattered to Bertie, Jock and I in the Celtic dressing room and, fortunately, it didn't end up mattering at Glenavon either.

Fallon's endeavour, ability and affability quickly overcame any petty prejudices, and his five-goal debut accelerated the process of integration. It also had a more tangible impact, convincing Glenavon's management that the full-back they had spotted in Sligo should start the season at centre-forward.

This was becoming an oft-used experiment, and it would not be the last time that Fallon would shelve his own doubts to embrace the role of attacking spearhead. The difference on this occasion was the level of success he enjoyed. With his other clubs, and indeed at international level, he merely served a purpose, unsettling defences with his physicality without ever becoming a prolific goalscorer. At Glenavon, he was something of a sensation.

By late September, this natural defender was the Irish League's leading goalscorer, having already reached double figures. Yet, for all this early success, Fallon remained convinced that it was only as a full-back that he would earn a move across the sea. And again, fate intervened on his behalf.

> I had a stroke of luck in December 1949, when the club sold their right-back, Charlie Gallogly, to Huddersfield. That gave me the chance to move back to my own preferred position and I began to really enjoy my football. The standard of matches was slightly higher than in the south but I felt I was more than holding my own and other people must have agreed because I was soon told that a few clubs from England and Scotland were watching me.
>
> When I heard that Celtic were one of those clubs, I think my heart nearly stopped. It was the move I'd always wanted, of course, but I still doubted whether I was ready – or if I would ever be good enough. But I just focused on my football, did my best to believe in myself – always so important – and concentrated on keeping up my performances for Glenavon. The rest, I hoped, would take care of itself.

Putting aside his nerves, excitement and insecurities was one thing. But Fallon had another self-imposed barrier to overcome. In snubbing the opportunity to turn professional to insist on part-time terms and continuing his trade as a confectioner, he had prepared for failure. Now, with success beckoning, he was close to exhaustion. And no wonder.

From Monday to Friday, he began work at 6am and clocked off 12 hours later. Saturdays were barely any easier, with another early start at the bakery followed by a midday finish and a race to join his team-mates for the 3pm kick-off. It was an arduous routine, and one which made Fallon's energetic and eye-catching performances all the more impressive.

> I had never worked so hard in my life. But I had no complaints. It was exactly what I'd asked for, and I was never scared of a bit of hard work. People might have thought I was being negative or pessimistic in not dedicating myself to football, but I felt at the

time it was a good compromise. I didn't know at that stage how good, or how lucky, I was going to be in Lurgan.

Glenavon had got me a job as a foreman confectioner and, although the hours were long, I enjoyed it. The bakery itself was good and, any job I did, I tried to do to the best of my ability. I wasn't just passing time. I would even go round telling people, 'I've heard that bakery up the road does the most fantastic cakes', just to drum up a bit of business for the place. And I was back on the wedding cake decoration, which I always enjoyed and which brought in some extra money to send home to Sligo.

I was certainly a busy man in those days, but I didn't mind because everything was going well, and I knew that I had made the right choice in coming to Glenavon. Lurgan's a small town, not much bigger than Sligo, but the club was well run and looked to be going places.

Glenavon were, in fact, every bit as ambitious as Fallon himself, and well on the way to becoming the first provincial club to win the Irish League. All three of the club's championships would be won within the space of the next decade, although their Sligo full-back did not stick around to see the trophy raised.

After all, a job in his own trade hadn't been the only assurance he had sought. Glenavon were never more than a means to an end for Fallon, and he candidly told the club as much during signing talks. A gentleman's agreement was sought, and received, that he would be allowed to leave should the right opportunity arise.

Celtic remained uppermost in his thoughts. But two quiet months had passed since their interest was first intimated, and Fallon feared that he had been forgotten. The opposite was true. Peter O'Connor, Celtic's scout in Northern Ireland, had been an unseen presence at Glenavon's matches, and each report to Glasgow was more glowing than the last.

O'Connor, a former player with Belfast Celtic, had recently recommended both Charlie Tully and Bertie Peacock, so his stock was high. Manager Jimmy McGrory was quickly convinced to take a look for himself. Fallon's date with destiny had been set, and it so happened that the date was St Patrick's Day. It was then that he would be watched by McGrory and 18,000 tricolour-waving supporters at Dublin's Dalymount Park. A more Irish occasion would have been impossible to imagine and yet Fallon found himself in the strange position of opposing the nation of his birth. The match was between representative teams from the League of Ireland and the Irish League – and the boy from Sligo had been selected by the north.

> Some people weren't happy about that. Those league representative matches were the biggest thing in Irish football at that stage and I was unique, certainly at that stage, in being a southerner playing for the north. Not everyone agreed with my decision, but I couldn't have cared less. Eligibility came from the club you played for, not where you were born, and I was proud that the Irish League considered me to be the best in my position.
>
> I had been reserve for the League of Ireland in the same fixture the year before and this was a chance to play, so why not take it? I had a great welcome from the boys in the Irish League team and I couldn't wait to play. I had heard a rumour that Mr McGrory would be there to watch me and, having heard and read all about him, I could barely contain my excitement.
>
> Unfortunately, the game itself was a let-down. We lost 3-1 and it was blowing a gale, so neither side was able to play much good football. What was worse was the fact I had played poorly. I was never a flashy player anyway but I felt I hadn't performed to my capabilities. I went away thinking that Mr McGrory would not have been impressed. I actually thought I had blown my chance.

Not for the last time, Fallon was – by some distance – his own harshest critic. This supposedly underwhelming performance had prompted a queue to form at Glenavon's door, and McGrory was at its front. Even years later, the Celtic manager retained vivid memories of his St Patrick's Day scouting mission and the impression his future captain had made. "His sheer enthusiasm for the game had to be seen to be believed," he enthused. "I simply had to sign him."

Yet even when McGrory travelled to Ireland for the second time in a week, with the sole purpose of meeting him, Fallon remained riddled with self-doubt. Indeed, he now feared that this face-to-face chat could be the death of his dream. And so it was that he was tempted into an uncharacteristic white lie.

> Because the move was so close, I didn't want anything to put

Celtic off. That would have killed me. I was nearly 28 and worried they might think I was a little old, so when Mr McGrory asked me my age, I told him I was 22. Now, that might sound dishonest but it was something a lot of professional players did in those days, particularly in Ireland. The clubs weren't interested in seeing your birth certificate and checking whether you were telling the truth. All they wanted to know was: could you play and were you fit?

Celtic seemed convinced that I could play and I knew myself that I was one of the fittest players in Ireland, so I didn't feel as guilty about the lie as I might have done. I knew that, God willing, I had a lot of good years ahead of me and that my age wouldn't be an issue. And so it proved. I played over eight seasons at Celtic and I would like to think I gave the club good service. They weren't disappointed with me, I know that.

Eventually, though, I had to tell the truth about my real age when the club was going on a tour and had to sort out new passports for the players. I was always getting pulled to the side wherever we travelled because of my Irish passport, so it was decided that I needed a British one like the rest of the players. Naturally, I didn't want to get caught out if the British authorities checked my date of birth against the official Irish records. I'd have got the jail! So I came clean. I was a bit nervous about telling Mr McGrory but I needn't have worried because he was such a kind man and accepted my explanation without any anger or disappointment at all. I think he knew by then that Celtic were getting their money's worth.

McGrory's understanding and forgiveness were matched only by his discretion. Fallon's secret was safe with him. There was the odd whisper and knowing wink, but for decades his true age remained unknown to fans, journalists and team-mates alike. Ian Paul, the former *Herald* reporter, once wrote that it was "kept as secret as a KGB code". Fallon's colleagues were certainly none the wiser, as shown by their contemptuous comments about Jock Stein's arrival. "They were all saying to me, 'Imagine signing an old guy like that. What use can he be?'" Fallon recalled, laughing. "What they didn't realise was that I was a few months older than Jock."

Even his closest friends – including Stein – remained in the dark. George Stein, Jock's son, remembers the subject being a consistent source of light-hearted sparring. "The pair of them used to laugh about it because Sean would insist, always with a smile on his face, that he was the younger of the two. My dad would just look at him and shake his head. I never did find out the truth until I heard about Sean's 90th. I could have imagined my dad looking down on the celebrations, saying 'I knew it!'"

Fallon's dubious date of birth might have been a running joke with Stein, but not everyone saw the funny side. Sean's daughter, Louise, remembers one particular rebuke arriving from the unlikeliest of sources. "We were all coming out of Mass one day when one of the passkeepers said: 'Mr Fallon, can I have a quick word with you please?' I think my dad probably expected that he was looking for tickets. But this man pulled him to one side and said: 'Mr Fallon, I work in the passport office and I was looking over your details the other day. I see that you have two different dates of birth on two different passports. That would lead me to believe that you're lying. There's a fine for that, so I would advise you to fix it as soon as possible.'" "I told him to mind his own business!" was Fallon's recollection of the same incident.

The fact that he went on to provide Celtic with sterling service, making over 250 appearances, ensured that Fallon's was a victimless crime. Nonetheless, misleading anyone – far less a man such as McGrory – was undeniably out of character. It underlined just how desperate and determined he had become. And yet, incredibly, Fallon very nearly walked away from the move he had sought for so long, even going so far as to reject the club's initial offer. The reason for this unexpected twist did, however, say more about Celtic at the time – and football in general – than it did about the player himself.

> I can still remember the excitement I felt when I heard that Mr McGrory was in the club rooms at Glenavon waiting to see me about signing for Celtic. It was a dream come true. I felt that I should tell him about all the great things I had heard about him and the club, but I also knew that I should ask some important questions, like what I would be earning at Celtic.
>
> When he told me that I would be starting off at eight pounds-a-week, going down to six in the close season, my heart sank. I was never someone who was motivated by money, but at that stage I was earning almost eight pounds-a-week as a foreman confectioner, plus six pounds for playing for Glenavon. Most of

that money was sent back to my family in Sligo and I didn't feel I could accept taking such a huge pay-cut, even if it was to move to Celtic.

I could hardly believe what I was saying, but I told him: 'That wouldn't be enough, Mr McGrory. I couldn't accept that.' I explained the situation and he said that he understood and would make a phone call to the chairman, see if anything could be done. A few minutes later, he came back and said the club would be prepared to make a final offer of 10 pounds-a-week. I didn't think I could risk negotiating any more. But it's amazing to think now that moving from Glenavon to Celtic left me four pounds-a-week worse off.

There were a few English clubs in for me at the time, all offering more money than Celtic needless to say, but they were wasting their time. As soon as Celtic came in for me, my mind was made up. Fulham and Leicester both came out to see me and so did Peter Doherty, who was player-manager of Doncaster Rovers. Turning down Mr Doherty was most difficult of all because I had been a big admirer of his when he played for Ireland and, like Mr McGrory, he was a true gentleman.

Even with that call back to Celtic Park – and I can't tell you how nervous I was while Mr McGrory was on the phone – it took just a few minutes to settle everything. When I walked out of that room, I was Sean Fallon of Celtic. In a magazine article a few years later, I said: 'I can never hope to find words to express my feelings at becoming a member of the Celtic Football Club.' It's become quite a famous quote, that one. And I still feel the same way. It was the realisation of a dream not only for myself, but for my dad. I was as delighted for him as I was for myself. People back home told me that he went off his nut when he heard the news.

Glenavon's fans reacted in a similar way, although it was rage that fuelled their fervour. Fallon had become a hugely popular player at the club, and supporters viewed the fee – £5000 up front, £1000 after six first-team appearances – as scant compensation. Besieged by complaints, the chairman attempted to assuage his critics in the *Lurgan Mail*, pointing to Fallon's stipulation that the club accede to a cross-channel move.

Glenavon had behaved honourably by their player, and made a tidy profit in return. They were also comfortable in the table; well clear of the relegation zone, but not close enough to Linfield to mount a title challenge. The fact that Fallon's departure could stir a response so passionate in such circumstances, and after such a short association, showed just what an impression he had made.

His time at Glenavon had been an unqualified success. The pace had indeed been upped and the target attained. After years of purposeless plodding, Fallon had sped his way through two career-defining moves in just seven months. A week later, he would board a boat from Belfast, little realising that his destination would be home for the next six decades. His was a story only just beginning.

Chapter 5
False Starts

For Sean Fallon, the final seven days of March 1950 were among the happiest of a full and remarkable life. Jimmy McGrory had permitted Celtic's new signing a week in Sligo before summoning him to Scotland, and a triumphant homecoming awaited. The Glenavon gamble had paid off handsomely and Sean's seemingly impossible dream – the dream of his father – had been realised. Intense satisfaction and delicious anticipation made for a potent blend.

"That was a wonderful time," recalled his sister, Marie. "Daddy was so proud. In those days, it was special for someone to achieve something like that. Nowadays there are more opportunities to travel and to achieve things in different places, but back then you didn't have many people from Sligo going out to be successful in other countries. Sean was the talk of the town."

It was a golden era for the Fallons. While Sean had been seeking out a route to Celtic Park, his father had been busy arranging a transfer move of his own. This one made for even bigger news. At the heart of the negotiations was the late WB Yeats, literary giant and favourite son of Sligo, whose body was being returned to his spiritual home after lengthy political wrangling. It had taken nine years since his death and burial in France, but Yeats' last wish – to be laid to rest in Drumcliffe churchyard – had been granted.

Sean was thrilled. Decades later, his children would joke that the only subject in which his knowledge of Celtic could be matched was the life and times of this esteemed Irish poet. That week in 1950, one of Yeats' most famous lines would have held added personal significance. *"I have spread my dreams under your feet. Tread softly because you tread on my dreams."* It might as well have been an entreaty from Fallon himself, pleading for reality to match his long-held Celtic fantasy.

> Signing for Celtic, well, it felt like winning the lottery. Going home, seeing everyone so happy and proud, brought home to me what I'd managed to achieve. But I knew that I'd done nothing yet, or not really. I didn't want to sign and then go over to Glasgow and be a failure. I'd built up Celtic so much in my head, read everything I could and listened to all my dad's stories. But I also had no real idea of what I was going into. I'd never been out of Ireland, never lived in a big city and never played for a big club. I didn't know how good Celtic would be and whether I'd be good enough myself. But, by this point, I was beginning to believe in myself more. That was vital. Confidence in yourself is essential at a club like Celtic, otherwise you'll just get swallowed up. You can forget about becoming a top professional if you don't believe in yourself. And by then I did; I knew I could play. But, still, I was just praying it would all work out.

Ultimately, Celtic surpassed all his hopes and expectations. Youthful fascination blossomed into lifelong adoration. But while Fallon and Celtic turned out to be a marriage made in heaven, the path to true love did not run smooth. Homesickness, a disastrous debut and a career-threatening injury removed any prospect of a honeymoon period, and divorce very nearly followed. But in March 1950, all those difficulties lay ahead, dormant, unknown and generally unexpected. Before he could begin facing them, Fallon first had to negotiate the crossing from Belfast, and even that was rough and uncomfortable. It also posed his first major challenge as a Celtic player: staying sober.

> That was easier said than done with Charlie Tully looking after me! Mr McGrory had arranged for Charlie to meet me on the boat, to make sure I would find my way in Glasgow, and I was

excited about it because I'd already heard a lot about this great player. But I don't think I made a good first impression. No sooner than he'd introduced himself, I was ushered down to the bar. 'What are you having, Sean?' he asked. 'I'll take a lemonade thanks, Charlie,' I told him. 'A *what*?' he said. 'A *lemonade*? Ah, don't tell me you're one of *those*!' I could only apologise. Charlie's tipple was always the same – a beer and a half of whisky – and I had no idea how he managed to put so many of them away. I must have had about 14 lemonades just keeping pace with him that night. And with the sea being so choppy, I've never been so sick in my life. I've not been able to look at lemonade since!

The two travel companions would become great friends, to the extent that Fallon was asked to sponsor Tully's son, Charlie Jnr, at his confirmation. But their personalities would never align. Extroverted and streetwise, Tully was in his element amid the bustle of Glasgow, and what he loved most was the reciprocation of his affections. The city had fallen in love with Celtic's mischievous maverick; the proliferation of green-and-white Tully cocktails, Tully ties and Tully ice-cream even spawning the phrase 'Tullymania'. Cheeky Charlie lapped it up.

On and off the field, Fallon was altogether less flamboyant. It was not the promise of fame that had attracted him to Celtic, but romantic notions of the club's charitable origins and commitment to cavalier football. And the same city that exhilarated Tully left him utterly overwhelmed.

Glasgow was a shock to the senses. I'd been used to living in small towns and had never experienced anything like it. I found it very difficult to adjust and suffered badly from homesickness. It's hard to imagine now, having lived here for over 60 years, but I found Glasgow to be a very lonely place at first. I would get out of the city at every opportunity I had, disappear out to the countryside and go for long walks. It would be up in the Cathkin Braes, places like that, and I'd be out there for hours. It became a habit. Even years later, when I was much happier and more settled, I'd still be walking 10, 15 miles most days. I can't imagine players these days would be allowed to do that.

I suppose it just showed that I was a country boy at heart and those early days in the big city were very difficult for me. I always remembered how I'd felt years later, when we had boys coming in to the club from Ireland and elsewhere. I would try to look out for them because I know it's not easy. I don't know how I would have coped, only I was fortunate enough to have an aunt living in Glasgow. Having a bit of family to help me through those times made all the difference.

This same Aunt Winnie had given a roof to his mother during the war but, with four children of her own, she was unable to make Sean the same offer. Instead, digs were arranged by Celtic, with a house just off Alexandra Parade selected on the recommendation of first-team coach Jimmy Hogan. What the homesick recruit needed was somewhere to settle; a refuge in this unknown and intimidating city. What he encountered nearly had him dashing for the first boat home.

The first night in these digs, I went out like a light. So I wake up the next morning, happy to have slept well, turn over… and there's a man in bed beside me. I nearly had a heart attack! I don't know what Jimmy Hogan had been told, but it turned out that the chap had four sisters and this was the only other bed in the house. When he'd finished work, he'd just crawled in beside me. So, after the shock of my life, I was on the move again. Fortunately, the chairman, Bob Kelly, got wind of the situation and made sure to sort out somewhere for me personally after what had happened. I think he probably realised that I was homesick and was worried about me chucking it altogether and going home. So he arranged for me to stay in a place in Rutherglen, and this time he made sure I'd have a bed of my own.

This house was perfect. Funnily enough, the woman who owned it, Mary McGuigan, was the niece of Jimmy McMenemy. That family were becoming quite an influence on my life. She was a wonderful lady and lots of the other players would come to stay with her from time to time. I loved it there. The fact that Bob Kelly had taken such an interest in making sure I was happy and settled always stayed with me. I even remember when we first arrived at Miss McGuigan's, he was looking the place over, even testing the springs in the bed. He kept on asking, 'Are you sure this will be ok, Sean?' I was embarrassed. It was way beyond what I would have expected of the Celtic chairman and I never forgot it. I remember thinking at the time how happy I was that Celtic had men like him and Mr McGrory running the club. And I was determined to repay him.

That small kindness, ensuring the comfort of a homesick player, was the beginning of an enduring and reciprocal respect between player and chairman. Nor was it the only lasting alliance formed by Fallon in those early days at Celtic. In Bertie Peacock, he made a friend for life. The Coleraine youngster was a kindred spirit and saw in the newcomer the same startled look he had exuded after arriving from Glentoran the previous May. Without Tully to guide him, Peacock had wandered the streets of Glasgow for fully two hours before summoning the courage to ask for directions. But empathy wasn't all he could offer. Crucially, Peacock was also in a position to guide his fellow Irishman through the antagonistic excesses of a divided dressing room.

> There were a few cliques in the Celtic team at that stage. Some of the older, more experienced players tried to be clever with me initially; they would make fun of me, tease me about my accent. Maybe they saw me as coming in to take the place of one of their pals, I'm not sure. A few of them certainly didn't make life as easy for me as they might have done. But Bertie looked out for me in those days, kept me right and also put one or two of the others in their place, in his own quiet way. He would even interpret for me when some of the other players – deliberately or otherwise – couldn't understand what I was saying. On and off the park, Bertie was a gem. There were no flaws in his make-up. He was a great wing-half – the kind of player who seemed to be doing four jobs at once – a tremendous professional, and one of the nicest guys you could ever hope to meet.
>
> We became great friends. In fact, he was my best pal throughout my time at Celtic – even after Jock arrived. Neither Bertie nor myself took a drink, so we would go out socialising together. They used to bring some great shows to Glasgow in those days; you'd have all the big stars, and we'd go along to see those together. Even years later, when he'd finished playing and gone back to Coleraine, we would meet up every year. He would bring a team of his pals over here for a golf tournament at my club in Pollok, and I'd put a team up against them. I would also take the family to see him every time we'd got the boat over to Ireland, and Myra and the kids loved him every bit as much as I did. You couldn't help but love Bertie.

Peacock had yet to establish himself in the first team by the time Fallon arrived, but the extent of his promise was apparent. Already a full international at just 21 – in his case, with a bona fide birth certificate – he was displaying all the attributes that would make him a much-loved player for club and country over the next decade and beyond. It had, in truth, likely been Peacock's early progress, allied to the spectacular impact made by Tully, that convinced Celtic to plunder the Irish League for the third time in two seasons. Fallon, therefore, arrived with a great deal to live up to. The official Celtic Football Guide in 1950 reflected this sense of expectation, predicting that the club's latest Irish 'youngster' "would prove a real acquisition". Nor was it merely faith that Fallon had to repay, with the same publication stressing the "substantial fee" that had been required to secure his signature. The *Daily Record*, meanwhile, highlighted the versatility of 'Johnny Fallon' – a name they persisted with for some time – and observed that both centre-forward and full-back were longstanding problem positions at Celtic Park.

Despite these high expectations, it was a few weeks before McGrory and Kelly saw fit to thrust their new boy into first-team action. Fallon's first appearance in the green and white came, in fact, not at a packed Celtic Park, but in a reserve match against Kilmarnock. Only a handful of spectators bothered to turn up and Sean's contribution was such that he would have preferred there to have been no witnesses at all. A low-key, inauspicious second-string match it might have been, but he had looked – and felt – completely out of his depth. Even years later, in an article for *Charles Buchan's Football Monthly*, he made specific reference to this match and its alarming, humbling impact. "It was during that game," he said, "I fully realised how much I still had to learn about football."

His sister, Marie, recalls Sean confiding these worries to their father the next time he returned home. "My father asked Sean how he was managing the transition to Scottish football, which was very well thought of in those days. I remember Sean telling him, 'It was a bit scary at first. I'd always felt I was a step ahead and fast enough in the teams I'd played in before, whereas at Celtic I felt like I was two gears lower than I needed to be'. The pace of the game was such a step up."

Fallon wasn't the only one left questioning whether he could make that jump. Concerns emanating from his error-strewn outing against Kilmarnock ensured that he was again left out for the next first-team match, away to Partick Thistle on April 10. But Celtic – already out of the title race and beaten by Third Lanark just a few weeks before – lost 1-0 without him. Changes were demanded and, ready or not, that meant Fallon coming in at left-back to face Clyde five days later. Memories of his torrid reserve debut were still fresh, but he calmed himself with the assurance that, whatever happened, this match couldn't go any worse. Surely.

For most of the first half, it did seem that Fallon would indeed get away with a performance that, while disappointing, was not proving disastrous. Willie Fernie had even given Celtic the lead on the sodden Shawfield pitch, and chances were that a Celtic win would gloss over any of the new boy's perceived failings. Then, with 34 minutes gone, calamity struck. Goalkeeper John Bonnar, speaking in Eugene McBride's *Talking with Celtic*, remembered the incident well. "I'm organising the defence. Sean's on the front post. I tell him, 'Anything your height, Sean, you head it'. Over comes the ball. Sean puts it straight in the net. Lovely header! McGrory himself couldn't have done better."

> What a start! Can you believe it? That can happen as a defender, of course – you go in to clear the ball, catch it wrong and it spins into the net. But to happen on my debut! It was one of those terrible moments. I just wanted the ground to swallow me up. It wasn't just the own goal either – it was a bad performance from me in lots of respects. From what I can remember, we needed a late goal from Charlie to save a 2-2 draw, and I felt responsible for the fact we hadn't won. I can only imagine what the people at Celtic must have thought. They'd have been wondering what the hell they had signed.

The sole consolation for footballers in such mortifying circumstances is the knowledge that there is always another game, with their chance to atone often arriving within days. Fallon wasn't so lucky. Pride hadn't been the only thing wounded at Shawfield. More worrying was the damage inflicted on an ankle that had been intermittently troubling the player for almost two years. It was an injury that dated back to a chapter in his career that already seemed a lifetime ago.

Remember that coaching course I went on to Dublin, while I was still at Longford? The one with George Hardwick? Well, on the last day of that course, everyone involved was put into a little match – just a bit of fun to finish things off. Unfortunately for me, someone came in to tackle me, fell and his weight all landed on my right ankle. I was in agony. It was probably the most painful injury I ever had, and it turned out later that I had suffered what they called a flake fracture of the ankle.

It bothered me on and off all the time I was at Sligo Rovers and Glenavon, and I mentioned it to Jimmy McGrory before I signed. Don't ask me why I was so up front about that and told him lies about my age but, anyway, he told me not to worry about it and said that Alex Dowdells, Celtic's trainer, would sort me out if it flared up again. And, sure enough, Alex worked hard with me after the Clyde match, got me on my feet again and I was back in the team within a few weeks.

But it was to prove a false dawn. Fallon did make his comeback, and it was a much happier occasion than his debut, with Third Lanark dispatched 1-0 at Hampden in the Charity Cup semi-final. He more than played his part too, and left the national stadium confident of retaining his place in the team to face Rangers three days later in the same competition. It would be his first cup final, his first Old Firm derby, and it would be remembered as one of the truly great games of that era. The Hollywood star Danny Kaye was presented to the players beforehand and stuck around to see Celtic – led by hat-trick hero John McPhail and the irrepressible Tully – beat the champions 3-2 in front of over 80,000 spectators. Among the victors was a young Peacock who, despite, going on to play in the legendary 7-1 game, named this final as the pick of his 453 Celtic appearances. Fallon? He watched it all from the stands, distraught. And missing out on one match, however memorable, was the least of his worries.

My ankle had flared up again and I thought that could be it for me; that my career could be over. Injuries like that could finish you in those days, and it wasn't looking good. The ankle had been bothering me for years and, if anything, it was getting worse. Alex Dowdells did his best but neither he nor any of the doctors could seem to get to the bottom of it. I could tell they were worried.

Fallon was not for giving up easily though. Having spent close to two decades dreaming about playing for Celtic, he was not about to settle for an association spanning just two matches. But nor did he spend his summer trawling the country in search of specialists and alternative medical options. Instead, he took a path that would be unthinkable for modern day footballers, and was remarkable even at the time.

Rather than check into hospital, Fallon took the boat to Belfast and headed for home. But as Sligo drew near, he diverted from his usual route and took the road north towards County Donegal and his final destination. He was on his way to an island in Lough Derg known as 'St Patrick's Purgatory', a place of pilgrimage where Ireland's patron saint was said to have witnessed a vision of hell. Fallon might not have been able to match that, but foreseeing a future without Celtic and football had been bleak enough. And so it was that that he entrusted everything – his health, his dream and his livelihood – to the same higher power that had comforted St Patrick.

> All I did at Lough Derg was pray and fast. I starved myself for three days in the end. But it was worth it. You never know that your prayers will be answered, but you leave it with God. I was so fortunate. When I came back from that pilgrimage, the ankle injury that was causing me so much bother, which no-one seemed to know how to fix, suddenly felt fine. In fact, after Lough Derg, it never bothered me again.

By mid-September, Fallon was back in the team and showing just why he had been signed. Though six months of physical pain, homesickness and on-field setbacks had left their scars, he felt a turning point had been reached. Had he been reading his beloved Yeats at the time, another of the poet's famous lines would likely have resonated like never before. *"Joy is of the will which labours, which overcomes obstacles, which knows triumph."*

Chapter 6
The Mad Monk

Seeking divine intervention at Lough Derg might seem extraordinary, but it was a course of action that fitted comfortably within its context. This, after all, was a summer in which Fallon had already been serenaded by Bing Crosby and greeted by the Pope. Miracles hardly seemed in short supply.

These unlikely encounters had occurred during a highly unusual close-season tour. Celtic based themselves in mainland Europe for the best part of a month, yet their itinerary included just one match. It was a brutal encounter, too, ill-befitting its friendly title, with opponents Lazio labelled "vicious" by Bobby Collins, who remembered the 0-0 draw as the most violent match of his 25-year career. The animosity at the end was such that Celtic's players and staff left the stadium in fear of attack. It made for a lot of aggravation for what was, in essence, a token gesture.

That Rome trip didn't really have anything to do with football. It was all Bob Kelly's idea. He was a very religious man and, wherever we went in Europe, the first place he would go looking for would be the chapel. So when the Pope declared 1950 as Holy Year, the chairman thought it would be good for the team to go over to experience it all. The players were delighted. The whole experience was tremendous. Everyone loved it, even the non-Catholics.

Because the chairman hated flying, we went by boat to Brussels, and it was on that journey we met Bing Crosby. Bertie and myself heard a rumour he was there, popped our heads into the bar, and John McPhail and Charlie Tully were already having a drink with him. Trust Charlie. Crosby had been over in Scotland playing golf, and he took to us straight away. He wasn't much of a football fan, but we turned him into a Celtic supporter. By the time we got to Brussels, he was looking to find out everything he could about the club. We even had him singing 'I Belong to Glasgow'.

It took Celtic five days to reach their destination, and the conversion of Crosby aboard the SS Royal Albert was just one of many incidents en route. They also travelled home via Dijon and Paris, spending three nights soaking up the French capital's delights without so much as looking at a football. But nowhere came close to Rome. The Celtic party had been guided through the eternal city by Ballieston's Monsignor Flannigan, who arranged a kick-about with the student priests of the Scots college and, more importantly, secured a prime spot inside St Peter's Basilica to meet Pope Pius XII.

It was an event readily attended by all players, regardless of religious affiliation, and they were rewarded with an experience excitedly set out in the official *1950/51 Celtic Football Guide*. "The Celtic club have been the initiators in many things, and in being called out in St Peter's, they rank as the only football club to have that honour. We left St Peter's inspired and thrilled."

That was one of the greatest experiences of my life. I can still remember it as if it was yesterday. The funny thing was that the Pope greeted us in Irish Gaelic. However it had been explained to him, he obviously thought we were all from Ireland. It was just as well I'd paid attention in my Gaelic classes at school. That whole experience, being in Rome, in St Peter's, meeting the Pope, and then coming back via Paris, was just beyond belief to me. I'd never been out of Ireland until a couple of months before and I can't tell you how grateful I felt to Celtic. The club could take only 14 players to Rome and, with me having that bad ankle injury, I wasn't even considering being one of the group. Really, I didn't deserve to go. All I had done for Celtic at that stage was play a couple of games and score an own goal. The club owed me nothing.

As the journey neared its end, Fallon's mind was a tumult, torn between conflicting emotions of joy, gratitude, guilt and worry. Thrilling as this European expedition had been, he fretted about whether injury would prevent him from justifying Celtic's faith and kindness. It was only after Lough Derg, and the improbably quick improvement in his ankle, that the process of repayment could begin. Fortunately, the speed of his return from injury was matched by the rate at which his contribution increased.

Fallon was back in the team by September, a gap of less than four-and-a-half months, and his season began as it would end: with a defensively flawless 1-0 win over Motherwell. The visit to Fir Park arrived three days before an Old Firm derby and, on this occasion, he managed to steer clear of injury to sample the fixture for the first time. The only way in which history repeated itself was in the scoreline: another memorable 3-2 win for Celtic, with Fallon left to revel in the celebrations sparked by Peacock's decisive late goal.

Finally, he had some momentum. And he wasn't merely playing; he was playing well. The early uncertainties had been overcome on the training ground, and everyone was now seeing the player who would remain a first choice for the remainder of his Celtic career. The fans, particularly the diehards, liked what they saw.

In those days, everyone talked about the Jungle at Celtic Park. That was the famous terracing you saw as soon as you came out of the tunnel, and it was the area that all the players focused on. If the boys in there liked you, you were made. If they didn't like you, chances were you wouldn't last long. I was very lucky that, rightly or wrongly, they loved me. And I always appreciated their support. The thing is, the fans aren't stupid; they can see what a player is giving. The ones who come week in, week out know an awful lot more about the game and their club than most people give them credit for. I always told the players who played under Jock and myself to respect that and to make sure those fans had nothing to be unhappy about.

The supporters who watched me would have seen I wasn't a great natural talent. Some players, like Jinky, Charlie Tully, Willie Fernie, are born footballers. Others, like myself, needed to work very hard at it. But I always made sure I did that. There was never a day in training when I gave anything less than my best, and

Bertie and myself would often come back in the afternoon for extra practice. Sometimes it would be more physical work but more often it would be trying to take the ball off Willie, who was a superb dribbler. That helped me find my feet at Celtic. Playing with all these great players added to my game and I liked to think I brought something to the team once I settled down.

I wasn't particularly tall, but I was solid and a strong tackler. I was also a good striker of a ball with both my right and left foot, and my reading of the game was always a strong point. And although I wasn't the most skilful player, I always looked to keep the ball; to make sure that my pass went to a green-and-white shirt. I also think I had the kind of mental strength you need to play for a club like Celtic. Pressure didn't bother me. Once I was out there on the pitch, I shut my mind to everything else and just focused on the game and my direct opponent. If he had a few tricks up his sleeve, I would want to know about them in advance and have an idea of how I was going to handle them. And if he was one of those players who didn't like getting hit – and there were a few of those – you can probably guess what I did to him the first chance I had.

Overplaying the brutality of his game was a favourite joke and method of self-deprecation for Fallon. All the same, there was many a true word spoken in jest, and plenty of witnesses to the Irishman's ability to terrify. Doug Baillie, a former adversary with Rangers and Falkirk who went on to write for the *Sunday Post*, was one of many who described him as "the hardest tackler against whom I ever played".

Team-mates were also left in awe. Billy McNeill was hardly averse to a physical joust, but confessed to having been dainty and half-hearted in comparison to a man he encountered first as fan, then as a colleague and later as a pupil. "I've never played with or against anyone harder," he said. "My big memory of Sean as a player is of watching him clatter folk and then walking away, that big chest all puffed out. Even people standing in the crowd would be wincing. He was always fair and honest, but he must have been a nightmare to play against. I'm glad I didn't have to do it." Others weren't so lucky. As one report a couple of years after his retirement put it: "When Fallon hung up his boots, every winger in the country went back to believing in Santa Claus."

Such uncompromising, unyielding toughness might not have marked him out as a classic Celtic player but, in 1950, it was just what the club needed. Jimmy McGrory's team were mixing occasional brilliance with frequent incompetence and had come to be seen as a soft touch. The contrast could hardly have been starker across the city, where Rangers had built an aura of invincibility on the foundations of their legendary 'Iron Curtain' defence. Had Celtic wondered where they were going wrong, they need only have looked at how the Ibrox club had beaten Hibernian to the 1949/50 title despite scoring just 58 goals to their rivals' 86. It was their meagre tally of 26 goals against that had proved all-important, this in a season in which McGrory's Bhoys conceded 50, more even than the likes of East Fife and Partick Thistle.

The extent of the team's fragility was such that no one player, not even a defender as formidable as Fallon, could inspire a transformation. But the Irishman's acquisition represented a significant step towards at least addressing this crippling Achilles' heel. As early as March 1951, in his first full season, the new boy was the subject of an article in *The Bulletin* under the self-explanatory headline, 'Solves Celtic's Back Problem'. "Right-back has been a problem position for Celtic for several seasons now," the story began, "but the acquisition of the Irishman, Sean Fallon, has removed all anxiety. Since his arrival at Celtic Park last season, Fallon has gradually settled down from his sometimes too-adventurous inclination to become one of the safest tacklers and cleanest kickers in the Scottish game."

The dressing room, too, had been won over. Evidence of the esteem in which he was now held by his team-mates arrived a few months later, when captain John McPhail ascribed to him an astonishing title. "We must pay tribute," he wrote in his newspaper column, "to that stout-hearted stalwart whose motto, 'They shall not pass', meant for us so much. I mean Sean Fallon, the most lion-hearted Celt of all." This high praise was echoed on the terracing, where courage, endeavour and unstinting commitment to the cause quickly established Fallon as a cult hero.

"The fans loved him," remembers Brian Quinn, the former Celtic chairman, who was 15 and a regular match-goer when Fallon broke into the side. "Before he earned the Iron Man nickname, the fans actually called him the Mad Monk, just because he was so utterly fearless. From what I recall, he was a better footballer than he was given credit for. But what distinguished him from other players was his bravery – that willingness to go into challenges almost any other player would shy away from."

Fallon took great pride in being remembered for these attributes and few comments gave this old Irishman greater satisfaction than McNeill's description of him as "the most wholehearted player I've ever seen… brave as a lion". Retrieving an old Ian Paul assessment – "Sean Fallon would be regarded as the most honest player of his generation" – also had him beaming, though he was soon protesting that Peacock and others were just as deserving of this accolade.

Paul, a former *Herald* journalist, had justified his statement by observing that: "No-one was more prepared to give his all – and then some more". For Fallon, that was the very least that should be expected of a professional footballer. He felt equally strongly that honesty should extend to the way in which the game was played, and jealously guarded his reputation for being hard but scrupulously fair.

> I could take the physical stuff and dish it out, but always within the laws. In every game I played, I was able to look my opponent in the eye at the end and shake his hand, knowing I'd played fairly. That was why I never had any bother from referees. I was never sent off in my life and only ever had one talking to from a referee. There was the odd mistimed tackle, naturally, but I even seemed to get away with those. It helped that I got on well with refs. I wouldn't try to kid them, but I'd stay on their good side just by being polite. If I hit a fella hard and didn't come away with the ball, I wouldn't say anything to the player himself but I'd go over to the referee and say, 'Sorry ref, I mistimed that one. Won't happen again'. It always did the trick.
>
> The refs knew I wasn't dirty. I had no time for those kind of players; the kind who would go over the ball looking to hurt you. I got a name for being hard but I always used my shoulder. I never went in with the flat of my boot and I never, ever tried to put an opponent out of the game. I was just a naturally competitive player who enjoyed the physical side of football. That was why I always hated training games. I only knew how to play football one way, and that was to win the ball, whatever it took.

One of the victims of this single-mindedness was a young Clyde winger by the name of Norrie Innes. He would become a great friend of Fallon's, and recalls that the Irishman's approach earned him admirers even among the players whose legs he turned to jelly. "I'll never forget the first time I was tackled by Sean," said Innes. "It felt like my body had cracked from head to toe like a jigsaw puzzle. But immediately he was over making sure that I was all right, and after the game he made a point of coming to check on me again and to wish me well. And it hadn't even been a foul. The tackle was perfect. But that was why Sean was so well liked. There wasn't anyone in Scottish football at that time more popular among his fellow players."

Gratifying as this might have been, Fallon hadn't come to Glasgow to win popularity contests. He desperately wanted to make his mark, to be remembered, and knew the only way to do that was to restore some of Celtic's lost lustre. His vision of the club had, after all, been based largely on listening to the stories and experiences of his father, and he quickly realised that the Celtic he had joined was not the Celtic with which John Fallon had fallen in love.

That legendary inter-war side had been the nation's foremost footballing power, winners of four successive league titles and with a manager, in Willie Maley, at the peak of his powers. Celtic's class of 1950 were, at best, also-rans. Without a major trophy in 12 years, they had even flirted dangerously with the unthinkable – relegation – as recently as a couple of seasons before. Hibernian, who would win the championship in each of the next two years, were now the only credible threat to Rangers' dominance. This was a worrying situation that had been years in the making. Celtic had been stubborn on the issue of 'guest players' during the war, refusing the services of, among others, a young Matt Busby. Spurned by his boyhood heroes, the former Liverpool and Manchester City star went instead to Easter Road and helped lay the foundations for an era which would culminate in the emergence of the 'Famous Five' frontline. Busby's next stop was Old Trafford, where he made Celtic's star player, Jimmy Delaney, his first signing. The mood at Delaney's former employers was probably best summed up by the fans' withering nickname – 'The Five Sorrowful Mysteries' – for the forwards he left behind.

Improvement during Fallon's time at the club would not have been difficult to achieve. But silverware? The omens did not bode well. Never did that goal seem more distant than when the team began 1951 in stunningly inept fashion, losing five league matches in succession. The highlight of this particular January had been snatching a barely deserved 2-2 draw at East Fife in the Scottish Cup, which in itself merely emphasised the extent of the malaise. Yet it was on that freezing afternoon in Methil that a memorable Celtic success story began unfolding.

The Fifers were seen off in the replay, non-league Duns swept aside in the next round and Hearts beaten 2-1 in the last 16. Celtic remained unconvincing and could have lost heavily at Tynecastle but for an inspired performance from goalkeeper George Hunter. "I never saw a display like it in all my life," is how Fallon, decades later, remembered Hunter's masterclass in *Talking with Celtic*. Merited or otherwise, progression allowed the fans to dream. By the time Aberdeen and Raith Rovers were dispatched in the quarter and semi-finals respectively, there was a belief that, surely, an end was now in sight to the gloomiest era in the club's history.

It mattered little that the basis for such conviction did not stand much scrutiny. The faithful chose simply to ignore that final opponents Motherwell were the team in form, and had won 2-1 at Celtic Park in the sides' most recent meeting. Fallon was wary though, and had good reason to be. In direct opposition would be a player he named towards the end of his career as his most feared adversary. "Jinking Johnny Aitkenhead posed many a problem for me," he said at the time. "That dawdling, dandering style of his covered most effectively his subtle change of pace and deceptive 'drag' tricks."

But Fallon and his team-mates, while far from assured of victory, did have one significant advantage. A crowd of 131,943 had turned out to watch the final and, without segregation, those in green and white outnumbered their claret and amber counterparts by 25 to one. It was a show of loyalty that couldn't fail to inspire.

> That was the Celtic support for you. No matter how the team were doing, successful or otherwise, the fans would always be there. It meant so much to the players and I can still remember the roar when we came out of the tunnel. On a day like that, Hampden

could be awesome. For someone like myself, who'd grown up hearing about this famous stadium and 'the Hampden roar', it was a privilege to play there. You felt like pinching yourself. But I knew there was a job to do and that I'd have it tough against Aitkenhead, who always gave me trouble. I decided from the start, 'I'm going to make my presence felt here'. I didn't want to be chasing him about a big pitch like Hampden for 90 minutes, so I went straight in about him, not giving him any time to settle.

It wasn't a great game but we scored a good early goal thanks to John McPhail and managed to see it through. The relief at the end, the delight, was immense. We were so pleased for the club, for ourselves, but most of all for those fans. I was delighted too, because it seemed like half of Sligo had come over to cheer me on that day. My family and so many of my friends were there and I couldn't wait to get back over to Sligo with them to celebrate and show off my Scottish Cup badge.

While home, he would also have read a gushing *Sligo Champion* article in which he was proudly described as having established himself, just one season into his Celtic career, as "one of the top-ranked defenders in Scottish football". Such praise would require justification in the seasons ahead. But with Aitkenhead having been subdued and a clean sheet secured, Fallon had undoubtedly played his part at Hampden – and done so in his own inimitable style. In *Celtic's Greatest Games*, David Potter provided a vivid account. Fallon and fellow full-back Alex Rollo had, he wrote, "kicked everything that came over the halfway line – paper bags, stray dogs, trainers and their own men included. The wind didnae even get by them".

The best-known image of that sunny April afternoon is of Fallon, a picture of bliss, carrying shoulder-high his captain and match-winner, John McPhail. But while photographs often trump words in expressing the sheer ecstasy of such moments, Sean succeeded in finding a description that was both eloquent and emotive. "As I walked off Hampden Park, I felt I had got everything out of life I had ever wanted."

Chapter 7
Political Football

Courting controversy was never Sean Fallon's style. Mixing sport and politics still less so. He was therefore the unlikeliest candidate to be caught in the middle of an almighty Irish row, pitting north against south, and ultimately causing a schism between the two. Yet that was the fate which befell him in the autumn of 1950. Add to the scenario dirty tricks, threats against his family and an ethical dilemma, and it amounted to the most unpleasant experience of his career.

All this fuss and fury emanated from a single letter, sent to the Celtic full-back on September 27. "I have pleasure in informing you," it read, "that you have been selected to play in the international match: Ireland v England." On the face of it, this was sensational news. Fallon, uncapped and barely back in the Celtic team, had been asked to pull on the green jersey and do battle with, among others, the great Stanley Matthews.

There was only one problem. The return address was not in Dublin, but Belfast, and the team calling him up was one of two squabbling over the right to be known as Ireland. This was a tussle dating back to 1921, the year before Fallon was born, when the Football Association of the Irish Free State (FAIFS) split from the Belfast-based Irish Football Association (IFA). An uneasy peace had followed in the intervening decades, with both associations fielding international teams under the banner of Ireland, and each picking players from every part of the island.

During that time, close to 40 players turned out for both the IFA and the FAIFS's successor, the Football Association of Ireland (FAI), including legendary figures such as Johnny Carey. But it could not go on forever. English clubs were becoming increasingly irritated at the demands dual representation placed on their Irish players, and sought an assurance that the associations would "restrict the selection of their players to that area over which they have jurisdiction". That demand was made by the FA in July 1948, just as Fallon was signing for Glenavon. By the following year, Ireland had shed its status as a dominion of the British Empire, and both associations were committed to participating in the 1950 World Cup qualifiers. FIFA, faced with players representing two different teams in the same competition, was forced into action.

The outcome was inevitable, with the IFA informed that it could no longer select players born south of the border without the FAI's consent. That should have been that, and the Belfast authorities – though still clinging to the title of Ireland – adhered to FIFA's directive for their opening two matches of the World Cup qualifiers. Yet all it took were two heavy defeats, 8-2 and 9-2 against Scotland and England respectively, to bring about a turning back of the clock. For the visit to Wales in March 1950, Northern Ireland called up and fielded a quartet of southern players.

The FAI reacted furiously. Motions were tabled requiring that players sign undertakings not to represent other associations and threatening bans on those tempted to do so. Ultimately, everyone fell into line. Or almost everyone. Fallon, having not been capped by mid-1950, was not required to nail his colours the mast. That would happen if and when he was picked, and would only become a problem in the interim if the IFA risked the wrath of the football community by calling him up first. Even then, Fallon would still need to accept. In Dublin, each scenario must have been considered equally improbable. However, in dismissing the possibility, they reckoned without the esteem Fallon had gathered during his time at Glenavon, and his gratitude towards those in the north. They also failed to take into account that both parties had already committed a lesser act of rebellion.

The England match caused all the uproar, but what people didn't seem to realise was that I'd already played for Northern Ireland by then. I was the last player from the south to do so in fact. It had been a friendly match earlier that same September at Windsor Park against the British Army, who had John Charles in their team. It wasn't an official match so I wasn't given a cap for it, but when they asked if I would play in it I said I would be more than happy to. I'd been treated very well in the north and been picked for the Irish League. The fact was, they'd shown faith in me much earlier than the people in the south. There was also the fact that two of my best friends, Bertie [Peacock] and Charlie [Tully], played for the north, as did my old pal from Glenavon, Wilbur Cush. He was actually in the team when I played against the British Army and, although I was the only southerner that day, everyone made me feel very welcome. Playing against Charles was a thrill too. What a great player he was. That said, the main thing I remember about playing against him is that he caught me with an elbow, just below my heart. I was in agony. I could hardly breathe for about 20 minutes.

I must have done well enough though, because the IFA asked me afterwards if I would play in the match against England. 'Certainly,' I told them. 'I'd be delighted to.' They were talking about me being up against Stanley Matthews and, again, that was all very exciting. I didn't see what the problem would be. Johnny Carey, Con Martin and all the others had played for the north, and I felt that it could even do a bit of good to have the two sides mixing and coming together. The letter the IFA sent through was basically just confirming what we'd already spoken about and what I'd agreed to. But that was when the politics started. There was a family, the Cunninghams, who ran Shamrock Rovers and were very influential within the FAI. Joe Cunningham sent me a letter, telling me that under no circumstances was I to play for the north. Then he phoned me to say the same thing. Both times, I told him: 'I'll be playing. I've given my word and I'll be playing.'

I would have played too, but then they started bringing my dad into it. I was told that they would create bother for him politically, stir things up, if I went ahead and played. I spoke to my dad about it and he told me that I had to play and not to worry about him. Bob Kelly was very supportive and said that he and Celtic would back me all the way. But then I got word from Sligo that there had been a threat made against my family; that their house would be burned down if I played for the north. My dad was still telling me to play, not to let the hoodlums have their way. 'But I'm not there,' I told him. 'It's not me who'll be facing the consequences'. In the end, I felt I had to pull out. I felt terrible though. I knew I had let the people in the north down after giving them my word I would play. It was one of the hardest decisions I ever had to make and I still wonder if I did the right thing. But can you imagine if I'd gone ahead regardless and some headcase had carried out that threat? I couldn't have lived with myself. The whole thing left a very bitter taste.

Fallon wasn't the only one who had trouble forgiving and forgetting those responsible. His refusal represented a public humiliation for the IFA, who were incensed by the tactics of their counterparts in the south. It didn't help that the Irish media framed Fallon's reluctant withdrawal as a snub. The *Sligo Champion* made a great deal of Fallon's "patriotic action", reporting that it had represented "a severe rebuff" to Belfast and caused "a major sensation" throughout the game. The dispute also made headlines on the other side of the Irish Sea, where the *Daily Record* predicted – correctly – that the IFA would break off relations with the FAI and cancel all inter-league matches. The irony is that even now, 63 years on, bickering continues between the associations over issues of eligibility, with no mutually acceptable compromise in sight. The obvious solution has been the one continually spurned.

> There should have been an all-Ireland team. That would have solved a lot of problems and it might even have made things easier off the park too. The rugby boys have it right. It's a small island and you need all the players you can pick from. Football could have gone exactly the same way as rugby and the reason it didn't, as far as I'm concerned, was down to the committee men at the FAI and the IFA. It wasn't about the team itself; it was about not wanting to go from two committees to one and them losing their privileges and foreign trips. That's why the situation has stayed as it is for so long, and it's real a pity. Most of the players would have been in favour, I'm sure of that. I know I would have loved to have played alongside Bertie and Charlie in an all-Ireland team.

Even better would have been to line up beside these fellow Celts at a World Cup. Yet that was a stage which, unlike Peacock – who made it all the way to the quarter-finals in 1958 – Fallon never graced. Even with their newly imposed restrictions, Northern Ireland remained the stronger and better organised of the island's national teams for decades, qualifying for three World Cups before the Republic reached their first. But Fallon, having spent so long doubting his ability to make it at the top level, was simply grateful for any international career at all. And wary though he was of the FAI hierarchy, there was no prospect of him rejecting their advances.

> Not at all. Every boy dreams of their country, and I always wanted to play for the south in any case. I was Sligo born and bred, so it was only natural. It was just that the north asked me first, and I didn't like being told that I couldn't do what other players had been doing for years. But I wasn't going to let that situation spoil things for me when I eventually did get the call from the FAI. Any time I walked out with that shirt on, my chest would be puffing out with pride. The whole of Sligo seemed to come down for those games at Dalymount Park, and they could be great occasions. The Irish team was pretty poorly organised back then but we had some good players. Just not enough of them to qualify for a World Cup, sadly.

It took just a month-and-a-half after his aborted call-up for Northern Ireland for Fallon to win the first of his eight caps. A memorable debut it was too, with the Irish coming from two goals down to claim a well-earned draw with Norway. He had travelled as the team's 12th man, but a late injury to Con Martin handed him the chance to line up alongside Carey, his former tutor. Fortunately, he succeeded in making a considerably better first impression than he had at Celtic. Among those impressed was the *Irish Independent's* W.P. Murphy, who wrote of having "liked newcomer Fallon, a trenchant tackler and strong kicker". Those attributes weren't sufficient to keep him in the team for the Republic's next two matches, but Sean – by now a Scottish Cup winner – was recalled for the visit of West Germany in October 1951. It was to be the highlight of his international career.

> The Germans were a great side. They were on their way to winning the next World Cup and no-one gave us a prayer. But

we just rolled up our sleeves, got in about them, and showed that old Irish spirit. It was a great game, the best I ever played in for Ireland, and we ended up winning 3-2. I took a sore one from their keeper – he'd caught me when I'd tried to charge him, as you were allowed to in those days – but all that pain disappeared when the final whistle went. The Germans actually thought they'd equalised from a corner, but it turned out the referee had blown the final whistle while the ball was in the air. It was bedlam at the end. All the fans were spilling on to the pitch and it was a pleasure to be part of it all.

Fallon had again played his part, earning fresh acclaim for a diligent man-marking job on the German winger, Richard Herrmann. Yet his great hope – that the victory would signal the beginning of an exciting new era – was quickly dashed. The full-back's next three matches for his country, all between May and June of 1952, were lost by an aggregate score of 15-0. However, it was during this humbling three-match series in Austria, Spain and Germany that he first encountered Frank O'Farrell. The West Ham United wing-half, best known for a short-lived spell as Sir Matt Busby's successor at Manchester United, would become his closest ally in a clique-ridden camp.

We found that the Dublin boys tended to keep to themselves, city boys together. A few of them seemed to think they were head and shoulders above the rest of us. With Frank being a Cork man and another 'outsider', we palled around together during those trips away. It was very clannish in those days and we felt that there was a definite Dublin bias. It was folk from the Dublin clubs, Shamrock Rovers in particular, who ran the association at that time, so they picked their own boys. They had too big an influence as far as I was concerned.

The fact that, to this day, Shamrock Rovers have supplied more players to the national team than any other club suggests this was not merely small-town paranoia. With no manager in place and the selection committee all-powerful, objectivity was far from guaranteed. O'Farrell, still going strong at 85, remains convinced of its impact. "I was capped only nine times, and Sean eight. When you think that we were both playing regularly for top club sides, that's a pretty disappointing total. Sean was certainly deserving of more recognition. My memory is of him always geeing up and encouraging those around him; he was a great leader of men. He was one of those great competitors, an excellent tackler who also used and distributed the ball very well. That made him a natural at full-back. I could never understand why Ireland often played him at centre-forward." Fallon shared this sense of bemusement. And yet it was in attack, where he won three of his eight caps, that he enjoyed his most memorable moment in a green shirt.

> The France game? That was something. They came to Dublin calling themselves the unofficial European champions and they had the great Raymond Kopa in their team. But we managed to get a 1-1 draw, and I scored our goal. Ireland had me up at centre-forward to unsettle the French defence and keeper, and that was exactly what I tried to do.
>
> The papers said I was like a battering ram that day and I could believe it because, my God, I was sore all over when I came off. I think they had a few bruises too. The keeper wasn't happy with the attention I was giving him, I know that. At that time you could pressure and challenge keepers more, knock them off guard with your shoulder. And he got annoyed with me, had a kick and grabbed me by the throat. I didn't care, though. I never minded getting a bit of that kind of rough stuff as long as I was helping my team.
>
> That was a great day and I was delighted that my dad and all my family were down to see it all. There was a funny moment in Jury's Hotel later, during the official reception. Someone came up to us, shook my father by the hand and congratulated him for 'scoring such a grand goal'. I don't know how old they thought I was. Maybe they heard I had been lying about my age.

Credit was at least apportioned correctly in the media, with Ireland's makeshift striker making headlines on both sides of the Irish Sea. 'Fallon found flaws in Wonder French XI' was the headline in the tabloid *Daily Sketch*, whose correspondent, John Graydon, was effusive in his praise. "With a speedy and strong centre-forward, such as Celtic's Sean Fallon proved himself to be, the Frenchmen always took their eye off the ball and waited, worry written all over their faces, for the arrival of the broad-shouldered

Fallon among them. Their concern seemed to be not clearing the ball, but getting out of the way of the husky Eire leader." The *Daily Record*, meanwhile, wrote that the "fiery Celt" had been a "terror", sharing Graydon's view of the visiting defence "fearfully watching Fallon and not the ball". The boy from Sligo was the toast of Ireland. And yet it was around this time, during a visit to his homeland, that he came perilously close to making the most powerful of enemies.

I was never much of a gambler, but I was quite keen on the horse racing. One time, Bertie [Peacock] and myself decided to go back to Ireland for a big race. As it happened, Eamon de Valera, the famous Irish President – who was Taoiseach at that time – was there and came over to speak to us. While we were chatting about Celtic and all sorts, he was called away by one of his entourage, so he asked if we would look after his little grandson while he was gone. And didn't we somehow manage to lose this grandson of his. The racecourse was packed and I can't tell you how panicked we were. We couldn't find the wee fella for quite a while – it seemed like hours – and we're thinking, 'This is us. We're going to end up in the jail'. Fortunately, he finally turned up, absolutely fine. I don't know if I've ever been so relieved in all my life.

A potential disaster having been averted, Fallon began looking forward to his next international outing and the beginning of Ireland's 1954 World Cup qualifying campaign. He was met by silence. Despite his heroics against France and ever-rising status at Celtic, he found himself suddenly and inexplicably shunned by the national selectors. Another three years would pass before he was recalled, and his comeback was to double as his curtain call.

Johnny Carey was manager by then, but he didn't have much of a say. None of the managers did. There was too much power in the hands of the selection committee, guys who'd never kicked a ball in their lives. That wasn't right, and the team suffered because of it. My card was marked because I had a go at one of the committee members after a match in Germany [a 2-1 defeat in which Fallon had scored]. He'd come away with something stupid to one of the younger players, having a go at him for swapping his jerseys, and I had a go back to speak up for the lad. The FAI were miserable back then and wouldn't allow us to swap our jerseys after matches. They wanted them back to wash and keep on reusing.

I wasn't normally one for talking back or causing trouble, and I don't think I had a single run-in with any of my club managers or chairmen. But the way those selectors dealt with things was beyond a joke. I played on for a few years with Celtic after that but I never got a sniff in the national team. That was me out of the picture. It was disappointing, of course, because I loved playing for Ireland. But what can you do? I knew I'd done my best in every match I'd played and I couldn't have been more proud to pull on that jersey.

Chapter 8
Mr Kelly

"We have the players. But it appears we haven't got a team." The words of Bob Kelly in 1949 were uttered as an analysis of the season just passed. Little did he know they would be ringing true for the next decade-and-a-half, and that he would be the man held responsible. The following summer, while Fallon was focused on Rome, Lough Derg and his troublesome ankle, the chairman was to be found shaping Celtic's destiny. He was doing so by allowing two of that era's great football minds to slip through his fingers.

The consequences of that catastrophic summer would permeate Sean's Celtic career. There would be flashes throughout the 1950s of what could – and should – have been. But these served merely to tease; to show what was possible and then snatch it away. It was to be a decade of missed opportunities and false dawns. The 1951 Scottish Cup final was just the first of many. Brian Quinn, who was among the fans at Hampden that day, remembers the excited consensus that "a rebirth" had been witnessed. When Celtic returned from a memorable pre-season tour of America, Glasgow's Central Station was packed with cheering fans. Fallon and his team-mates needed a police escort to squeeze their way through the sea of adulation.

That exalted team ended the following season ninth in the table, having won just a third of their league fixtures. The Scottish Cup, the great symbol of revival, had been surrendered in the meekest of fashion, with a 2-1 defeat at Third Lanark in the opening round. Most depressing of all was the knowledge that this was not an exception to the rule. It was the rule. Celtic had been seventh in 1950/51 and would finish eighth in 1952/53. Winning the odd cup did not alter the fact that this once-dominant club were now an established mid-table outfit. Had Fallon taken stock, he would have found that, astonishingly, more league matches had been lost than won in each of his first three full seasons.

Yet it wasn't only the supporters who had experienced this surge of optimism in the spring and summer of 1951. The players felt it too, and so did Jimmy McGrory. The manager's report in the *Celtic Football Guide*, normally a gloomy catalogue of apologies and half-hearted excuses, had a decidedly bullish tone. "I won't say that we have a team to compare with the giants of the past," he wrote, "but give these lads a chance, I am sure they will go places. They have the ability, stamina, youth, enthusiasm and above all the real old Celtic spirit, and I for one predict that in a year or two we will have a team that will not only compare with those in the past but do even greater deeds."

That statement would appear ludicrous in the harsh light of the two seasons that followed. But McGrory was no fool. He knew the stuff of successful teams and realised that with the raw talent of Tully and Fernie, the industry of Peacock and Collins, the spirit of Fallon and Evans, Celtic should have been a match for anyone. And, at times, they were. It was the infrequency of those moments that was intolerable, and McGrory – uncomfortable as it was to admit – was part of the problem.

> Everyone liked Mr McGrory. He was a very modest man, especially when you consider that he had been such a magnificent player. You would never hear him boasting or see him angry. As a manager, though, he was too nice. He hated to hurt anyone, and in that job you sometimes need to be hard on people who take advantage of you. Some players ended up taking it too easy because of his good nature. All the same, even with his temperament, I thought he could have been a better manager than he was. The main problem for me was that he didn't get involved enough. You wouldn't see him at all during the week at training. Then on Saturday he wouldn't say a great deal. There

was nothing about tactics or organisation; that was something we had to discuss among ourselves. Before the game he would say something like, 'It's going to be a hard game today, lads'. Then nothing afterwards. There wouldn't be any advice on how to do things better.

I always felt that was a shame, because he had so much experience to pass on. When I was played at centre-forward, I felt like a fish out of water and I always thought that he, having been one of the best centre-forwards there had ever been, could have helped me a lot. I knew I would never be as good as him, but I was always ready to learn. But he never thought to take me aside and point me in the right direction. I do remember one time when he did come on to the pitch during a training session. He was in his suit and the ball was crossed in his direction. He got his head on to it and it went into the net like a bullet. Everyone just stood there, mouths open. I felt like applauding. And I thought, 'If only he would come out here more often and teach us how to do that'. But he didn't. It just wasn't the way he did things.

Fallon's is one of the more sympathetic critiques of McGrory's management. Plenty of others didn't see the unrealised coaching potential in Celtic's greatest goalscorer, and Bob Kelly – in his 1971 book, *Celtic* – delivered the most stunning assessment of all. "He would never in my opinion have been an outstanding success as a manager," wrote the Celtic chairman. "In a few words, he was too modest and gentlemanly to have made a real success of the job."

The sentiments expressed were not unique or particularly contentious. What made Kelly's evaluation so remarkable was that he had been the man keeping McGrory in his post for the best part of two decades. Had it taken him until 1965 to realise that this great Celt was ill-suited to the job of manager? Far from it. All signs point to Kelly having arrived at that realisation by April of 1948, the month in which his first season as chairman nearly culminated in relegation. Celtic's top-flight status was in jeopardy until the last game of the season, when they travelled to fourth-placed Dundee needing a win to be assured of staying up. "I knew inwardly that if Celtic lost I would have to resign," McGrory said in his biography, *A Lifetime in Paradise.*

But Celtic won 3-2 and the manager kept his job. Officially at least. A significant change took place nonetheless, and John

McPhail was among several players to notice it. "Just about that period, I think Jimmy let go of the reins," McPhail told Jim Craig in *A Lion Looks Back*. "He felt he hadn't been making good choices. I liked the old chap enormously, but he wasn't a dominant figure and, without any great fuss or announcement, Bob gradually took control." It had been a bloodless coup, but a coup all the same. Kelly had made up his mind on McGrory, but rather than change the manager, he instead changed the management structure. From now on, he would be in charge. It was a move that would define the next 17 years of Celtic's history.

Fallon would rightly point out that, like everything Kelly did, this decision was taken with the best of intentions. "Of one thing was I certain," the chairman later reflected. "We would never again, whatever the circumstances, reach the depths of 1948." But Kelly, while undoubtedly a more imposing personality than McGrory, was no football visionary. On all things Celtic, he was a hopeless romantic. As the son of James Kelly, the club's first captain, he considered himself to be the guardian of its traditions. On the field, that meant a cast-iron commitment to gentlemanly conduct and all-out attack. In *Celtic*, he wrote proudly of having "turned aside from win-at-any-price tactics". Bonuses were even paid for defeats when he deemed the players to have shown the virtues he prized above all others: fair play, sportsmanship and a fierce passion for the club.

But the outcome of treating results as secondary was inevitable. Rangers, for whom winning was everything, strengthened their grip on Scotland's silverware. Players who should have been considered prize assets – Bobby Collins, Bertie Auld and Paddy Crerand to name but three – fell foul of Kelly for flashes of temper and displays of devilment. Asked what the biggest change had been after Jock Stein's appointment, Auld replied: "Being given the chance to compete." He added: "Before, if you were a naughty boy and won the ball and went through someone, you weren't appreciated at higher levels at Celtic Park." Fallon, too, felt uncomfortable with Kelly at the controls.

The chairman was very set in his ways. He was a football man through and through, and a great Celtic man. No-one could ever say otherwise. But he liked to pick the team. Although that was quite common with chairmen back then, it wasn't a good way to do things. Mr Kelly had idolised Jimmy McGrory as a player, but he was the stronger of the two characters and that meant he ended up being in charge of almost everything at Celtic Park. It wasn't out of badness, you understand; he thought he was doing what was best for Celtic. He wasn't always right though. He could have done with being more practical. The Willie Goldie incident has become well known in that respect. It wasn't that Bob didn't know his football; he just thought so much of people who loved the club as much as he did.

The case of Willie Goldie is not so much well known as infamous. To Kelly's critics, it encapsulated his reign. Mike Jackson, a player at the time, takes up the story: "We were on our way to a game at Airdrie and as we got near the ground, we spotted Willie, who was reserve team goalie, with his Celtic scarf on, walking to the match with his pals. So we're battering the window, shouting on him, and Bob turns round from his seat at the front and asks what's going on. When we told him, he shouted: 'Stop the bus! Get him on. That's wonderful, a young lad like that going to see the Celtic.' Willie was delighted – he thought he was getting a lift. Then we get to the game – and he's playing!" Unfortunately for Celtic, Goldie had been out dancing until 3am that morning, thinking – not unreasonably – that he had a day off ahead. Airdrie went on to win 2-0, with both goals attributable to goalkeeping errors. Goldie never played for Celtic again.

The chairman hadn't seen the reality; only the potential fairy tale of a player arriving in a scarf and leaving as a hero. It was by this quixotic logic that he would thrust raw youngsters into Old Firm matches and cup finals, and play specialists – Fallon among them – in the unlikeliest of positions. He would cling to the rare successes this approach yielded, ignoring the frequent failures.

Kelly remains the most divisive figure in Celtic's history. For every supporter or former player scathing in their criticism, there will be another lavish in their praise. "His arrogance in determining every aspect of Celtic's policy bordered on the pathological," was the forthright opinion of Tom Campbell and David Potter, both eminent club historians, in *Jock Stein, the Celtic Years*. "I always feel the chairman was never really given the credit he deserved for the success of the club," was the very different view taken by Bertie Peacock. Even McGrory, who had more reason than anyone to harbour ill will towards Kelly, readily sang his praises. "If you knew him like I did, you could have nothing but respect for him," he said in *A Lifetime in Paradise*. "He was never wealthy because he gave so much to charity. Principles meant everything to him."

This was the other side to Bob Kelly. This was the man who made and steadfastly stuck to a commitment that, every year, Celtic would pay more to charity than to directors and shareholders. It was this same man who, in 1967, arranged for representatives of the Marist Brothers to be the club's guests in Lisbon. The unyielding principles that rendered Kelly too idealistic to be an effective de facto manager made him an upright and highly-respected administrator.

When the Soviet Union invaded Czechoslovakia in 1968, he was the first to demand that UEFA act. And when Celtic came under extraordinary pressure from the SFA to lower the Irish tricolour, they had a man able to withstand it. As Archie Macpherson wrote of Kelly: "It would be erroneous to see him as simply the chairman of the club. He was also spokesman for a community. He championed Celtic causes when strong prejudicial tides occasionally turned against them and might have swamped them had his stern advocacy not been readily available." This was the Kelly whom Fallon respected and admired.

Bob Kelly fought Celtic's corner everywhere he went. No-one was better at that. He was also one of the most honest men you could meet. He might not always have been popular, but he always did what he thought was right and never did anything crooked or underhand. He was respected throughout Scotland, and he sorted out the SFA back when they tried to make Celtic take down the flag. That was his finest hour as far as I was concerned.

It was a ridiculous thing to demand of us, and the players were all very proud of the fact he fought it and won. It gave everyone in the club a big lift at the time. I remember him telling me that he would close Celtic Park rather than take down the flag. And I'm sure he meant it. There was even talk that we would play Gaelic games rather than soccer if the SFA didn't back down. I might have been a useful player for that Gaelic Celtic if it had ever happened. But I was delighted that the chairman stood his ground. It proved what an important figure he was for the club.

The only problem, at least until Jock came in, was that he tried to do too much. He didn't have any children, so Celtic became his family. But the main reason for the way he was at Celtic was that Bob would have loved to have been a player himself. I'm sure that him taking such an central role in everything at the club back then, especially with the team, was his way of making up for the fact he hadn't been able to achieve that ambition.

By the time he died, Kelly was 'Sir Robert', and remains to this day the most famous chairman in Celtic's history. He would also surely be the most beloved had he possessed, before 1965, a manager strong enough to curb his autocratic tendencies, and skilful enough to coach a successful team. It took Stein, emboldened by his spells at Dunfermline and Hibernian, to achieve the former. Yet the latter had been within Celtic's grasp a great deal earlier. After all, when Fallon arrived, training was led by a man described by Len Shackleton as "the greatest coach football has ever known".

Jimmy Hogan had been appointed during that quiet revolution of 1948, and arrived with a CV like no other. He would become best known for his work in Hungary, having established the revolutionary style of football that stunned England and the wider football world in 1953. But he was also a hero in Austria, where he forged the great 'Wunderteam' of the 1930s with Hugo Meisl, and in the Netherlands, Switzerland and Germany. Helmut Schon, who led the West Germans to victory in the 1974 World Cup, described his former mentor as "the shining example of the coaching profession". The DFB said he had been "the father of modern football in Germany".

Yet the Englishman was a prophet without honour in his own country, where arrogance and insularity reigned. Suggesting a shift of emphasis towards passing, movement, control and teamwork, and away from Britain's obsession with strength, stamina and individuality, had been bad enough. Warning, as he did from the 1920s onwards, that 'the continentals' would soon surpass the game's self-proclaimed masters made him a target of ridicule. Hogan saw the same tired mantras being repeated and shook his head. He watched players running endlessly round a track, not a ball in sight, and explained why it was madness. He witnessed those same players eat and drink what they pleased, and preached the importance of diet.

He was a true pioneer, decades ahead of his time. He was someone who could educate and inspire, coach and cajole. He was well of aware of it too, even signing his autographs, 'Jimmy Hogan – The World's No.1 Coach'. He was, in short, just what Celtic required.

> Jimmy was coaching the team when I first arrived at Celtic, and he impressed me greatly. It was obvious from the start that he was someone who really loved his football and knew the game inside-out. Bob Kelly was picking the team but Jimmy was doing all the work on the training ground and behind the scenes. He wanted us to play perfect football if that was possible. But like any great coach, he never asked anyone to do anything beyond their capabilities. It was all about teamwork, and about everyone using their individual abilities for the benefit of the team. He used to emphasise the fact it takes 11 players to make a good side, but that individuals within that 11 could inspire those around them to improve.
>
> He was a proper football man with a lot of exciting ideas about the game. If you look at the history of the great teams back then – Hungary, Austria, Germany – Jimmy Hogan was influential in them all. And that was in the days before foreign travel became so common. Players and coaches moving between countries was very rare, so Jimmy was something exceptional. He was a fair age when he came to us but his enthusiasm was incredible. The coaching was much better that what I had been used to, and I enjoyed it thoroughly. Most of all, I felt he would make me a better player.

Fallon never had the chance to find out. By the time his trip to Lough Derg had worked its magic, Hogan was gone. He was 67 by that time but in good health and in no mood to retire. He would live until 91, and went on to work for several years at Aston Villa, where a young Ron Atkinson was among those who cited him as a major influence. The fact that he had lasted just two seasons in Glasgow said more about Celtic than it did about Hogan.

There had been no desire on his part to leave. A devout Catholic – he would sprinkle holy water on the players before matches – Hogan felt a natural affinity with Celtic, telling the *Daily Record* that joining the club "felt like coming home". But he admitted in that same interview to having detected suspicion among certain players, "as if each and every one was saying 'what can this old codger show us?'" And herein lay the problem.

John Paton, who was one of his disciples, recalled the difficulties Hogan endured in *Prophet or Traitor? The Jimmy Hogan Story*. "What stuck in my mind was his remark one day that the club didn't need a groundsman because, 'We'll cut the grass with the ball'. The senior players laughed, but he was trying to get everyone into the mentality of keeping it on the floor, moving it quickly, making it simple and, when not in possession, getting into position... The problem was the players didn't have the discipline to take it in... The attitude to Jimmy was, 'You're going to teach me how to play? I can play this game'. But could they?" The answer to that could be measured in trophies. The unheralded departure in 1950 of an unappreciated giant was a damning indictment of the culture pervading Celtic Park.

> Most of the players respected Jimmy for what he had achieved. I know I did. But it's true that some of the more experienced lads didn't buy into what he was trying to teach us, mainly because they thought they didn't need to be taught. That was a pity because you can always learn and Jimmy had so much experience to pass on.

There was a fitting postscript to the shabby treatment of Hogan. It came three years later, when he was at Wembley to see Hungary inflict a famously stylish and emphatic 6-3 win on England. Also in the crowd that day were the Celtic players, having been dispatched by Kelly with the ironic purpose of broadening their football horizons. They watched, wide-eyed, as the Magyars showcased a new and superior way of playing. Later, they read Gustav Sebes, Hungary's coach, explain the secret behind his team's revolutionary approach. "We played football as Jimmy Hogan taught us," he said. "When our football history is told, his name should be written in gold letters." Perhaps it was then that the penny finally dropped. But by then, of course, it was too late.

In spite of the sneering scepticism of senior players, Hogan had succeeded in adding style and sophistication to Celtic's play. According to Tom Campbell: "The signs of his arrival were evident in various ways on the field: defenders trying to pass the ball, the use of the goalkeeper to start attacks, innovations at free-kicks, and a dramatic improvement in the play of Bobby Evans. After he left, Celtic began to deteriorate again."

It didn't help that, within weeks of Hogan's departure, a potential replacement also bade farewell. Chic Geatons, who had been coaching the reserves, tendered his resignation, having lost patience with Kelly's running of the club. "It is all wrong that the chairman should take over so much managerial direction," he later explained in the *Weekly News*. "The chairman should chair the directors, the directors should direct and the manager should manage." Few could fault his logic, but nothing changed. Not until Stein, at least. A more immediate problem, with Geatons and Hogan gone – and Kelly seemingly disinclined to recruit a replacement – was the gaping void left on the training ground.

> Alex Dowdells was our trainer after Jimmy Hogan left, but he was more of a physio than a coach. He did a lot for the players, but there was very little if anything in the way of actual coaching. He was just there to keep us fit, get us running and make sure that we ticked over from Saturday to Saturday. The quality of the sessions definitely went downhill and some players began easing off. That wasn't Alex's fault – it wasn't his speciality, after all – but it was a shame not to have someone like Jimmy still around the club. There was a lot of talent at the club, but someone to organise us and get us playing as a team was the one thing we always lacked.

The result was wasted potential which could have been realised had their chairman not declined to pursue Matt Busby. The future Sir Matt was, by this time, already Manchester United manager. He was, though, a Celtic supporter, and the *Daily Record's* 'Waverley' reported in 1949 and again in 1950 that he had intimated his desire to return to Scotland. Desmond White, then club secretary, felt sufficiently confident of securing Busby as manager to submit the appointment to the board. In doing so, he seemed to be presenting Kelly with a silver bullet; a ready-made solution to the team's many problems.

"But Bob would have none of it," explained Lisbon Lion and Celtic historian, Jim Craig. "He was very angry about the idea. He even ended up falling out with his brother over the issue because David Kelly had taken Desmond White's side. Bob and David never spoke again." Fallon, decades later, was left to ponder what might have been.

> The Matt Busby thing is amazing to me because I hadn't long joined Celtic at that stage and had no idea any of this was going on. It would have been interesting if the chairman had gone for it because Busby was a great figure. He had been one of the first to promote the idea of a manager controlling everything on the football side: signings, coaching, picking the team. He ruled the roost down at Manchester United and it became obvious from his success that if you had a football man in the manager's job who knew the game and did his job well, you were best to leave him in charge. We could definitely have done with that kind of set-up at Celtic.
>
> I often felt if we'd had a manager like Busby, or Jock, when I was playing, that team could have achieved so much more. We definitely should have gone on to win a lot more trophies than we did. We had some brilliant individuals, but they played as individuals at times. Rangers were definitely more of a team than we were. What we needed was someone to really organise us because Mr McGrory – lovely man though he was – just wasn't cut out to do that. Busby could have done it. I can only imagine he would have been a star at Celtic if they'd brought him in.

No-one will ever know for sure. Nor will we ever discover whether Kelly's intransigence on the issue emanated from loyalty to McGrory, or his desire to retain control of team matters. Either way, losing a ground-breaking coach and rejecting one of the game's great managers did not make for an auspicious start to the '50s.

But Celtic's chairman was to be afforded one final shot at redemption. Within 18 months of spurning two potential saviours, he was presented with another. For Kelly and Celtic, it would be third time lucky. The Stein years were beckoning.

Chapter 9
Jock Who?

"What the hell have they brought you in for?"

This was how the most revered figure in Celtic's history was welcomed to the club. There was no playful nudge. No knowing wink. Jimmy Mallan, a tough and long-serving defender, was deadly serious. What's more, he was only saying what everyone else was thinking.

Celtic were 12ᵗʰ in the league table when Jock Stein arrived in December 1951. They had taken just 10 points from their opening 11 matches, raising fears of another relegation battle. What the fans craved was an injection of quality; star quality preferably. What they were presented with was a journeyman centre-half from non-league Llanelli. As Kelly acknowledged years later: "The club was almost boycotted because I bought Stein."

The signing baffled not only Mallan and the Celtic support, but Stein himself. "Celtic, after me? It was laughable," was his recollection of hearing of the club's interest. Even the player's father was incredulous, considering his son to have found his level in the lower reaches of the game. Fallon, in fact, was one of the few not to be found asking: Why? But he did have one question: Who?

I had never even heard of Jock Stein. I was told he had played for Albion Rovers but I honestly had no idea who he was at that stage. I reserved judgment for that reason, but a few of the players definitely weren't happy about the signing. Jock was seen as having no pedigree whatsoever. Plus, he was going on 30, so folk thought he was washed up. Charlie was one of the worst. 'Him? That old fella could be my grandfather,' he'd say. The fans were exactly the same. Everyone wrote Jock off before they'd even seen him play. I thought he at least deserved a chance to prove himself. But I can't say I was excited by him coming to the club. No-one was.

I can still remember the day he arrived at Celtic Park and was taken to the reserve team dressing room. I actually think that was what Bob Kelly had in mind for him. We had four or five centre-halves already at the club at that time, so Jock was coming in – as I understood it – to help develop the young players by bringing a bit of experience to the reserves. Even so, it was seen as an unusual signing. You have to give credit to the people in charge for knowing better than everyone else.

The man responsible was well known to Fallon. Jimmy Gribben might have been reserve team coach, but he was an influential and respected figure among the first-team players. His knowledge of the Scottish game was all-encompassing – hence his memories of Stein – and, unlike McGrory, he would counsel players on areas for improvement. "Jimmy's advice to me was always the same," Sean recalled. "'Play with more brain and less brawn'. He was quite right." Stein, meanwhile, described Gribben as "my mentor", and made a point of taking the European Cup directly to the former Bo'ness player's boot-room on returning from Lisbon.

This gratitude was well merited. Having been a miner and part-time footballer before leaving for Wales, Stein fully expected that he would be returning to more of the same. It was Gribben who kept him out of the pits and, with the help of one or two others, Fallon included, set him on a course towards fame and glory. Yet Sean's understanding of the signing had been correct. Years later, Kelly confirmed that neither he nor Gribben expected Stein to feature in the first team. However, that plan had to be rewritten within a week of his arrival, when three defenders – Mallan among them – were sidelined by injury.

Jock made sure he took that chance, and once he got himself

in the team he never looked back. The thing is, people underestimated him as a player. I honestly thought he was a great centre-half. The fans might not have seen it but what impressed me most about him was his reading of the game. I liked him from the start, both as a player and as a person. There was no nonsense about Jock. He was down-to-earth, straightforward; a good professional who wanted to train well and was serious about his football. I always admired those kinds of qualities, and I like to think I had them myself. So Jock and I hit it off right away.

Having not been expected to make a single appearance, Stein went on to rack up 148. Fallon was alongside him for most of those, and joked that their on-field relationship was based on a simple understanding: "Anyone he didn't kick, I did." There was, of course, a great deal more subtlety involved. With no direction from the manager, a small group of the more diligent and forward-thinking Celtic players began formulating tactics in private. At the heart of discussions were Stein and Fallon. A strategic partnership had formed.

"Sean and my dad were interested not just in going out to play, but in thinking how the team should play," said George Stein, Jock's only son. "Celtic didn't have a great deal of leadership in that particular area and it was only really my dad and Sean, along with one or two others, who were focused on doing something constructive. The two of them spent a lot of time together even at that stage, talking about how things could be changed and improved."

We'd always get together in Ferrari's restaurant at the top of Buchanan Street. All the Celtic players would go there for lunch and, afterwards, Jock, Bertie and myself would sit there for hours, talking football. We were a bit of a trio back then, and would work on moves and systems for our area of the park. We'd also talk about games coming up and any players we felt were dangerous and could steal a goal. It all helped. When you're not quick – and neither Jock nor I had much pace – I think it forces you to think more about the game. Jock and I were similar in that we could read situations and read opponents. Pace was our weakness, but our opponents had weaknesses too. We made it our job to find them.

Neither of us was a drinker or big socialiser, so football was our big passion. We'd never tire of talking about the game and I was always impressed by what he had to say. We had very similar ideas about football. Jock was clever and a great communicator too – much better than I ever was. We became good friends very quickly. Our ritual was always the same: lunch in Ferrari's, talking football, and then off to the Paramount Cinema across the road to see what films were showing. We both loved westerns, although that was one area we did have a bit of a disagreement. Jock thought no-one could beat John Wayne, whereas I was more of a Gary Cooper man.

Yet the Stein-Fallon partnership was forged on more than just idyllic afternoons comparing cowboys and talking football. Together, they endured an underperforming team, suffered crushing defeats and picked up serious injuries. They also encountered tragedy. On September 20, 1952, both featured in a 2-1 victory over Rangers. It was the club's first derby win in two years and the first of Stein's Celtic career. Yet there were no celebrations, and for good reason. The day had begun not with a light breakfast and talk of the game ahead, but with the funeral of team-mate Jackie Millsopp. This versatile and popular player had died a few days earlier, having collapsed after a training session. He was just 22.

That was a dreadful time. Jackie had been taken ill with appendicitis but everyone thought he would recover, so it was a terrible shock when he didn't make it. I'm not ashamed to say that I shed a few tears. I had got to know him well because we'd shared a cabin on the boat over to America for our tour the summer before, and he was a lovely lad. Everyone at Celtic liked him, and it affected us all for a long, long time. But on the day of the funeral itself, we just got on with it. It's hard to believe now that we had an Old Firm match the same day, but what happened to Jackie ended up bringing us together.

Sadly, the Celtic team wasn't always so united on derby day. After one particular defeat to Rangers – and there were plenty during that era – Charlie Tully provided an infamous analysis of the club's Old Firm inferiority, declaring: "There are too many Protestants in this team." Stein was one of several to react with justifiable fury. Amid the pushing and shoving that ensued, a fist-fight was avoided only by Fallon – in the words of Archie Macpherson in *Jock Stein: The Definitive Biography* – "rising above it all and quelling any violent backlash". At first, that meant using his physical force to keep the warring factions apart. Later, it entailed utilising his diplomatic skills to heal the rift created by Tully's barb.

> Charlie wasn't normally that kind of person but he was obviously frustrated that day and came out with a stupid, unfair comment. You shouldn't forget he had been brought up in Belfast, which was very divided back then, but there was still no excuse for what he said. At the time, he was looking for me to back him up as a fellow Catholic, but there was no chance of that. I had nothing but respect for the Protestants in our team, and one of the things I admired most about Celtic was that, unlike Rangers, we signed players from any background.
>
> I always liked Charlie but what he said that day created a division, and that was the last thing we needed. I could understand why Jock wasn't happy. He might not have been brought up a Celtic supporter but he had taken the club to his heart and was a complete professional who never gave anything less than his best. To have that questioned, well, it was a red rag to a bull. Jock was never Charlie's greatest fan anyway. He appreciated his talent, as did we all, but he didn't feel he was a team player. I don't think Charlie would have lasted long had Jock been in charge back then.

On such matters, Fallon had no need to speculate. He knew only too well that this was one of the earliest subjects on which he and Stein would agree to disagree. Tully might have been the darling of the supporters and Scottish football's most precocious talent, but his lifestyle and work ethic earned only disdain from the club's newly arrived centre-half. While manager, Stein admitted: "I would have had to chase Charlie away as a player in my Celtic team." Fallon would have made him a focal point. His view was that Tully's flaws, while frustrating, were a price well worth paying.

> For pure skill, Charlie was the best footballer I ever played with. That said, he was the worst trainer. We'd be running round the park and he'd be struggling at the back, shouting at me: 'That

won't make you a better player, Fallon!' But what a great talent
he was. He could be lazy, no doubt about it. But the way I saw
it, supporters went along to be entertained – and Charlie was
just the boy to do that. He was a real artist on the ball, had great
skill and touch, and defenders were scared to come near him in
case he made a fool of them.

I always remember him giving the Aberdeen full-back, Don
Emery, a terrible time of it one afternoon. Emery was a tough
player but he couldn't get near Charlie. Late in the game, Charlie
pulled a ticket out of his pocket and said, 'Look, Don… would
you not be more comfortable watching me from the stand?'
Only Charlie would have had the cheek to do something like
that. That was why the fans loved him. I still think he's one of
the greatest players to wear the green and white.

Fallon, selfless and unspectacular, might have been the archetypal
team player, but he placed a high value on the unpredictable
genius of great mavericks. In 2002, this love of individual talent
was underlined when he named Tully, Jimmy Johnstone and Paolo
di Canio in a list of his 10 favourite Celtic players. Stein would
have shuddered at the mere thought of that trio in the same team.

Yet areas of disagreement between the two men were few. Where
they did exist, both were able to differ while still understanding
and respecting the other's position. Stein admired Fallon as a
man of principle and, according to Macpherson, never forgot his
decisive intervention following Tully's divisive declaration. Nor
was he alone in spotting the Irishman's ability to unite and, where
necessary, reconcile. Frank O'Farrell's opinion of Fallon as "a great
leader of men" was gaining more subscribers and, in December
1952, it was recognised with the Celtic captaincy. The incumbent
skipper, John McPhail, had been on the slide ever since his winning
goal in the 1951 cup final, and was now beset by weight problems.
When Celtic took the decision to send 'Hooky' to a health farm in
Tring to shed some pounds, they also removed the burden of the
armband. Fallon was seen as the natural successor.

What an honour that was. And what a surprise. I had been at the
club only a couple of years and had no expectation of becoming
captain. That was beyond my ambitions. I was a bit concerned
at the time about Hooky's reaction but he didn't seem to mind

and, if he was upset, he obviously didn't blame me. The two of us always got along very well. Everyone seemed very happy for me and being Celtic captain was a responsibility I took very seriously. I always gave everything on the field anyway, but there's more to being a captain than that. You've got to lead by example as a person too, and I made sure that I always tried to show the club in the best light off the park.

It would be a short-lived thrill. Fallon's time as skipper began on December 13 with Celtic's most emphatic win of the season, a 5-0 trouncing of Dundee. It effectively ended just a week later, when a 3-2 victory at Falkirk came at considerable personal cost.

The great Jimmy Delaney was playing for Falkirk that day and, during the first half, we both went in for a tackle. He did nothing wrong but my forearm got squeezed between his hip bone and my hip bone. It broke in two places. I came in at half-time and I knew it was bad, but there were no substitutes in those days so I didn't want to go off. The doctor took a look at it, held my arm up to his ear and gave it a little shake to see if he could hear anything – not very scientific, I know. He said it wasn't broken and that was good enough for me to get back out there and play out the rest of the game. By the end of the match, though, the sweat was lashing off me and the pain was unbearable, so I asked to be dropped off at the Royal Infirmary on the way back home. Sure enough, the X-ray showed the two breaks. That arm gave me a lot of problems from then on. I broke it another few times, mainly through coming back too early, and it never really healed properly.

Delaney, though blameless, was horrified. After hearing the news the following day, the first thing he did was write to Fallon, pledging his prayers for a quick and full recovery. His letter concluded approvingly: "The fact that you played right through the rest of the game proves you have the old Celtic spirit." Buoyed by these words and determined to hasten his return, Fallon spent five hours a day squeezing a rubber ball in his left hand to strengthen the muscles in his arm. The injury, though a setback, should not have been serious enough to end his season or cast doubt over his role as captain. Yet some poor medical advice, a couple of botched, over-eager comebacks and two more breaks ensured that Fallon played only a handful of matches over the remainder of the campaign.

The consequences for Celtic underlined his growing worth to the side. A team he had led to within a point of top spot, ahead of Rangers, ultimately finished the season eighth, 14 points adrift of their old rivals. "The quiet man from Eire who plays with such fire and fervour on the field has been missed badly by Celtic," stated one report, capturing the general consensus. When Celtic were drawn to face the Ibrox side in the Scottish Cup, legendary former manager Willie Maley – notoriously sparing with his compliments – previewed the match in his newspaper column with an unusual tribute. "I will miss Fallon, a natural footballer, brave and strong, with just an over-touch of the rashness of his countrymen," he wrote. Fair as this assessment might normally have been, the Irishman's only rashness that particular season lay in his consistently hasty comebacks. The last of these came in mid-April, and was ended at Dalymount Park in a friendly against an FAI select, when a flailing boot struck his weakened arm. It cost him his place in the Coronation Cup side, and involvement in Celtic's greatest triumph in a generation.

Fallon watched as his team-mates swept aside Arsenal, Manchester United and Hibernian en route to lifting the trophy, and knew instinctively that his time as captain had passed. Yet he realised, too, that the tournament, and the armband, had served a greater purpose. His loss had been another man's gain. It had been the making of Jock Stein. The same player who had been the most unwelcome of additions just 18 months before, and who was never intended to play a first-team match, was now a conquering Hampden hero. There would be no looking back. Stein would spend the ensuing months taking the trophy on a tour of supporters' clubs with Bob Kelly and, while doing so, formed a relationship described as "like a father and son" by close friend Tony McGuinness. The importance of this bond would only be realised years later, during the greatest period in the club's history.

Yet Stein's elevated position was indebted to more than just Fallon's broken arm. Even with the Irishman injured, there would have been other, higher-profile and seemingly superior replacements. Stein, after all, had not merited a single mention in the 1952/53 *Celtic Football Guide* and was not even considered a guaranteed starter. Bobby Evans and Bertie Peacock, both long-

Fallon of the Rangers: Sean's father, John, poses with sister Agnes during his days in the Connaught Rangers. Fallon Snr fought in Gallipoli and Serbia for the British and Allies during the First World War before being injured and discharged in 1917

Aspiring priest: For much of his youth, Sean – pictured on the day of his first holy communion – envisaged himself going into the priesthood

Little Celt: The earliest known photograph of Sean, aged two (front row, second from left) with the Sligo Celtic team of season 1924/25. The club had been formed by his father (back row, fourth from right) after his return from Glasgow

National sport: A keen and successful Gaelic footballer, Sean (front row, third from left), with his club team Craobh Rua, went on to represent his county before being banned by the GAA

Irish Rover: Sean (third from left, back row), represented his hometown team during a single season with Sligo Rovers in 1948/49. At 26, it was his first campaign in a national league

The lifeguard: Fallon, a trained lifesaver, teaches a young boy how to swim during a visit to Sligo with his Celtic team-mate and best friend, Bertie Peacock (right)

'Everything I had ever wanted': Sean (second from right) carries aloft goalscorer John McPhail after a 1-0 win over Motherwell in the 1951 Scottish Cup final at Hampden Park. It was the first trophy of his football career

Hampden hero: Fallon slots home the winning goal in the 2-1 1954 Scottish Cup final win over Aberdeen at Hampden Park before a crowd of 130,060

Head Bhoy: Fallon going for goal against Partick Thistle during one of his stints at centre-forward

Class of '55: Sean (second from left, front row) is flanked by Bobby Collins (left) and Jock Stein (right) in this Celtic line-up in 1955

Steel and skill: A stern-faced Fallon poses with two of the great Celtic entertainers of the 1950s, Willie Fernie (left) and Charlie Tully (right)

RECORD STARS

AS SALLON SEES THEM

★

FALLON, CELTIC

I LIKED Sean Fallon. I liked his rugged features, ready smile, and that determined jaw.

Here is a man of iron, a man who will give everything he has no matter what job he tackles. A tough fellow, Sean — with a big heart to go with the toughness.

Cartoon hero: Fallon's features and personality – "a man of iron… with a big heart to go with the toughness" – are depicted in the *Daily Record* by renowned caricaturist Ralph Sallon

Derby duel: Sean pressurises Rangers keeper George Niven during a 2-1 Old Firm derby win at Celtic Park on September 20, 1952. Players from both sides are seen sporting black armbands in honour of Celtic's Jackie Millsopp, whose funeral had taken place earlier the same day

Club mates: Sean at Bonnington Moor golf course in Eaglesham with Celtic colleagues (from left) John Bonnar, Mike Haughney, Charlie Tully and Bertie Peacock

The passport: Sean had to come clean on his real date of birth – after knocking six years off his age to seal a switch to Celtic – when applying for a British passport

International honours: Though his involvement with Republic of Ireland was blighted by controversy and conflict, Fallon wore the green jersey with great pride on eight occasions

Love and marriage: Sean laughs as Bertie Peacock leans in to kiss Myra following the Fallons' wedding on May 4 1959. Sharing the joke (from left) are Myra's brother Billy Craig, Neilly Mochan and Jock Stein

The Iron Man: Sean earned his reputation as one of Scotland's fittest and strongest players with hours of hard graft in the gym and on the training field

Blank canvas: Fallon was the central figure in player recruitment during Celtic's glory days

SKULL
Split twice

EYEBROWS
Split twice

TEETH
Two broken

COLLAR-BONE
Broken

SHOULDER
Torn

ARM
Three fractures

KNEE
Torn

ANKLE
Broken
Torn ligaments

INSTEP
Badly bruised

In the wars: A newspaper feature highlights the variety of injuries collected by Fallon during his Celtic career *(left)*

Pain game: Despite sustaining several serious injuries as a consequence of his fearless style of play, Fallon never once failed to complete a match *(above)*

serving fans' favourites and full internationals, would have headed a substantial cast of likelier contenders. That he jumped the queue was down to one man and one man alone. As Bob Crampsey wrote in *Jock Stein: The Master*: "How did the workaday Stein ever become club captain? The answer is that he did because Sean Fallon did."

Fallon's time as skipper may have been short, but it included a decision of immense significance to both Stein and Celtic. When asked to select his deputy, the Irishman looked beyond Evans, a Scotland stalwart, and Peacock, his closest friend, to the bit-part centre-half signed less than a year before. It was a decision none of his team-mates saw coming.

> I don't think anyone, including Jock himself, expected it. A few players weren't happy because there were still a lot of people who didn't really rate him. A few of the others would certainly have expected to be given the job of deputy ahead of Jock. Bertie wasn't one of those people – he took it all in his stride – but it hurt me not to ask him because he was a great friend and a great Celt. No-one was happier than me when he went on to become captain a few years later.
>
> But my reasoning with Jock was very simple: I saw him as being the best man for the job, and the best for Celtic. He wasn't a star player but, as a man, I thought he had something special. He was a natural captain for the same reasons he was a natural manager: he was clever, determined, a leader and a winner. I liked the way he spoke about the game too; whatever he said, it just made sense. He had good ideas, clever ideas, but practical too – and he could put them across very well. He was serious about football and I could see already that he was completely committed to Celtic. There were a few who didn't believe in him like I did at that stage, but he won them round in the end, as I knew he would.
>
> I do think it was an important moment for Jock, being made vice-captain. It gave him a new status at Celtic, especially when I had to drop out of the team through injury. He became very close to Bob Kelly after the Coronation Cup, and that was very important in the years ahead when Jock became coach and manager. Making him my deputy strengthened our relationship too. Jock and I already got on well but after that we were very close. I think he always appreciated that I took a big step in doing what I did, especially as it wasn't the popular thing to do.

On reflection, the decision was typical Fallon. His uncanny ability to identify greatness was as evident here as it would be later in his career, spotting hidden potential in aspiring footballers. It was also every bit as invaluable.

"Jock was always immensely grateful to Sean for his support in those early days," said Archie Macpherson. "And becoming captain was very important to him because it created that initial bond with Kelly and the Celtic supporters. It was admirable, too, that Sean didn't just pick the obvious candidate. With Sean, the impression was that the club always came first, above himself and above any individual whose nose might be put out of joint. No doubt he looked at Jock and saw that here was a man of stature – not necessarily the best player, but a man with ideas. Someone you could count on."

Fallon's faith would, of course, be thoroughly vindicated. As for Jimmy Mallan, he was released by Celtic a few weeks before the Coronation Cup campaign, his question having been forcefully answered. Silverware now sparkled on the horizon. With Fallon at his side, Stein's critics would become an endangered species.

Chapter 10
The Iron Man

"From what I know of Sean Fallon, he's got a hide like a rhinoceros, an appetite like a horse, the heart of a lion and the stamina of a marathon runner. Nothin' can hurt the Sligo Slasher. He chews bolts and spits rust. He's a rarin' tearin' son of a gun that all the injuries in the game can't hold down."

They don't make them like Malcolm Munro any more. Amid the *Evening Citizen* man's vivid metaphors and liberal use of artistic licence, his point was unambiguous. Fallon wasn't merely a footballer; he was a force of nature. So imposing was his on-field aura that another venerable former journalist, Bob Crampsey, remembered the full-back as "Herculean". "My recollection of Fallon in the hooped jersey," he wrote, "had him as about 7ft tall and built proportionately." Crampsey was not alone. Whether it was as the Sligo Slasher, the Mad Monk or, ultimately, the Iron Man, the myth of Sean Fallon became as formidable as the man.

Wherever he went, his reputation preceded him. "Players would often be watching me and not the ball," he recalled with a chuckle. And, far-fetched as some of the accounts might have seemed, his was a legend unembellished. When it came to putting his body in harm's way and playing through even the most excruciating pain, Fallon was every bit as fearless and selfless as those stories suggested. Testament to this is a frightening catalogue of injuries.

As well as the usual strains, gashes and knocks that punctuate a footballer's career, he suffered five breaks to his left arm, fractured an ankle, broke his nose, tore ligaments in both legs, cracked ribs, broke his collarbone, and very nearly lost an eye. Yet never once did he fail to complete a match.

Packie Bonner, one of Fallon's last signings and a close family friend, would revel in his countryman's tales of commitment bordering on insanity. "Any time I would ask Sean how he was doing, he would always get on to telling me about one of his old injuries," said Bonner. "My favourite story was the one about his bad eye, which I heard so often I almost know it by heart. He'd tell me: 'I got that one at Dundee, and it was Jock's fault because he was playing inside me that day and went astray. The ball was crossed over for the big striker Jock should have been marking. He was about to head it in the net and I couldn't get to the ball in time. The only way for me to stop the boy scoring was to put my face into the back of his head. Well, son, I woke up and I didn't know where I was. My nose was broken, my teeth were missing, and this eye has never been the same since. But Dundee didn't score, I know that. And naturally I played on once they'd woken me up a bit.' That was Sean. Fantastic. Where would you get stories like that in football these days?"

It was remarkable even at the time. John McPhail dedicated his newspaper column to the incident, with the headline – 'It's no cushy job being a pro!' – reprimanding those who portrayed footballers as having it easy. He wrote: "I would like to introduce them to a face – the face of Sean Fallon, Celtic's Irish international left-back – quite a handsome face too until last Saturday when it was involved in a collision with the bone-crushing skull of Jim Chalmers of Dundee. I saw the results the other day – men have escaped from a Marciano bout with less. Eyes cut, bruised, swollen, nose broken and discoloured, mouth gashed – the only trace of the old Fallon was the cheery Irish brogue."

That was a bad one. I came close to losing my eye and it's never been right since. I still get a kind of mist over it. But I'm lucky I don't have worse really. I would go in against guys who were bigger than me and sometimes I came off ok, sometimes I didn't. But even when I was really hurt, I was never carried off. I would always look to get back on my feet and play on. It's a man's game and you should act like a man. Even back then, you would see players going down as if they were dead. I hated that. I picked up some nasty injuries but I would always try not to let on. Showing an opponent that you're hurt is a weakness as far as I'm concerned. That's why I always played on.

I used to come home black and blue though. I'm pretty lucky these days, but I still can't fully turn my left arm, plus my right knee gives me some problems and there's the bad eye. But at least I know I gave everything for my team; that I never shirked a tackle that I could have won. That's something. I know the fans appreciated it. The Iron Man, they used to call me. They knew that although I didn't have the talent of some of the boys we had out there, I'd need to break a leg before you'd catch me limping, never mind going off the field.

Pat Crerand was one such appreciative supporter. "Sean was incredible," said the Manchester United legend. "He is one of the greatest ever Celts, without question. I used to go to watch Celtic everywhere back then, and he would take plenty of punishment, especially when he played up front. But the courage he had stood out a mile. The fans loved him."

Fallon would have dismissed such grand praise, doubtless with a self-effacing joke about "only being good for kicking folk". But Crerand's was far from a lone voice. Matt Lynch, a beloved figure at the club during the 1930s and '40s, described the Irishman as "the epitome of a real Celtic player". "He knew the history of Celtic and showed it in his play," added the former winger.

This latter comment struck upon a key element of Fallon's make-up. Courage and competitiveness came naturally, but it was a fanatical devotion to his club and its cause that underpinned the full-back's propensity for self-sacrifice. "He had a genuine love for Celtic," said Bertie Auld, who observed Fallon as a player, coach and assistant manager. "As a player, there has never been anyone more dedicated or wholehearted. What a warrior he was. If there was a 50-50 tackle, you'd put your house on Sean winning it."

The 50-50s were rarely the problem. It was when the odds were heavily stacked against him, the situation seemingly hopeless, that Fallon caused himself greatest damage. Take October 24, 1953. This was the day Celtic beat title rivals Hearts 2-0 and took a major step towards their first league championship in 16 years. It was also the day on which Fallon earned his Iron Man moniker.

> I picked up another bad injury that day and, believe it or not, that one was Jock's fault too. It's a wonder we got on so well after the problems he caused me! He'd had a chance to clear the ball but hesitated and allowed Davie Laing to steal it and run through on goal for Hearts. I tried to cover but I wasn't in quite the right position so, as Laing got ready to shoot, I had to throw my body in front of him. I blocked the shot but his studs followed through and crunched into my arm and shoulder. You can still feel the hole it took out of my collarbone. I knew it was broken, and my wrist too. There was no doubt. But it was a big game and I felt that if I could get strapped up at half-time, I could play on – at least fill a space, keep someone busy. So I went back on with a sling. I would have been useless in defence though, so they put me up at outside-left. I always remember the Hearts full-back telling me, 'Injured or not, Sean, I'll be going for everything'. We even managed a bit of a joke about it. But I can't say I enjoyed playing the rest of the match like that. I remember being sick with the pain.

It might not have been a personal highlight, but that injury was a pivotal moment in Fallon's playing career. And astonishing though his stoicism was, it was the Irishman's reaction to the ensuing praise that ensured its place in Celtic folklore. He had secured a vital win, playing on in agony with an injury that should have ended his season – and might have ended his career. It was plainly heroic, and everyone acknowledged it as such. Everyone but Fallon. His assessment? "Ach, it wasn't as if it was a broken leg." But his protests were in vain. Waving away the plaudits, claiming not to know what all the fuss was about, did nothing to diminish recognition of his gallantry. Nor did it alter the gravity of the potential consequences. After all, while the damage to the collarbone and wrist was not in itself catastrophic, it followed three prior breaks – all to the same arm, and all within the past 10 months.

> The doctor said I was lucky that my body produced a lot of calcium, more than usual – otherwise I'd have been finished. It

was the same doctor I'd seen about the previous breaks and he was worried about me. He said that the body can only produce so much calcium and that I was asking too much of it. I just wanted him to tell me when I could get back playing again, but he said that I should forget about football and go back to Ireland for a long rest, steer clear of any physical activity. He wrote to Celtic and told them the same thing, that the arm couldn't take any more abuse. So I was sent back to Sligo and told to take it easy.

For a restless competitor such as Fallon, that was easier said than done. He had returned just in time for the Henry Cup – the race he had twice won – and was convinced by sponsors to swim part of the course. "Stupid, I know," he recalled sheepishly. The plaster protecting his arm was left sodden and it took a favour from a friend of his father's at the local hospital to arrange a replacement without Celtic's knowledge. Not that the club was closely monitoring his progress. The full-back had been written off for the remainder of the campaign and returned to Glasgow in the spring only to be cleared for another period of rest and recuperation. But the story of his and Celtic's season was about to take a fateful twist.

> I had a flight home all sorted. I was going to watch the team play at Hamilton, but my bags were already at the terminal and I was to go there straight after the match. But as fate would have it, John McPhail picked up a very bad groin injury in the game. It left the club struggling for players. Just as I was due to leave to go to the airport, Bob Kelly called me over and asked if I would be willing to stay and try to play after all. I knew the doctor wouldn't have been happy about it, but there was no way I was going to refuse.

So it was that Fallon, inactive for five months and seemingly out for the season, was back in the starting line-up four days later. But there was one key difference: his position. Having been injured at left-back, he was restored to the team at centre-forward. It made an already difficult task all the more daunting.

> I played wherever Celtic asked me to without ever complaining, but I would never have picked myself at centre-forward. To be honest, I hated playing there. I didn't have any great finesse and I wasn't quick. My best qualities were reading of the game

and tackling and, as far as I was concerned, that made me a defender. I think my team-mates and the supporters would have agreed with that. The problem was that most of our forwards were on the light side, so the club stuck me up there to rumble up the opposition and create a bit of space for the others. I was just there to upset the defenders, knock them about and not give them a minute's peace. And I made sure I did that. If I wasn't a great striker, I at least wanted to be a handful for anyone marking me.

He invariably succeeded. If anything, in fact, Fallon was a victim of his own success. Unlike his previous clubs, Celtic had initially proved reluctant to field him at centre-forward, and it was only during the 1951 summer tour of the USA – due again to an injury to McPhail – that he was first thrust forward as a temporary stopgap. Had he not scored the winner, it might have been a short-lived experiment. But that goal, and his bustling, all-action performance, established Fallon as an automatic replacement when McPhail's problems flared up once more during that July's St Mungo Cup. By the time he had scored twice in the quarter-final replay and then twice more to inspire a memorable comeback in the final against Aberdeen, people were asking whether he was merely a stopgap after all. Willie Maley even likened the Irishman to one of the club's all-time great strikers, writing that he displayed "the same never-say-die spirit as Jimmy Quinn". Fallon should have been thrilled. Instead, he felt like a fraud.

It had been the same at Glenavon. For a while, I scored quite a few goals because people didn't know how to handle me. I wasn't a typical centre-forward and that caused defences problems at first, but they were soon wise to me. The truth was, I was very limited as a striker, and I knew that better than anyone. I was good for a bit of shock value at first but, once teams realised I didn't have any real pace or skill to get past them, the goals would always start drying up. Being spoken of in the same breath as Quinn, who'd scored hundreds of goals for Celtic, just made me feel uncomfortable. I knew I could never be that kind of player for Celtic.

For once, Fallon's downplaying of his own abilities was justified.

His attacking potency had a shelf life and he was shrewd and humble enough to recognise it. Yet if his life and career prior to 1954 had taught him anything, it was surely to never say never. Odds would have been long on him returning from injury in 1954, rusty and out of position, and inspiring a turnaround in the title race. But as he knew only too well, stranger, more miraculous things had happened.

A few weeks earlier, Celtic had fallen eight points behind leaders Hearts with defeat at Tynecastle and seemed resigned to another year of failure. With just two points for a win, a run of consistent brilliance represented this notoriously inconsistent side's only chance of salvation. As it transpired, Celtic weren't just brilliant; they were flawless. Their league campaign culminated in a run of seven successive wins and underpinning this unblemished streak was the prolific form of their makeshift Sligo centre.

In hindsight, the date of Fallon's comeback – March 17 – should have been taken as a sign. Just as in 1950, when he wowed McGrory at Dalymount Park, it would be a momentous St Patrick's Day. Simply emerging injury-free would have represented success, but he managed to mark his return with a goal as Celtic beat Airdrie 6-0 for their biggest home win of the season. Better was to follow. By the time April arrived, the gap at the top was down to a point, Celtic had two games in hand, and Fallon had scored four times in three appearances. The high point of the intervening period had arrived on March 20, when he helped bring about a turning point in the season. With Hearts losing at Pittodrie and Celtic seemingly poised to blow the chance this presented, it was Fallon's second-half brace that turned a 1-0 half-time deficit against Partick Thistle into a priceless victory. His performance at Firhill even evoked a familiar association, with Tom Campbell writing of him "galloping through the Thistle defence, shrugging off tackles like Jimmy Quinn".

This "very limited" striker was in the process of firing Celtic towards a historic title. By the time Falkirk were beaten 3-0 in April, with the Bhoys' suddenly free-scoring centre claiming a now-predictable goal, there was no way back for Hearts. The first and only league championship of Fallon's playing career had been secured in spectacular style.

That was a special season. No-one expected it to end that way, least of all myself. I thought I was finished and heading home until the summer. But although it was great to play my part in such a tremendous achievement, I can honestly say that success was all about the team. The balance was right all over the park that year. And the thing I remember most about that season was the spirit we had. Obviously winning helps, but it went deeper than that. We were so united as a group of players, and that hadn't always been the case.

Real camaraderie has to go through the entire club – the young boys, the old ones, the reserves – and that season it did. It wasn't any coincidence that results improved. When you're playing as a team and playing for each other, the results will follow – provided the ability is there. And ability was never really a problem with that team. Later, when Jock and myself were manager and assistant manager, we'd talk about the '54 season. We knew how important it was to get the same kind of spirit, and that's exactly what happened. The Lisbon Lions weren't just a great team – they were like brothers. Both sides had great individuals, but it was always the team that came first, just as it should be. In terms of '54, I never played in a better Celtic team. That season, finally winning a title, meant a lot to all of us.

And, for Fallon at least, the best had yet to come. The concluding chapter of the 1954 fairy tale was to unfold at Hampden, in the Scottish Cup final, with 130,060 there to witness it. Sean's father was among that colossal crowd, and saw his son score a goal described by Bertie Auld as "the most important of that era" in Celtic's 2-1 win over Aberdeen. The mere mention of it never failed to raise a smile in the man responsible.

It's not every day you score the winning goal in a cup final. I never expected it to happen to me and it was something very, very special, especially with my dad there to see it. Celtic hadn't won the double for 40 years, so it was a bit of history. But I must thank Willie Fernie for that goal because he did all the hard work for me. He'd set off on one of those great runs of his, beating man after man, and I just tried to keep up, get into space and hope that he'd see me. When he cut it back, I was eight yards out and couldn't really miss. I say that, but there was a moment just after I hit it when I thought I might have got it wrong. But then Hampden just exploded and I kept on running, soaking it up. Willie was a good friend and we'd often laugh about it over the years. 'My name should have been on that goal rather than yours,' he'd tell me. 'A blind man could have put it in from there.' He wasn't far wrong. But I was proud all the same. And I'm sure my dad was too. I think we both could have died happy that afternoon.

Those were the days in which men tended not so share such emotions, and certainly not with each other. Sean, though, learned the full extent of his father's pride in an unorthodox way, when Sligo's town council staged a celebratory dinner in the wake of the cup final. John Fallon had been asked to deliver a toast and spoke of his son's Hampden winner as one of the happiest moments of his life, adding "there is no prouder father than I". Sean attended the event with Jimmy McGrory and, for someone with a soft heart – in contrast to his Iron Man image – he did well to hold back the tears. Described by McGrory at the same dinner as "a credit to Sligo on and off the field", Fallon used his speech to thank Celtic for exceeding his wildest dreams. "It is the greatest club in the world," he enthused. "And more than a club, it is a home and an institution."

Pride was evident everywhere he looked. A band had greeted his arrival in the town, and Tom Palmer, another speaker at the dinner, lauded "this truly great sportsman" for "bringing international fame to Sligo". The *Sligo Champion* even described Fallon's unmissable winning goal, slotted home from the edge of the six-yard box, as "a great shot from 18 yards out". As with Munro and his bolt-chewing depiction, the details mattered less than the substance. And whether the ball came from 18 yards or 18 inches, the outcome was the same: Fallon was a hero.

And yet it could all have been so different. Given how perfectly scripted the conclusion to the 1953/54 season was, it is impossible not to wonder how it would have unfolded had John McPhail avoided injury at Douglas Park. For Fallon, the outcome would surely have been missing out on the one league title his playing career yielded. The consequences for Celtic, considering his contribution to the club's only domestic double in a 53-year period, could have been every bit as grim.

Fortunately, neither player nor club was forced to confront this alternative scenario. Instead, indelible images of Fallon had been formed. The first was of a selfless stalwart, battling on, bandaged and in evident pain. The second was from Hampden. "I'll never forget his celebration after scoring that cup final goal," said Bertie Auld. "I can still see him running away, punching the air, battering the wind and the sky. And, as always with Sean, the chest was puffed out. Then there was that smile of his. He had a wonderful smile, Sean."

It had been well earned. This rarin' tearin' son of a gun had not been held down. Sean Fallon, the Iron Man, was already a Celtic legend.

Chapter 11
Hampden in the Sun

The home in which Fallon spent his final years is tucked away in a cosy corner of Glasgow's south side. Warm, welcoming and unpretentious, it fitted him perfectly. The walls of this flat are now adorned with photographs, all reminders of his glorious career and the immense pleasure he took in Celtic's success. But these are recent additions, hung in the months since his passing. While Sean was living there, the only pictures displayed were of Sligo and his beloved family, with football mementos conspicuous by their absence.

There was, though, one exception. Sitting proudly atop Fallon's television set was a small sculpture of a Celtic jersey, given to him in 2002 at the club's 'Greatest Ever Celt' awards. It wasn't for making the all-time best XI, a team in which he was beaten to a full-back slot – "quite rightly too," he would insist – by two of his signings, Danny McGrain and Tommy Gemmell. But it was significant enough to display all the same, and the inscription revealed why.

'Greatest Ever Old Firm Game
Celtic 7 Rangers 1
1957 League Cup final'

"The best of the best," he told me during one early visit, motioning towards the statuette. Certainly, we have never seen its like again. The 7-1 game remains the most lop-sided result ever recorded in a British cup final, and the biggest win for either side in the Old Firm derby's 125-year history. For most Celtic fans, only Lisbon ranks higher, while some – Bertie Auld included – find it impossible to split the two. "When you look at us winning the European Cup," Auld told *Celtic TV*, "for me the 7-1 game was every bit as big." Fallon was prepared to go a step further.

> I would say I enjoyed it even more than Lisbon. Both were magnificent, and it's not to say that beating Rangers 7-1 was more important than winning the European Cup. But in terms of pure enjoyment, the 7-1 game was hard to beat. The fact I was playing makes a difference. I loved every minute with Jock as manager, and we obviously had much more success during that period. But I'd still say my happiest times with Celtic were when I was playing. Nothing was ever as good as the feeling of pulling on that shirt and going out there on the pitch. I used to envy our players when I worked as assistant manager.

It was a match that would have been remarkable in any era, in any context. In 1957, it was utterly unimaginable. Rangers had won each of the last two league championships, while Celtic – after a near miss in 1954/55 – had returned to their inconsistent ways. Successive fifth-place finishes confirmed what the fans already knew: that the promise of their double-winning team had been squandered. Frustration on the terraces intensified and, before long, heroes were being turned into villains. Fallon was one such victim. Just nine months after his Scottish Cup winner, the announcing of his name at centre-forward in a match against Hearts elicited audible jeers from pockets of the Celtic support.

The catcalls did not go unanswered. Sean himself played as if unaware of their existence, but the press were not so forgiving. Tommy Muirhead, who had starred for Rangers and Scotland before moving into journalism, fronted a scathing response. "There is no greater club man in Scottish football than Celtic's Sean Fallon – and it is about time a misguided section of Parkhead supporters realised it," he wrote in an article "deploring" the "anti-Fallon 'wolves'". "Before the end of the match," he added, "the guilty ones should have been hanging their heads in shame. There are several reasons why Hearts lost this match 2-0. There is only one reason why Celtic won it – Sean Fallon." Given the Irishman's record of continually playing through injuries for his club's benefit, Muirhead viewed the fans' behaviour as a betrayal. Yet his sense of outrage was not shared by the player himself.

> You have to be ready to take the bad with the good in football, especially at a big club. You can't expect everyone to be praising you all the time because even the best players at Celtic – people like wee Jinky, Kenny, Bobby Murdoch – took a bit of stick occasionally. It didn't change the fact that our fans were tremendous, and never once did I forget that. Even if a few of them were getting on to me at that time, it was probably just because I was playing up front. And I could understand that. They knew their football, those supporters, and they could see as well as I did that I didn't belong there.

His form at centre-forward might have won Celtic the title, but Fallon had hoped the club's management would be savvy enough to quit while they were ahead. Instead, Bob Kelly persevered with him in a position in which his all-action approach had patently lost the crucial element of surprise. Fallon, having seen this coming, shared the fans' frustrations. Yet he also felt powerless; convinced that publicly voicing his misgivings would be an act of disloyalty and ingratitude. If remaining faithful came at the cost of his popularity, it was a price he was ready to pay.

Fortunately, those smattering of jeers never reached a tipping point. By the following season, Fallon was back in his natural defensive habitat and seemingly better than ever, having added experience and composure to his fearsome physicality. Among those who noted this evolution was Malcolm Munro, who wrote in the *Evening Citizen*: "He looks a really class player. There are two Fallons. The one with the rip-roaring style, the tough guy, the crowd pleaser. And the smooth customer who reads the opposition mind and places himself in a strategic position to counter their moves." There was soon tangible evidence to support such claims. By December 1956, the *Daily Express's* Harry Andrews was eulogising about Celtic's defensive record – "the best in British football" – and attributing it largely to Fallon's "astonishing" positional sense.

In the role he had vacated, the picture was not so rosy. Kelly's tinkering resulted in the fielding of seven different centre-forwards during the 1955/56 campaign, which ended in Alex Dowdells leaving for Leicester City with a telling parting shot. Celtic, he said, "didn't know the meaning of consistency". It is likely that Dowdells had in mind two successive Scottish Cup final defeats, both contributed to – if not caused – by the chairman's eccentric selection policy. Bobby Kirk, a member of the Hearts side which took the trophy in 1956, spoke of laughter echoing round their dressing room when news of Celtic's line-up filtered through.

There was mirth, too, when Kelly attempted to solve the club's striking problem with a rare foray into the transfer market. Billy McPhail and Sammy Wilson, the former notoriously injury prone and the latter a free transfer from St Mirren, arrived either side of the 1956/57 season. But while even the Celtic fans labelled this duo "the crock and the cast-off", Fallon's hopes were considerably higher.

> I felt Billy was exactly what we needed. I'd played against him when he was at Clyde and always thought he was a tremendous player. He was graceful on the ground, had a powerful shot on him and there was no-one better in the air in Scottish football as far as I was concerned. He had that amazing ability to hang in the air when he went up for a header, and the intelligence to knock the ball down for the players around him if he couldn't go for goal himself. That was where Sammy came in. He wasn't a great all-round player, but he was a natural finisher and he would feed off those knock-downs. Billy was definitely the main man in that partnership though. Having played up front myself, I could see he had all the attributes you need.

Not everyone shared this enthusiasm. Just as they had disagreed on Tully, so Fallon and Jock Stein took opposing views on McPhail. In *Oh, Hampden in the Sun*, supporter Peter Sweeney recalled discussing the former Clyde striker with Stein during a visit to Jackie Millsopp's grave. "To our surprise," said Sweeney, "Jock blurted out, 'They've signed the wrong man! McPhail's days are over. He has two dodgy knees and will never finish a match again'."

Fortunately for Celtic, Stein's pessimism proved unfounded. McPhail finished not just one match, but 57, and scored 38 goals in the process, five of which were spread across two triumphant League Cup finals. Yet although his mastery over John Valentine was arguably the central feature of the second and more famous of those finals, the pre-match coverage focused almost entirely on his shortcomings. Even McPhail's brother and Celtic predecessor, John – now working for the *Daily Record* – joined in the criticism of his younger sibling, asking: "What has happened to his footwork?" Another *Record* correspondent, 'Waverley', correctly identified the McPhail-Valentine duel as crucial, but predicted a positive outcome for the Rangers centre-half. "I have doubts about the Celtic forward line," he wrote, "and it has been made obvious that those in control at Parkhead share my qualms." McPhail might have buckled beneath such negativity. Instead, he thrived on it.

> I'd never seen Billy so confident. We were all confident for some reason. Don't ask me why as we'd been having a poor season and Rangers were going well. Maybe we knew this was the last chance to do something special for the supporters because quite a few of us were coming toward the end of our careers. Billy was feeling good because he knew Valentine from earlier in his career and felt he had the beating of him. We had also been working on tactics among ourselves and we decided that our approach was going to be to channel our play through the middle as much as possible, push Sammy close to Billy and see if we could take them by surprise. It worked very well, although Rangers helped us – you could have got a circus through the middle of their defence that day. Valentine ended up being made the scapegoat but I thought the full-backs were as much to blame. They gave him no cover whatsoever and Billy had a field day. He showed how important it is to have a proper centre-forward because one thing I do know: we would never have won 7-1 if I'd been up front. I was glad to be in my old full-back position. We didn't have too much to do in defence but I enjoyed being back there, tidying things up and keeping everything calm.

Those same duties had been occupying Fallon all week. Just 48 hours before kick-off, he had been breaking up a fist-fight between two of his team-mates, with Tully again at the heart of the skirmish. This latest dispute was sparked by Charlie's 'Tullyvision' column in the *Evening Citizen*, which included the assertion that only two Scotland internationals – neither of whom was Bobby Evans – would merit inclusion in a British select team. "The others," Tully added, "lack class." Evans' response was to initiate a flurry of blows that left both men on the floor before Fallon and others stepped in. "It was as well for Charlie that we did," Fallon recalled with a chuckle. "He was making a show of being held back, but Charlie was no fighter. Bobby would have murdered him." A couple of evenings later, this same duo – never the closest of friends – found themselves sitting together at the post-match reception. By then, they at least had common cause to celebrate.

> The two of them were outstanding in the game itself. Then again, we didn't have anyone below-par that day. You get games like that – not very often unfortunately – when everything goes right, everyone's in the mood and everything you do seems to go right. It was the greatest match I ever played in and one of the best performances I saw from any Celtic team. Rangers were the team to beat, the champions, and yet we destroyed them. We actually should have scored more than seven but we eased off a bit towards the end. Even the goal we lost, we only conceded because Bobby was off the field with an injury and we were a man down. The whole thing was magnificent. No-one ever dreamed of a day like that, and it's never been forgotten since. How did the song go again? 'Oh, Hampden in the Sun... Celtic seven, Rangers one...'

I can still see and hear Fallon now, singing that famous adaptation of Harry Belafonte's 'Island in the Sun', happiness etched on his face. While other matches faded from the 90-year-old's memory – even Lisbon, sadly, was a blur – that bright October afternoon remained gloriously vivid. The enjoyment he took, 55 years on, in sharing his reminiscences served the same purpose as the trophy adorning his television. It underlined that this match was different. Special.

His pride in having been a part of it was understandable. It had been a result so momentous, a performance so stylish, that it even prompted a tribute from the unlikeliest of sources. The 1958 *Rangers Supporters Association Annual* earned full marks for magnanimity with an article in which Celtic were lauded for proving "that the true art of football will triumph in the face of all opposition". The praise kept coming, even years later. Bob Kelly, writing shortly before his death in 1971, stated emphatically that the 7-1 team had "played with a mixture of skill and enthusiasm that has never been bettered by any side wearing the green and white hoops".

The match would be remembered for McPhail's hat-trick, and for a Willie Fernie performance so magical it earned comparisons with Patsy Gallacher. But Fallon, while less eye-catching, left Hampden content in the knowledge that he had played his part. His direct opponent, Alex Scott, was one of the most dangerous wingers of his generation; a Scotland international who would win an English title with Everton. "He was a good player, and a real flyer," Fallon reflected. "If he got a run on me I was finished." Yet Scott spent the final, in the words of the *Sunday Post's* Jack Harkness, "in Fallon's hip pocket". Not for the first time, the 20-year-old's speed and trickery were trumped by the astute positioning of a man 15 years his senior. Cyril Horne of the *Glasgow Herald* viewed the contest as a mismatch. "Fallon again reduced the ill-supported Scott to a hapless young man," he wrote, "prominent after the first 10 minutes only for unsuccessful attempts to provoke his stronger, wiser opponent."

This was Celtic's self-professed "ordinary player" at the peak of his powers. Restored to his natural position and enjoying the longest injury-free spell of his Celtic career, he had become the kind of dependable, experienced defender on which title-winning teams are built. This image of solidity was even conveyed in verse thanks to this poem on the 7-1 game in the 1958 Supporters Association handbook:

> *Fallon, the strong, who undismayed,*
> *Fronted the hostile roar,*
> *Staunch as the rugged rocks that guard,*
> *His native Sligo's shore*
>
> *...*
>
> *Time shall not dim your lustre,*
> *And none your right gainsay,*
> *To measure your feat with the brightest page,*
> *In Celtic's history.*

The 1957 League Cup final had been a defining match in Fallon's career. But according to contemporaries, it was not *the* defining match. That honour, they insisted, belonged to a game played almost 14 months earlier. Again, the opponents were Rangers and, again, it was a high-scoring affair. But this time Celtic were on the receiving end of a 4-3 defeat, and it was a stray pass from Sean that led to the winning goal. That he earned eternal esteem in such circumstances was down to one incident, and one man. That man was Sammy Baird.

Sir Alex Ferguson, who joked about the clash in his eulogy at the Irishman's funeral, remembers Fallon's fellow protagonist well. "Sammy was Rangers' hard man in those days, and he could be a wily character. He never went for 50-50s; always delayed just so he could get in there second and take the man. Sean was tough – my God, he was tough – but he played in the same honest way he lived his life. Sammy was more cunning." Ferguson's was a diplomatic description. Celtic fans of that era generally opt for more colourful adjectives.

> The supporters didn't like Sammy at all and I could understand why. The only players I had no time for were the ones who would go over the ball looking to hurt you, and Sammy could be guilty of that. He was a good player and a hard player too, both qualities I admired, and he was actually a nice guy off the field. But for whatever reason, he had a nasty streak in him that meant he didn't do everything within the laws. You had to watch him because he'd put you out of the game as soon as look at you. That night we're talking about, he'd gone after Tully. But I sorted him out in the end.

At the time, it seemed like an instinctive act. In *Oh, Hampden in the Sun*, Fallon was described as having been "so incensed by the cynical fouling committed by Baird that he gave him an even stronger dose of his own medicine". But Fallon's retribution had not been the product of momentary indignation, or an uncharacteristic flash of temper. It had been years in the making. Revenge was served ice-cold.

> It went back to an incident a few years earlier when Sammy was playing for Clyde. I was up against him and at one point I fell in the box. Next thing I know someone's kicked me in the back

of the head. So I look up and there's Sammy, running away, chest puffed out. I didn't react at the time but I thought, 'Ok, I'll remember that, Sammy'. Very soon after that, though, before we had the chance to play Clyde again, he got a transfer to Preston. It was a while before Rangers came in for him and brought him back to Scotland, but I hadn't forgotten. When the chance came, I taught him a bit of a lesson.

Ferguson was there to see what happened next, having been taken to the match by his Celtic-supporting father. "The ground was brick hard and there was a 50-50 in midfield; actually, more like a 60-40 in Sammy's favour. And then it was like one of these Batman comics: POW! WOW! BANG!"

Also on hand to witness this legendary tussle were three future Lisbon Lions: Bertie Auld, Jimmy Johnstone and Billy McNeill. "You could have heard it at Glasgow Cross," is how Johnstone remembered the almighty collision between these Old Firm hard men. What followed was a collective intake of breath. "There was this great hush to see which of the two of them – if either – would be able to play on," recalled Auld. "And needless to say, up came Sean, dusted himself down, puffed out his chest and ran on to get on with the game. Well, the roar that went up! Sammy was lying there, trying to call for the trainer. And Celtic Park was going crazy." Baird was duly stretchered from the field, his collarbone and shoulder broken. And Fallon, despite keeping up appearances, wasn't faring much better.

I felt like I'd been hit by an iceberg. I remember thinking: 'Something must be broken here'. But there was no way I was going to let on. The crowd went daft when I got up; Sammy was the one man they wanted. Hand on heart though, I never went in with the intention of putting him out of the game. My dad would have killed me if I'd gone in to injure a player and Bob Kelly would never have stood for it. I got a talking to from the referee for it, but there was nothing wrong with the challenge. It was a 50-50 and Sammy had made the mistake of coming in square to me. That was why he came off worse. I felt that I owed him one, but I didn't mean to break his collarbone and shoulder. I went in to see him after the game when I heard it was a bad one, and there were no hard feelings. Sammy was actually manager of Stirling

Albion when Jock and I were at Celtic and we always got on well.

If Baird declined to hold a grudge, it is because he had no reason to do so. A bone-cruncher it might have been, but Fallon's challenge was indeed perfectly lawful. The *Glasgow Herald's* correspondent spoke for many when he stated that the Celtic full-back had been "incorrectly penalised", adding that if anyone had been guilty of a foul, it was Baird. For Sean, such incidents – two fully committed players putting everything on the line for their clubs – were the stuff of which Old Firm derbies were made. "I loved everything about those games," he said. "Almost everything anyway."

The qualifying of this statement had nothing to do with matters on the field. Even Rangers' dominance could be grudgingly endured. It was the fixture's accompanying baggage – violence, religious tribalism and the hijacking of Irish politics – that Fallon found ugly and intolerable.

I've always hated that. Celtic and Rangers are two great clubs and the game doesn't need all the nonsense that goes along with it. You'd like to think it's getting better, but then I look at what Neil Lennon's had to deal with and I can't believe it. It's dreadful. People said that Glasgow was even worse for being anti-Catholic and anti-Irish in my day but I never had it as bad as Neil. You'd get people shouting things from the crowd or the odd idiot talking about 'the stupid Irish' or 'the dirty Irish', but they were very much in the minority. I felt that I was made very welcome in Glasgow generally speaking, and I'm proud to have brought up my family here.

The extent of the Catholic-Protestant issue surprised me when I first arrived though. My dad had warned me to watch out for it but, having played in a mainly Protestant area of Northern Ireland, I didn't expect Glasgow to be any worse. The fact that it was disappointed me because I had no time for all that sectarian stuff. For me, part of being a good Christian is that you accept other people's beliefs and treat them the same as you would anyone else. All the division and hatred – it was a load of nonsense. Rangers didn't help the situation by refusing to sign Catholics, of course. That was a disgrace, and it went on far too long. If Celtic ever tried to do the same, I would have been the first out of the door.

Whatever happened off the park, the relationship between

the players on both sides was always very good. We played hard against each other, but we were great friends and I often wished the supporters could have seen that. We would go out socialising together and I got on very well with the likes of George Young – big Corky we called him – and Willie Thornton. Willie Waddell would be there too – he and I were great pals right up until he died. His nickname was Deedle, and he was one of the best players I ever came up against. He was big for a winger but, naturally, I'd try to cut him down to size a bit. We got on very well. He even proposed me for Pollok Golf Club, which was very tough to get into in those days. He told me: 'I'll get you in, Sean. But no kicking me when we're out on the course.' I told him I was making no promises.

Waddell was someone of whom Sean spoke often. "Deedle felt the same way about his team as I did about mine," he would say admiringly. To Fallon, this devotion to a rival club made him a kindred spirit rather than an enemy. Naturally, the old warriors would rib each other on the golf course: Waddell about the five titles he won as a player, Fallon about 7-1 and the European Cup. But both knew that they were united by a great deal more than divided them. To the very end, Fallon believed passionately that this principle applied to Glasgow as a whole.

As such, he took no pleasure in Rangers' descent into liquidation. The Irishman said continually that he felt sorry not only for the staff at Ibrox, but for the players at Celtic Park. Those players, he insisted, were being denied one of the game's great thrills. He was mindful that his career had been shaped in Old Firm battle – by 'Hampden in the Sun' and his clash with Baird – and that he had never grown tired of playing in that famous fixture. Little did he know, walking off the pitch after the 7-1 game, that his next derby would be his last.

Chapter 12
The Coach

It was in 1957 that Harold Macmillan, Britain's then Prime Minister, famously told the nation: "You've never had it so good." For Fallon, that would have been just about right.

By the end of the year, he could reflect not only on the most satisfying victory of his career, but the most accomplished performances. When the *Daily Record* named its team of 1957, Sean – "the toughest man in the game" – was a popular choice at left-back, seeing off competition from Scotland internationals Eric Caldow and Harry Haddock. "A stylist? Not on your life," commented the *Record*. "We shall never see him in ballet. But what a tackler! He's the main reason for Celtic's goals-against column being one of the lowest in the country."

Fallon's age – at 35, he was a veritable veteran – might ordinarily have caused concern, but the old white lie ensured the press and public were none the wiser. To the trusting masses, Fallon was 29 and just hitting his peak. Nothing in his performances suggested otherwise. "Sean got away with that dodgy birth certificate because he was one of the fittest players around," said Bertie Auld. "As a team-mate, he was a pleasure to play with – the kind of guy you knew you could rely on. He was a leader too; a great influence on youngsters like myself at that time. Even off the park, he led by example in the way he behaved, the way he trained, the fact he was always so immaculately dressed. His enthusiasm rubbed off on everyone." None of it was forced. If Fallon seemed to relish every moment, it is because he did.

> Every day was a joy for me. I just loved being a footballer. I'd been brought up running round the garden, my dad throwing the ball up and getting me to head it back, and I'd loved football ever since. To make my living from the game was a dream. And to do it at Celtic, well, I never forgot how lucky I was. If anything, it became more enjoyable later in my career because I became a better player. You're learning all the time in football and by that stage I had the knowledge and experience of how to exploit other players' weakness. Although I was getting on a bit, I didn't have to worry about losing my pace – not when I'd never had any in the first place. My overall fitness and stamina was still very good because I'd always looked after my body well. The only vice I had was cigarettes. Other than that, my lifestyle was good. I still took long walks, ate a raw egg a day and went swimming in the evenings, although I had to keep that a secret from Jimmy McGrory. I remember him saying to me: 'What's this I hear about you going swimming?' 'Well,' said I. 'It's better than going to the pub'. But he wasn't keen and told me I should stop. 'It'll slow you up,' he said. 'And, Sean, you're slow enough as it is.'

Fallon would chuckle at the memory of this exchange, happy to acknowledge the truth in his manager's uncharacteristically harsh remark. It neither fazed him nor kept him away from the pool. He knew he was no speed-merchant, but felt comfortable that – like so many accomplished defenders – his experience and positional nous could negate this disadvantage. Nor was he concerned about his levels of performance, motivation or fitness. All three were as high as they had ever been, and suggested that he could be of use to Celtic well into his 40s. But even the Iron Man had his weaknesses. His heart and lungs might have corroborated that bogus date of birth, but the joints didn't lie. By the summer of 1958, he had the knees one would expect of a battle-scarred 36-year-old. Time was running out.

> I had problems with both my knees but the right ended up causing me most trouble. I'd twisted it badly and needed an

operation, but they made a bit of a mess of it and left a piece of cartilage floating about in there. It took a couple more operations to get it sorted and I ended up with about 30 stitches. These days, it would all have been sorted by keyhole surgery and I could have gone on a good while longer. But every time I played after that, the knee would fill up with blood. I had to go up to the Royal Infirmary before every match to get the blood drained just so that I could play.

Fallon resorted to cortisone injections to fend off retirement, but knew he was merely delaying the inevitable. On March 22, 1958, less than three months after being named in the *Record's* team of the year, he made his 254th and final competitive Celtic appearance in a 4-2 win over Airdrie. After eight years of living his boyhood dream, it was over. The club kept faith and retained his registration for the 1958/59 season, but an attempted comeback in the public trial match of August 2 ended in him being helped from the field. The knee had again broken down and, for once, so did the man. Tears welled in Fallon's eyes as he limped towards the touchline.

With Billy McPhail sustaining a career-ending knee injury in the same match, it looked like the end of an era. But though McPhail confirmed his retirement within weeks, Fallon couldn't yet bring himself to throw in the towel. Just a couple of months later, he was back in the hoops and back at Celtic Park – this time lining up for the reserves. That meant playing under Jock Stein, who had been given the job of coaching the second team after being forced out of the game by an ankle injury. Stein, according to Fallon, "was already in his element", and he proved supportive too, doing everything within his power to coax his old friend back to fitness. But it was to no avail. This was a losing battle in which, eventually, even Celtic's old warrior had to admit defeat.

I was in terrible pain but I didn't want to give up, so I kept on going back to the surgeon – Mr McDougall was his name – to have the knee drained and get my cortisone injections. The last time I went to see him, I was struggling and he told me: 'Son, I'm not happy giving you these injections.' The dangers of cortisone weren't as well known then but he told me – quite rightly – that I was putting myself in danger. 'You could lose your leg if you keep going this way,' he said. 'Take my advice and call it a day.' After that I could see I had no other option. But I was heart-broken. It was difficult for me to picture a future without playing football. It had been such a love of mine and I missed it terribly. Plus, I had no idea what I would do next. Everything was up in the air.

There had been a time, not so long before, when Fallon's post-retirement plans seemed far from unclear. The subject was broached as early as 1954, when Peter Farrell, the former Republic of Ireland and Everton captain, interviewed him for the *Empire News and Sunday Chronicle*. "One thing is certain," wrote Farrell. "Fallon will return and settle in Ireland." This had always been the plan. Sean would reminisce that, whenever a season ended, he, Charlie Tully and Bertie Peacock would race to the docks for the first available boat home. "None of us could wait to get back." But while Peacock and Tully returned to settle in Coleraine and Belfast respectively after hanging up their boots, Fallon – initially the most homesick of the three – stayed put.

In tracing this change of heart, one date – February 24, 1957 – stands out. That was the night on which Sean was cajoled into attending a young team-mate's family party at the Irish club on Sauchiehall Street. He had been sorely tempted to give it a miss. Billy Craig, the colleague in question, was 14 years his junior, and the party wasn't even for him. Sean had never heard of Myra Craig, whose 21st birthday was being celebrated, far less met her. But she was to leave a lasting impression.

I don't remember too much these days with this old head of mine, but I do remember meeting Myra for the first time. That's one night I'll never forget. As soon as I saw her, I thought, 'That's the girl for me'. I wasn't one for going with the girls much and I hadn't thought a great deal about settling down before then. I was actually starting to get a bit of ribbing in the dressing room because I was the only one of the older players still not married. Until Myra, I never felt I'd met the right woman. But once I met her, there was no doubt in my mind. I had a lot to thank John McAlindon for there because he was a pal of Billy's, and it was through him I ended up going to the party. John was a great friend of ours for many, many years. Billy was a nice lad himself, a very fast outside-right – the kind I would have tried to slow down if I'd been playing against him. I spoke to him first before asking

Myra out but he didn't seem to mind at all. I think he knew I was an honourable sort.

Craig also learned that there was no danger of his team-mate moving in too fast. Sean's sights might have been set on his future bride but, as with his early football career, the pace of progress wasn't exactly rapid. As Myra recalled: "My 21st was in the February and we didn't meet again until that November. All I would hear now and again from Billy was, 'Sean was asking for you'. Then I heard he'd been asking where I usually went dancing at the weekend. It was one night when I was out with a group of my friends that we met up again. I liked him from the start. He was quite shy in some ways but, typical Irishman, he also had the gift of the gab. He was always very calm too, never flustered. He put people at ease. And, as he'll tell you himself, he was a very good dancer." This would indeed be readily – and regularly – confirmed by Sean. "The tango was my favourite," he'd say. "And Myra was a great dancer herself. We'd go in for all the ballroom dancing competitions in those days."

My interviews with Sean generally took the form of meandering, unstructured chats, and Myra would often join us, connecting the dots when her husband's memory occasionally faltered. A better, kinder couple you could not imagine. What I will remember most about being in their company is the fun they had together; the cheeky comments that would have both in uproar. When their initial meeting was first mentioned, Sean leaned back, seemingly thoughtful, focused his gaze on his wife and said: "By God, you were lucky, weren't you?" Laughter would erupt, and before long Sean would find himself the butt of the jokes. "When we were first married," Myra said, "the handle fell off the door and I asked him to screw it back on. He told me, 'Myra, that's a job for a man who fixes door handles for a living'. I knew then I didn't have a handyman for a husband." Sean grinned broadly, shrugging his shoulders in half-hearted protest. But often, when Myra left the room, he would lean in my direction. "That was a prize I won there, son," he'd say quietly. "I don't know how I managed it, but thank God I did. I wouldn't change her for the world."

An old interview with Bertie Auld came to mind at those moments. "Forget your Dalglishs and McGrains," Bertie said.

"Myra was the best signing Sean ever made. What she seen in that old fella was a mystery to me."

The young Miss Craig certainly had not been wowed by Fallon the footballer. As she said: "I remember him asking me, 'Did you think I was a good player?' And I had to tell him, 'Sean, I didn't even notice you.' I had been a few times to watch Billy but I didn't remember Sean at all. Then, by the time we got together properly, his career was almost over." Indeed, it was in the summer of 1958 – just before that ill-fated public trial – that Sean took Myra to Sligo for the first time. "He brought me to see his family and then proposed at Rosses Point. That was on July 7, and afterwards we went on to Dublin to buy the ring. Lovely memories." The following May, at St Mark's Church in Shettleston, Myra Craig became Mrs Fallon. Sean, meanwhile, had undergone a title change of his own.

> By then, I was coach rather than a player. Just as I was retiring, Celtic told me that they wanted me to stay on and take care of the third team. The club had just bought Barrowfield, and youth development was becoming a big focus for Bob Kelly. The job involved bringing through young lads towards the first team, working with Jock – who was in charge of the reserves – and helping to sign some young players. I was delighted. More than anything, it was a big relief because I knew by that stage that I didn't want to leave Glasgow. I was settled in the city and had met Myra, so I was hoping there might be a chance for me to stay in some capacity. And the job they gave me was perfect. Working with young players, bringing them in and then developing them, was what I always enjoyed most – even when I was up with Jock in the first team. It was a great honour for me and I felt within myself that I could do the job; that I wouldn't let the club down.

It was an appointment lauded in the dressing room, on the terraces and in the media. When Jimmy Sanderson of the *Scottish Daily Express* broke the story on November 29, under the headline 'Fallon to be Celtic's top coach', he wrote that the club "were to be applauded" for keeping hold of their "30-year-old" Iron Man. "Fallon's bubbling enthusiasm and hard, scrupulously clean play have made him one of the most popular players in Scotland," added Sanderson. "It was thought that at the end of his playing career the much-injured Sean would go back to Ireland as a manager. But he has never hidden the fact that he considers Celtic, 'the greatest club in the world'. His appointment as coach will be hailed not only at Parkhead but throughout Scotland."

"Everyone was behind it," is the recollection of Bertie Auld. "Sean was well liked, well respected and had that great passion for Celtic. He was one of the club's great leaders at that times, someone who would look after the young players and not only give them great advice, but show them how to conduct themselves through his example. Sean was the kind of guy you'd never want to lose from your club. The players loved him." Celtic were certainly determined to retain his services and that desire owed to more than his sterling and steadfast service as a player. Even before hanging up his boots, Fallon's natural inclination towards coaching and scouting had become apparent and Billy McNeill was among the first to witness it. "When I signed in 1957, it was Sean and big Jock who came out to my house in Bellshill," said McNeill. "Sean was still a player and a big part of the team at that stage but he was obviously already working with big Jock, and I remember him coming into the park in the evenings to help take training. Quite a few of the boys at that period were part-time and trained at night and Sean was always around the place to pass on advice and help you settle in." The work was unpaid and unseen to the wider public, but Fallon – having been enthused by Stein's plans for the club's youngsters – relished the opportunity to work with an old friend.

Jock was doing a great job already. He had retired a couple of years before because of a bad ankle that bothered him for the rest of his life. But he often said that the injury was the best thing that ever happened to him because it gave him the chance to move into coaching. Bob Kelly had decided to start up a youth policy, and there was no-one better than Jock to head that up. The young players loved him. People talk about how hard Jock was, and that's true, but the main thing about him was his enthusiasm and his knowledge of the game. He made players think about football, understand the jobs they would be doing, and why those jobs were important. The way he communicated his ideas was first class, right from the start. I could see he was going to be a tremendous manager. I found that I even learned a lot from him myself.

Despite this ready acknowledgement of Stein as the senior partner, Fallon's appointment prompted speculation that he had leapfrogged his former vice-captain in the coaching hierarchy. It was a supposition that, initially at least, appears to have been based more on perception than reality. Their respective salaries in 1959 – Stein earned £1000 per annum to Fallon's £780 – certainly seem to confirm the former's pre-eminent place in the pecking order. Sean's role, meanwhile, was outlined by the duo's former team-mate, John McPhail, in an article for the *Daily Record*. Its headline – 'Fallon? He's the Celtic star-finder' – was to prove prophetic. "Celtic's fortunes are not high right now," wrote McPhail, "but playing his part in the revival is the quiet man, Sean Fallon, an ex-Eire internationalist, and one of the grandest fellows ever to wear a green and white jersey. The particular post of the Irishman is to coach Celtic's youngsters in the evening, on Saturday to manage Celtic's third team, to study youngsters' potential, and to report progress to the Parkhead board."

This made for a fairly modest set of responsibilities. At this stage, Fallon was no immediate threat to either Stein or McGrory, and had no wish to be. He was both grateful for, and fulfilled by, a role in which he had the freedom to cultivate what he described as an "experimental" side. Its purpose, Sean stressed, was not the winning of matches, but the unearthing of hidden gems. "We play boys from boys guild football, amateur football and juvenile football," he explained in the *Record*. "It's a case of giving them a chance to see how they work out in the higher grade." It was an approach that, from the very start, yielded notable success stories, with Charlie Gallagher and John Fallon featuring among Fallon's earliest line-ups.

"Sean was great to work with," said Gallagher. "The thing that stood out for me, and which was particularly comforting as a young lad, was that you knew you were dealing with a good man – someone with real honesty and integrity. Sean never embarrassed you or shouted and bawled at you. If there was something he felt you should be doing better, he would take you aside and make his point, firmly but in the right way. He wouldn't stand for any nonsense, and he demanded that your standards were high. But he was decent and kind-hearted, and players responded to that. There was a great trust there for Sean. If you ever had any problems, he would be the man you would speak to. You knew that, first and foremost, he'd want to help if he could, and also that he would never betray a confidence."

The key ingredients in Fallon's subsequent successes – the ability to identify talent and to inspire esteem and affection in players – had quickly become apparent. Evidently, the chairman was among those impressed. Before long, McGrory and Stein were looking over their shoulders, and with good reason. Fallon might not have coveted their jobs, but he was someone for whom Kelly was formulating big plans. Those designs, and his subsequent rise through the backroom ranks, have become the source of retrospective sniping, with Fallon portrayed in certain quarters as having benefited unduly from his chairman's patronage. It has even been questioned whether he merited, or had earned, the position to which he ultimately ascended.

In respect of his perceived status as a favourite of Kelly's, Fallon is guilty as charged. Nor can it be disputed that the pair's long-standing mutual respect grew even stronger after the Irishman's move into coaching. Yet to extrapolate from this, as some have, that he was appointed and then promoted for purely personal reasons is to ignore his evident talents and, more pertinently, all that he went on to achieve. Even discounting the popular view, espoused by Davie Hay, that the Irishman was "the perfect assistant manager" – and comfortably Celtic's greatest – how could anyone dispute that he was worthy of that rank? It's worth remembering, too, that Fallon wasn't Kelly's only favoured son. Stein was another looked upon paternally, and acknowledged himself that the post of reserve team coach "was a job basically created for me". Preferential treatment? Absolutely. But, frankly, what did it matter? Of all Kelly's decisions, favouring Stein and Fallon proved to be the most inspired.

> The chairman and I always got on well, although I'd say that Jock's relationship with him was closer than mine. The two of them got on exceptionally well and had a lot in common. But he didn't favour Jock, or myself, because he thought we were good people. He took to us because he thought we were good at what we did and good for Celtic. If he didn't think that, we would have been out. Celtic was everything to Mr Kelly. If I was in a job, it's

because he thought I would be good for the club. And I'd like to think I didn't let him down. Bob Kelly was a straight man, very honest. He never looked for us to do his dirty work for him or report back from the dressing room.

Jock and myself would never have betrayed a confidence in any case, but the chairman wasn't interested in that sort of thing. He might not have been popular with everyone, but he had great principles. We had a very high regard for the man. He had been very supportive of me in my early days and I never forgot it. He was also very fond of Myra and once we were married, the two of us would help out wherever we could. Bob wasn't fit enough by that stage to take his dog for a walk, so I would take it out to the Braes as part of my evening run. That didn't end too well though. One day when we were coming back, the dog wandered out on to the road and was knocked down by a car. I had to tell the chairman it was dead, and I knew that Lady Kelly doted on that poor thing. It's a wonder I didn't get sacked after that.

This wasn't to be the only calamity he would suffer in attempting to assist the chairman. Myra told of another incident, which occurred when she and Sean stopped by to check on the Kellys' house while the couple were on holiday. "As soon as we walked into the dining room, we could see a puddle on their table and water dripping down from above," she said. "Sean ran upstairs to take a look and, the next thing I knew, there was this almighty crash. He had gone to see at where the leak was coming from – and fallen straight through the ceiling. The whole thing collapsed and he ended up on his back, rubble all around him. He was lucky he didn't kill himself."

Fallon lived to fight another day, and just as well. There was much work to be done in this new role of his. Yet he was to find that the foundations of Celtic's future were as flimsy and precarious as the floor through which he had plummeted. A naive and ill-conceived revolution was already in the works, and the club's management structure was to become more dysfunctional than ever. Demoralising days lay ahead.

In hindsight, the warning signs were there even in that *Daily Express* article heralding Fallon's appointment. So enthused was the author that he suggested the move, "could help make Celtic the Busby Babes of Scotland". This, it soon became clear, was exactly what Bob Kelly had in mind. Sadly, and not for the first time, reality would not match Kelly's romantic vision. From having "never had it so good", Fallon was about to endure the famine and frustration of Celtic's lean years.

Chapter 13
The Kelly Kids

A round the time Fallon was being injected with cortisone at the Royal Infirmary, morphine and the last rites were being administered in the Rechts der Isar Hospital in Munich. It was there in that snowbound Germany city, on February 6, 1958, a month before Sean's final Celtic appearance, that a plane crash claimed the lives of eight Manchester United players and left Sir Matt Busby fighting for survival. "Awful. Just tragic," was how Fallon remembered the Munich air disaster. "No-one in football talked about anything else for months."

The Busby Babes were a national obsession. Even before it was propelled violently into the realms of romantic tragedy, their story was so inspiring, so poignant, that it stirred all but the most hardened cynics. And Bob Kelly was no cynic. To an idealist such as the Celtic chairman, the tale of a young, home-grown team reviving a battered and once-great club wasn't merely to be enjoyed and admired. It was to be replicated.

He might have turned up his nose at Busby in 1950 but, on the basis that imitation is the sincerest form of flattery, Kelly was about to pay him the ultimate compliment. Or attempt to at least. Less than two years after the 7-1 game, seen as the last hurrah of an ageing team, came the first coining of a phrase that would have thrilled the Celtic chairman. "The Kelly Kids have arrived," wrote

Robert Russell of the *Scottish Daily Express*. The name would stick but, sadly for Celtic, little else in Russell's 1959 report stood the test of time. Kelly's new team, he wrote, "would one day surpass the fame of the Busby Babes… bring a new flag to Parkhead, and a new pride to Scottish football". Others were similarly bullish. Jack Harkness of the *Sunday Post* famously predicted that, by 1961, Celtic would have "the finest team they've had in many years, and one that will rank with the best in Britain".

Such optimism had been sparked by the emergence of some genuinely exciting young players, all coaxed through the ranks by Stein and Fallon. But in tipping them for greatness, the pundits seemed to be forgetting something. Celtic might have had the babes; they didn't have a Busby. The naming of the team after Kelly provided ample proof that not only was he calling the shots, but that everyone knew it. Consequently, comparisons with Old Trafford, where Busby and Jimmy Murphy's careful, insightful planning underpinned the Babes' rise, were always fanciful. Celtic's chaotic management ensured the Kelly Kids were always destined to be a disappointing tribute act.

> The ability was there in that group of players, and a lot of them went on to prove that. But it was a hard time for everyone. The organisation and planning wasn't right and too many of those boys ended up being thrown in too early. A few were ruined. We could really have done with some old heads in there to help them but, unfortunately, the club had got rid of almost all the older players and not replaced them. That became a problem when things got hard because there was a lot of impatience in the crowd. That got to a lot of those younger lads, when a bit of experience and character in the team would have made all the difference. Even still, we should have done better with those Kelly Kids. If you'd told me after the 7-1 game that we would go eight years without a trophy, I would never have believed it.

There is a school of thought that it is precisely because of the 7-1 game that the ensuing years were so gloomy. The manner of Celtic's victory seemed to embolden Kelly, strengthening his conviction that he knew best and could plan for the future accordingly. Following the Busby model evidently excited him and he told the 1959 AGM that Celtic was "in its most promising position" for three decades. Yet that same season was, statistically at least, the second-worst in the club's history, ending with the team in ninth position, having won just 12 of their 34 matches.

Kelly had embarked on a thorough clear-out of Fallon's former team-mates, offloading the influential trio of Bobby Collins, Bobby Evans and Willie Fernie to Everton, Chelsea and Middlesbrough respectively. The money raised was spent not on acquiring replacements, but on erecting floodlights. By May 1960, Bertie Peacock was the only survivor of the 1957 League Cup winners, and even he was being gradually phased out of the side. The Kelly Kids were on their own. In focusing exclusively on youth, Kelly had seemingly forgotten that even the Busby Babes had leant heavily on the experience of players such as Roger Byrne and Johnny Berry. Robbed of that kind of guidance and leadership, and subject to the unsettling influence of Kelly's incessant tinkering, Celtic's youngsters wilted.

Frustration at this was heightened by the knowledge that it could all have been so different. In Stein and Fallon, Celtic already had on their staff two men who – as they later proved – could have been for the Kelly Kids what Busby and Murphy were to the Babes. As Paddy Crerand said: "In those days, you were actually better off in the reserves with Jock and Sean because you got some proper coaching. There were systems of play and different ways of doing things. In my case, I remember they would lay out these long benches in different areas of the pitch and I had to hit them. There would be ones at different ranges: 30 yards, 40 yards, 50 yards. What it did for your passing was incredible. The first team was miles behind." There, players trained much as McGrory had in his 1920s pomp, with lap after lap of the Celtic Park track. The manager himself was, by his own admission, "getting a bit tired and torn", while Kelly conceded that the players of the 1960s "looked on me as an old man". Stein, by contrast, was energetic, popular, evidently talented, and eager for the chance to manage. Later, reflecting on that period, he would say: "We're all egotistical enough to think we can do the job better than someone else."

Kelly, though, was not prepared either to relinquish control or to move McGrory aside. The opportunity Stein so craved came not at Celtic Park, but at East End Park. He left for Dunfermline in March 1960, having been told by the chairman "that I had gone as far as I could be expected to go at a club like Celtic". Striking out on his own was crucial to Stein's subsequent rise and there were those who felt that Fallon should have made a similar move, if only to avoid becoming mired in the looming misery. "I'm sure if Sean had got away from Celtic and maybe gone down to England, he'd have been a big success as a manager," is the view of John Gorman, who came through the ranks under the Irishman during the 1960s. "He certainly had all the attributes." Yet it would be wrong to suggest that he decided against following Stein's lead. For Fallon, there was no decision to make.

> I never even thought about leaving. I admired Jock for going out on his own, but we had different priorities. For him, being a manager was everything, and rightly so – he was someone who was born for that job. But I didn't have the same ambition. Being part of Celtic was more important to me than becoming a manager. All the way through my career, I could never see past Celtic. Maybe on a professional level it would have done me good to go away for a while and learn my trade. Jock certainly came back a better manager, more experienced and confident in himself. But I was happy where I was. Jock was too – he didn't want to leave Celtic. He might not have grown up a Celtic supporter but he became as passionate about the club as anyone. Deep down, I think he was hoping that the club would fight to keep him. I remember talking to him in the dressing room the day he got a letter saying he could go. He was very disappointed. He'd hoped the club might see him as a future manager but, at that stage, it didn't seem to be the case.

In fact, Stein's departure owed largely to a belief that Celtic already had their next manager in mind, and it wasn't him. It was Fallon. As Stein's wife, Jean, said in *Jock Stein, the Authorised Biography*: "The old chairman (Kelly) used to suggest that he had simply let John go out for experience and that it was always the case that he would go back to Celtic, but I don't think that was right. John didn't think so either. He thought that Sean was going to be the next Celtic manager." By the early 1960s, this had become Scottish football's worst-kept secret. And yet the supposed heir apparent knew no more than the man on the street.

Everyone would tell me the same thing – that I had been earmarked for the manager's job. But it was a strange situation because the one person who never discussed it with me was Bob Kelly. It wasn't even a case of him not making any promises – he didn't even mention it. And there was no way I was going to ask him because I had too much respect for Jimmy McGrory to go asking about his job. I'm sure Mr McGrory must have known the board was looking at a successor, though, because he was quite suspicious of Jock and myself when we first started as coaches. That was a shame because I wouldn't have hurt Mr McGrory for all the world and at that stage I didn't even have the ambition to become Celtic manager. I was quite happy working with the young players and I was disappointed when Jock left because I felt that, in the reserves and third team at least, we were doing things the right way. But it turned out to be the best move he ever made.

Fallon and the players knew what Celtic were losing, and those in the boardroom would learn the hard way. The process of proving Kelly wrong – both on the manager's job and on the chairman's warning that Dunfermline were doomed to relegation – began for Stein with a 3-2 debut victory over his former employers. An unprecedented run of six straight wins followed to keep the Pars up and, within a year, the club was celebrating the first major trophy of its history. Again, Celtic were Stein's victims. The sight of him bounding on to the pitch at the final whistle, his white raincoat billowing in the wind, became the defining image of the 1961 Scottish Cup final. When the Pars players returned to the dressing room, they found their manager already celebrating in the bath, still wearing that same jacket.

Before the final, John McPhail had written an article for the *Daily Record* in which he not only tipped Celtic to win, but singled out Fallon as "the Parkhead secret weapon". "Sean has accomplished a first-class job since taking over from Jock Stein," he wrote. "His vast cup experience is invaluable to the Celtic kids and that kindly Irish tongue of his can help more than criticism to eradicate a fault... Dunfermline have the cup-seasoned Stein, who knows what he wants. But Celtic have the equally shrewd Fallon and the even more experienced Jimmy McGrory. These are the two men Stein fears most."

Fear? From all we know of Stein, it seems highly unlikely.

Yet McPhail remained close enough to the Dunfermline boss and Fallon to highlight the immense mutual respect that was maintained throughout their years apart. Indeed, according to his son, Stein felt at the time that Celtic had erred in delaying Fallon's accession to the manager's office. "I know my dad was surprised that Sean didn't get the job a few years before he ultimately came back," said George Stein. "Jimmy McGrory wasn't really up to running a football team by that stage, and my dad felt that the club would have been better getting on with it and giving Sean full control."

Stein would have appreciated that, whatever else, Fallon was a man of ideas. After all, the pair had spent much of the previous decade putting the game to rights in Ferrari's, discussing the changing football landscape, where Celtic were going wrong and how, given the chance, they would do things better. "We were modern-thinking, Jock and I," said Fallon. "We'd disagree about the odd player, but our basic ideas on football were almost identical." Their shared philosophy also reflected not only their mutual passion for organised, attacking football, but the influence of the same team – and the same epochal encounter.

Hungary-England in 1953 opened our eyes in a lot of respects. It was an education, that's the best way I can describe it. The Hungarians were magnificent; they made the English look stupid that day. Jock and I spoke about that game constantly because, at the time, it was a new type of football altogether. In those days, most people in Britain just assumed that everyone played 2-3-5 and in roughly the same way. The Hungarians changed everything in terms of their system and the way they played the game. It was all about skill on the ball and movement off the ball. You look at how much work the Lisbon Lions did off the ball, creating space – all those ideas came from watching teams like Hungary and the great Brazil and Real Madrid sides that came later.

We knew that we couldn't copy those teams completely – you have to bring your own characteristics – but they definitely gave us a few things to think about. You would have to say, too, that Bob Kelly deserved a lot of credit for taking us to see those games. He even paid for the entire squad to go to the World Cup in Switzerland and, again, that taught us so much. You never got any overseas football on TV in those days, so those games were fantastic for us. Real football people will tell you that they never stop learning. Whether it's by watching a game in the World Cup or a kick-about in the park, you're always picking up something. It just happens that some games are more special than others, and Hungary at Wembley definitely fell into that category.

It was a match that awoke British football from its smug slumber. "Here, indeed, did we attend, all 100,000 of us, the twilight of the gods," was how *The Times'* Geoffrey Green reported on the end of England's seeming invincibility. For Stein and Fallon, the memory continued to inspire. The former kept a film of the match in his house, while Fallon devoted an entire newspaper column to lauding the Magyars for bringing about "a further burst forward in football evolution". The article saw the Irishman identify three categories – "greater speed", "greater accuracy of the pass" and "team movement" – in which the "improved continental game" was leaving British football behind. Over six decades later, those areas of deficiency seem painfully familiar.

"Surely we have to learn not to be satisfied by our present performances," wrote Fallon, "but always strive to play the ball faster, and by training and coaching to play it more accurately. And we must remember, forever, that it is the intelligent play of the man not on the ball that makes the man on the ball a better player, and makes 11 individuals into a real team." Then, as now, it made for a cohesive and intelligent argument. Yet Fallon did not plan on resting simply on ideas and ideals; he knew that training-ground techniques were needed to put what he preached into practice. In *The Management*, a book on Scotland's great football managers, there is a chapter on the SFA's world-renowned coaching courses at Largs. Dave Russell was course director in the programme's early days, and his son, Robin, remembered one student in particular "making copious notes and then buttonholing Dad" after a session on Brazil's pioneering 4-2-4 system. That student was Sean Fallon.

As a player and a coach, I was someone who always wanted to improve myself so that I could make the most of what talent I had. That was why I went down to Largs to take my coaching badges. I thought it was very important because, throughout my time at Celtic, I worked a lot with the club's young players and felt a great responsibility to make sure they were getting the best education possible. Football was moving on. Celtic needed big changes and, the way I saw the situation, it was important that we try some new things. I definitely had my own ideas about what the club needed at that time.

Early evidence of Fallon's intentions came in the first close season following Stein's departure. In his sights was the ludicrous practice, which pervaded British football at that time, of keeping the ball out of training 'to make players hungry for it on a Saturday'. When the *Evening Times* reported on the start of pre-season, it was under the headline: 'Celts on the ball! Yes, ALL 28 of 'em.' "A revolution is taking place at Celtic Park," wrote the article's author, Gair Henderson. "A training revolution which is likely to make the Celtic team one of the fittest, toughest and smartest set of ball players in the league... Every player still works hard – maybe harder than ever – but they work with a difference. They work non-stop with a BALL AT THEIR FEET. Today 28 players checked into Parkhead... And what the astonished football scribes saw was this: Sean Fallon issuing each and every man with a football."

Fallon was described as the "ringmaster" and explained to Henderson: "The Celtic aim first and last is to produce ball players. This is the way we aim to do it." Again, his logic was sound. But this embracing of modernity wasn't to last. Before long, Celtic's players were again monotonously lapping the track under the guidance of trainer Willie Johnstone, the much-lauded "revolution" seemingly discarded. The criticism Sean drew for allowing this to happen was both understandable and, frankly, justifiable. "That's the only slightly negative thing I can say about Sean," said Charlie Gallagher. "He maybe took too long to get out of the traditional way of doing things, although you could see he was trying at times." Jim Craig arrived later in the decade but he, too, was underwhelmed by Celtic's training regime – and considered Fallon at least partially responsible. "Sean had carte blanche to do something before Jock arrived," was Craig's view. "But there was no great tactical input and the training was fairly uninteresting. The guys who played in the early '60s are fairly condemnatory of how it was all run. And yet, curiously enough, they all love Sean."

Perhaps they had an inkling of the unseen difficulties Fallon was encountering. Though the public viewed Stein's departure as boosting the Irishman's prospects, the reality was that it had left him in a near-impossible position. In McPhail's cup final preview, Sean's only contribution had been to make this point: "Now, some folk seem to think I dictate the team's tactics. That's entirely wrong." And so it was. But it begged the question: what did he do? The truth was that no-one – not even the players – knew the extent of Fallon's responsibilities. Bertie Auld, for example, considered him to be "effectively the man in charge", while Tommy Gemmell described him as "Bob Kelly's right-hand man". Gallagher, on the other hand, felt that "Sean had no real say during that time" and Bobby Lennox saw the Irishman's role as "basically a helper". Such confusion and conflicting opinions were understandable, particularly as Sean himself was often unsure about how far his remit extended. Merely taking on Stein's position in charge of the reserves would have been preferable as it would have permitted him the freedom to implement the kind of techniques and plans he'd spent a decade forming. As it was, a thankless promotion to work alongside McGrory left him treading on eggshells.

> That was the most difficult time I had at Celtic. Some people said I was assistant to Mr McGrory, others said I was coach and some even said I was effectively managing the team. None of them was right. The truth was, it wasn't clear what my responsibilities were, so I just tried to do what I could. I would have liked to have done more but I felt hamstrung. Bob Kelly had promoted me to work with the first team and wanted me to have more influence, but he still wanted the final say on the big decisions and to keep on picking the team. He also asked me to be careful around Jimmy McGrory so as not to upset him. That was difficult at the time because Mr McGrory had the idea that I was trying to push him aside and take over.
>
> I remember one time I suggested changing a couple of things to improve the way the team was being run, just to bring us more up-to-date. Football was changing at that time and we weren't moving with the times. But he lost his temper with me, and I'd never seen that happen before with Mr McGrory. 'You seem to be trying to take over, Sean. Don't forget I'm the manager here,' he told me. I tried to set him straight, to explain that it wasn't like that. I said: 'I'm just trying what's right for the

club, for the young players, and for you yourself, Mr McGrory.'
But after that I had to be very, very careful in everything I did,
whether it was in training or in the way I addressed the players.
I couldn't be seen to be over-stepping my authority. What people
maybe don't realise, because of the way he took over picking the
team, is that Bob Kelly absolutely idolised Jimmy McGrory. It
wouldn't have been good for me to get in a situation where the
chairman had to choose between one of the two of us.

The whole situation saddened me because all I wanted to
do was help the man. I knew McGrory loved Celtic as much as
I did but there were things needing improved for the benefit
of everyone. I thought I knew what the team needed at that
stage but I was held back from doing too much. It was a shame
because I think the two of us could have worked fairly well
together. I'd always got on well with Mr McGrory as a player
and had nothing but affection for him. After all, he was the
man who signed me for Celtic and allowed me to realise all
my dreams. But it was only later, once Jock came back, that he
seemed to understand the situation and realised that I hadn't
been trying to take his job after all. We always got on very well
after that.

The extent to which wounds healed was confirmed by Gerry
McNee, McGrory's biographer, who revealed another side to the
difficulties of the early '60s. He said: "I know for a fact that Jimmy
held Sean in the highest regard, not only as a player but as a man,
so I'm surprised it got as bad as it did. But I hope Sean didn't take
any of those incidents personally because Jimmy, frankly, wasn't
himself during that period. Celtic were struggling badly and he
knew the end was coming, so the strain was beginning to tell."

The wariness between the pair, as with so much during that
era, seems to have been entirely unnecessary. Celtic suffered as a
result and so, too, did Fallon's reputation. The diplomatic tightrope
he was treading with McGrory had been a substantial mitigating
factor but, all the same, he had not covered himself in glory. No-
one realised this more than Fallon himself. His son, Sean Jnr, said:
"I don't think my dad has many regrets, but I know he wishes he'd
implemented more of his own ideas in the early '60s. It wasn't
an easy environment though. What was needed at that time was
massive change; a complete overhaul of the team's management.

To do that from within, as a junior coach, was close to impossible. It needed someone with Jock's personality and record of success – someone completely sure of his own abilities – to come in from the outside and demand the changes necessary."

Sean Snr would echo his son's basic sentiments. He was not, however, as forgiving in assessing his role in a desolate era. His view was that, even if revolution had been impossible, bringing about a little evolution should not have proved beyond his capabilities.

I take my share of responsibility, most definitely. I should have done more to change things. It was an awkward situation but I should have taken more chances for the good of the club and not worried so much about upsetting people. I didn't want to go over Jimmy McGrory's head but, because of that, no-one took any big decisions apart from the chairman. That wasn't a good situation for anyone, especially the supporters. They could see that things weren't being handled well. The training was definitely one area we should have done a lot better in, and I knew that. Jock and I had always talked at Ferrari's about how it needed to improve a lot. But it took until Jock came back for that to happen.

Nonetheless, while the much-heralded training revolution was needlessly postponed, not everything was put on ice until Stein returned.

In another key area, Fallon had set about providing his old friend with a handsome inheritance and laid the foundations for the greatest years in Celtic's history. Stein would provide the missing magic, but the process of turning Kelly Kids into Lisbon Lions was already well under way.

Chapter 14
The Lean Years

.

'Good cop, bad cop' was an expression I heard repeatedly from the men who played under Fallon. Almost invariably, it would crop up in explanations of the dressing room dynamic, with Sean remembered as the yin to Stein's belligerent yang. "Jock would come in at half-time, give someone a real volley and then storm out," recalled Jim Craig. "Then Sean would come over, put an arm round whoever it was and build them back up again. He'd say: 'Don't worry about him. We know what you can do. Just up your game a wee bit and you'll be fine.' That's an important job, keeping footballers happy and confident. And Sean was excellent at it."

That he should be so comfortable in this role is hardly surprising. Making those around him feel good about themselves not only came naturally, but was one of Fallon's great pleasures in his life. "That's the thing about Sean – he was just a great man," said Billy McNeill. "He didn't need to play up to the role as the nice guy because that was just the way he was. As players, we knew he was completely genuine in only wanting the best for us."

Yet football being the sport it is, integrity and likeability are not always viewed as strengths. Think of Jimmy McGrory, and Fallon's description of him as "too nice" for the position he held. The Irishman, another thorough gentlemen, could easily have followed in his manager's diffident footsteps. Yet there was steel behind his soft-hearted exterior and most who mentioned the 'good cop, bad cop' analogy did so to dismiss it. "Sean could be the bad cop too," was a common observation.

In the early '60s, that was the role forced upon him. McGrory would never chastise, while Kelly – despite being the principal decision-maker – issued his instructions from afar. Fallon was bad cop by default, and players during that period remember him as such. When I asked Pat Crerand what kind of manager the Irishman would have made, "tough and strong" was his unhesitant reply. "There would have been no messing about with Sean, just as there was no messing about with him as a player," added the Manchester United legend. "He and Jock were very similar – both extremely strong characters who wouldn't take any crap from anyone."

Crerand spoke from experience. After all, he had made the mistake of pitting himself against Fallon in a notorious dressing-room row that, ultimately, cost him his Celtic career. It erupted on New Year's Day 1963, at a time when the Scotland midfielder was undoubtedly the most accomplished player at his club and, arguably, in the country. But on this particular day, he – like everyone else in green and white – was enduring an afternoon to forget. It was not, in his defence, a day for footballers, with a rock-hard Ibrox pitch inexplicably declared playable despite a treacherous covering of ice. Rangers, always the more physically powerful of the two sides, had adapted better to the conditions and deservedly led 1-0 at the break. With McGrory silent, Fallon attempted to rally the players, instructing them to be more direct in their passing while admonishing Crerand for straying out of position. Frustrated and angry, having deflected in Rangers' goal, the midfielder forcefully disagreed with these directives. When Sean held his ground, Crerand refused to return for the second half.

> He went back in the end. He had to – we had no subs in those days. It became blown up a bit over time, but those kind of arguments happen a lot in dressing rooms. Basically, the conditions weren't right for playing the kind of short passes that Pat preferred, but him being the headstrong character he is, he wouldn't accept it. We had a lot of pace up front and, with the conditions so icy, I

wanted to utilise that. The Rangers defenders were big but weren't the quickest to turn. It was made out later that I just wanted us to play long-ball football, but that wasn't the case. When the surface is good, I would completely agree with Pat – the ball should always be kept as much as possible and the passing game is best. One thing I always stressed to the players was that if there was an easy pass on, they should make it. But that wasn't a day for football. Pat and I disagreed, and I was annoyed with him at the time. But we had it out later and, as far as I was concerned, it was over and done with.

Crerand, too, felt that a successful reconciliation had been achieved. "I fell out with Sean, but I never lost my respect for the man," he said. "I always thought he was a magnificent servant for Celtic and we shook hands the same day. He's been a great friend ever since." But although the protagonists might have considered the issue resolved, there were two barriers to Crerand's outburst being forgiven and forgotten. The first was the fact that he had continued to rage after the final whistle, this time focusing his ire on 19-year-old John Hughes. "The worst moment of my career," was how Hughes remembered it seven years later. "He said that if I was included in the team again, he wouldn't play. It was the cruellest remark I have ever heard. You can imagine what effect it had on my confidence."

But Crerand had bigger problems than Hughes' hurt feelings. The second, ultimately insurmountable, barrier to absolution was the presence of Bob Kelly in the Ibrox dressing room. The Scotland midfielder had been a favourite of the chairman's, and was even made the club's highest-paid player shortly before that Ne'erday clash. Kelly, though, considered his conduct intolerable. Crerand found himself dropped from the team and, within two months, was on his way to Old Trafford.

That was a pity. You couldn't afford to make an enemy of Bob Kelly back then because he ran the club from top to bottom. But I felt he was wrong on that one. I would definitely have kept Pat at the club if it had been down to me. He could frustrate me at times because he had a hot temper, but I appreciated his talent and never wanted to see a player with that kind of ability lost to Celtic. No-one was sorrier to see Pat go than I was. The team needed him at that time, and we struggled without him.

Celtic were making a habit of selling such players. In 1965, the same year Crerand won his inaugural championship at Old Trafford, Bobby Collins became the first Scot to be voted England's Footballer of the Year. Fallon's old team-mate had reinvented himself as an intelligent and influential midfield general, and was the captain to whom his Leeds United team-mates looked for inspiration. "Bobby would have killed his mother for a result," is Jack Charlton's memory of him. "He introduced a 'win at any cost' attitude and, because we had a very young side at the time, he was a huge influence." Collins, in other words, was just the kind of player Celtic needed.

Bertie Auld might have provided some of the personality and mental toughness the Kelly Kids were lacking but he too had been sold. Temperament had again been the deciding factor, with Kelly said to have never forgiven Auld for cheekily ruffling the hair of Harold Davis after the Rangers defender scored an own goal. Devoid of experience and leadership, Celtic appointed 25-year-old Dunky Mackay as club captain in March 1961. Within two months, the same player was openly declaring that he wanted a move to England.

This might have been symptomatic of a wider malaise, but it was an act that Fallon would have struggled to understand, or forgive. As John Fallon, Celtic's goalkeeper at the time, said: "You couldn't have met anyone who loved Celtic more than Sean, and he hated it when players didn't show that same passion. He would always tell us, 'Don't ever forget what a great thing it is to be playing for this club'. He'd be raging if he ever thought anyone was selling Celtic short." One player who would have guaranteed Fallon the unwavering commitment he demanded, and who became available in 1961, was the Leeds United midfielder Billy Bremner. Kelly, though, balked at the asking price of £30,000. "He would have been a bargain if we had got him at that," Sean reflected. "I told the chairman that Billy was a big Celtic fan and would fancy the move. But he didn't believe in spending money at that stage."

Recruiting and rearing young players was the policy to which Kelly remained almost exclusively committed. Yet it was a rule with one prominent exception. In 1964, and completely out of the blue, Celtic attempted to sign a 36-year-old. He also happened to be the greatest player of his generation. The approach for Alfredo di

Stefano came four years after he had wowed Hampden with a hat-trick in Real Madrid's legendary 7-3 win over Eintracht Frankfurt in 1960. That remarkable match, which Fallon had watched alongside Stein, was the fifth successive European Cup final in which the Argentine had played, scored and emerged victorious.

Reserve centre-half John Cushley, who spoke Spanish, had been dispatched with Jimmy McGrory to Madrid, supposedly with the aim of bringing home a legend. But it was a plan with a significant flaw. "Di Stefano had already gone to his holiday home in the north of Spain," said Cushley. "In the end, we had to track him down on the phone. Mr McGrory was telling me 'Offer him this'. I couldn't believe the figures – it was more than the rest of us put together were getting. But in any case, Di Stefano said that he had already agreed a deal with Espanyol, so it was a bit of a wasted trip."

Normally thrifty to the point of notoriety, Celtic had promised the Argentinian £200-per-game, twice what the highest-paid player in Britain at the time, Johnny Haynes, was earning. Yet the fact they had arranged for three journalists to accompany McGrory and Cushley convinced Fallon that it was a trip geared more towards obtaining headlines than acquiring a star player.

> I always thought the Di Stefano thing was a publicity stunt. I would have loved nothing more if he'd said yes because it would have been tremendous to have someone like that at Celtic. But the board knew there was no chance. If he had accepted their offer, they would have had a heart attack. There just wasn't money for a player like that floating around at the time. It was a story that got the fans excited but that wasn't a good time for the club and I felt it was put out there to relieve a bit of pressure.

Lower profile, but of considerably greater significance to Celtic's future, was the recruitment drive Fallon had been embarking on. So successful were his efforts that, famously, 10 of the Lisbon Lions were already in place by the time Jock Stein arrived. What is not so well known is that the picture should have been rosier still. Joe McBride, Stein's first major signing, and the man who played half a season in 1966/67 and still finished top scorer, explained why.

"If it had been up to Sean, I would have been a Celtic player six or seven years before I ended up signing," he said. "There were actually three separate occasions when Sean came in for me, and the board made a mess of it every single time. When I was at Kilmarnock in 1959, he spoke to me and said, 'Joe, I've told the chairman that you're a good player and just what we need. We'll be in for you'. Billy [McNeill] said that all the players knew about it and were desperate for me to come. But Celtic didn't want to cough up the £12,500 that Wolves paid for me. It was the same story when I came back from England a year or so later. There were two clubs bidding for me – Celtic and Partick Thistle – and, again, Celtic wouldn't match Thistle's bid.

"The last time was the year before I eventually signed for Celtic. Sean came on the phone to me when my contract was up with Motherwell and told me, 'Joe, don't sign. We're coming in for you'. This was at the start of the summer and I didn't sign, but I wasn't getting any wages as a result. Celtic were in touch, but Motherwell were looking for a certain amount – nothing huge, no more than they paid for me the year after – and Celtic refused to pay it. It was left to Sean to phone and apologise to me. He even offered to square me up for any wages I'd missed out on, which shows you the kind of man he was. It was frustrating for both of us, but that kind of attitude summed up how tight Celtic were in those days. Funnily enough, when I did end up signing, it was Sean who phoned me up rather than big Jock. I actually told him to forget it at first, after the way Celtic had messed me about. But he assured me: 'Don't worry, Joe, it's different this time.' And, sure enough, it was."

Another man might have been bitter that it had taken Stein's arrival to force through this important and fairly modest purchase. 'Better late than never' was Fallon's philosophical response. He had felt for the best part of a decade that McBride was the missing ingredient in a forward line that, while talented, was over-eager in its play and chronically inconsistent. "Celtic can play well up to the 18-yard line. After that – it's bedlam," wrote the *Evening Citizen's* Malcolm Munro in 1961. "It's alright a team being inspired by its support. What's wrong with Celts is that they don't get so much inspired as excited." McBride, a quintessential predator who neither panicked nor hesitated with the goal in his sights, was the antidote to this affliction. No less an authority than McGrory, the club's record goalscorer, described him as "the best Celtic centre-forward I've ever seen". However long the wait, he was worth it.

> I've never worked with anyone who was as confident in front of goal or a more natural finisher than Joe McBride. It's just a shame we didn't get him earlier because I'm sure he would have made a big difference. The team in the early '60s had a lot of qualities but it was young and lacked a bit in composure or confidence. Bertie Auld and Ronnie Simpson made a massive difference in that respect in their own positions, and Joe would have been the same at centre-forward. He was desperate to come too. But maybe the board didn't feel they had to listen to me; I wasn't the manager. I only got any real say in signing senior players in the time just before Jock came back. Before that, my job had been mainly to sign young boys."

It was a job he did exceptionally well. Yet even there, for all his many spectacular successes, Fallon would lament the ones that got away. In the '60s, the most notable examples were Jimmy Smith, who went on to star for Aberdeen, Newcastle United and Scotland, and Eddie Gray. The latter, in particular, rankled. Gray had been pursued by 35 clubs and ultimately chose to move to Leeds United, where he would make over 450 appearances, bringing style and skill to Revie's notoriously uncultured side. "When he plays on snow, he doesn't leave any footprints," the Leeds boss said of his graceful winger. "An Eddie Gray comes along once in a century if you are very, very lucky." Fallon always maintained that Celtic should have been the lucky ones. "Even when I met Sean not long ago, all these years later, he was still talking about it," said Gray. "And still telling me I'd made a mistake."

> I wasn't joking when I told him that. I still think he should have been a Celtic player. He was the kind of player our fans loved to watch and he was a Celtic supporter himself. Unfortunately, although there was a will in the family for him to join us, the inducements Leeds were offering were much greater than anything we could put up. And I can't blame the board in this case because they made the boy a very good offer. I even convinced them to put down a couple of thousand pounds, and

I still don't know how I managed that. But we could not justify offering a young lad more than we would a senior player at that time, and that was what it would have needed.

Leeds, not for the first time, were grateful for Celtic's frugality. When the Yorkshire club named its 100 greatest players in 2006, Bremner, Gray and Collins came in first, third and fourth respectively. Had Kelly loosened the purse-strings even slightly, it is likely, given the players' allegiances, that all three would have linked up in green and white. Yet just as Leeds fans would shudder at the thought of their club without this towering trio, so Celtic supporters would struggle to imagine theirs without some of the players who could – and, but for Fallon, would – have ended up elsewhere.

The Irishman might be best known for snatching the Rangers-supporting duo of Kenny Dalglish and Danny McGrain, but equally significant were his earlier efforts in keeping Tommy Gemmell and Bobby Murdoch from Motherwell. Gemmell had wanted nothing more than to pull on the claret-and-amber of his hometown club, describing them in his autobiography as "the one team I wanted to play for". Motherwell, though, seemed oblivious to the potential that Fallon quickly identified. The Irishman would be at Gemmell's side at Celtic Park on October 25, 1961, when, along with another young hopeful by the name of Jimmy Johnstone, he signed his first contract. He was then a regular at the full-back's Coltness Juniors matches, and saw enough to recommend that he be recalled and promoted after just one season on loan.

Motherwell would doubtless have cursed themselves over Gemmell, but in Murdoch's case, they could not have done any more. The Lanarkshire club even took the remarkable step of offering the youngster, who was then just 14, a full-time contract at the not inconsiderable wage of £8-a-week. But David Potter, writing in his biography of the player, *Bobby Murdoch, Different Class,* explained how they were again left disappointed. "It was Sean Fallon who did the persuading and the hiring," he wrote. "Sean was a charming Irishman who allayed any fears that the boy's parents might have had, guaranteed that he would be looked after and allowed his own deep love for the club to become infectious." Those who saw Fallon in such situations insist that no-one has ever played the role better.

I never made any promises to parents that their son would make it and I always stressed how important it was that the boys keep up their education. There was no hard sell – I just told them how much joy I had taken in playing for Celtic, and that I hoped their son would experience the same. There isn't a better feeling in football than signing a young lad at 15 or 16 and then seeing him go on to enjoy great success. And with Tommy and Bobby, they couldn't have done any more. I always felt that Bobby wasn't as famous around the world as he should have been in those great days. He was a magnificent natural footballer, and someone with the ability to control and dictate matches. He had a lovely first touch and he would always make himself available to receive the ball if his team-mate was under pressure, and get up to support the forwards. When he got on the ball, he was a head-up player with a superb range of passing, able to pick out anyone on the pitch. A lovely lad too. He never gave Jock and myself a minute's trouble.

Tommy was cheekier and more sure of himself, but he was a great trainer all the same and a tremendous player. He wasn't actually a great tackler but he was quick, good in the air and his support play for our attacks was such a great weapon. He was a magnificent striker of the ball – one of the best around – and there aren't many full-backs who can say they've scored in two European Cup finals. We were lucky to get Tommy, although it was more than luck really because we got most of the good players back then. I get some of the credit but you need a lot of people to be doing their jobs well for it to happen like that. It was a scout, Eddie McArdle, who recommended Tommy, for example, and it was actually Bob Kelly who first spotted Bobby Murdoch. He had noticed him playing in a local game and told me, 'I think this lad would be worth a look'. So I went down to Overtoun Park in Rutherglen to watch him play and, sure enough, he was more than worth a look. You're always excited when you see a player like Bobby for the first time.

Fallon's role, which continued and was strengthened under Stein, involved following up on such recommendations and deciding which players to pursue. "There's no doubt it was one of Sean's great talents," said Jim Craig. "He obviously had an eye for a player and a good set of contacts about the country who would give him a nod when they'd seen someone worth a second look. Sean seemed to make the right call more often than not. The signings he made brought Celtic a lot of success, and a lot of money."

Craig was himself one of those signings, with Fallon – acting on a recommendation from scout Joe Conner – an unseen presence at the right-back's matches for Glasgow University. Even players not known as Sean Fallon signings turn out to have been indebted to the Irishman. One such example is Charlie Gallagher, who explained: "It was Sean who put in a word to get me signed on my 18th birthday. That was 1958, and Jimmy McGrory was the manager, but I know it was Sean who told Bob Kelly that I was worth taking on. I'm one of many who owe him a lot."

But Fallon's laying of the foundations for the Stein years did not begin and end with assembling a playing squad. He had also been the driving force in gathering together a backroom team on which his old friend would later rely, and which the players universally lauded. The arrival of Bob Rooney from Cambuslang Rangers in 1961 had been agreed with Bob Kelly and, three years later, he managed to convince the chairman to bring back Neilly Mochan as trainer. 'Smiler' had never been a favourite of Kelly's – due, it was rumoured, to picking up a fine for not holding a valid radio licence – but Fallon argued successfully for his return. Mochan rewarded that faith by forging a reputation as one of the finest trainers in the game, with Celtic's evidently superior fitness in Lisbon compelling evidence of his skills.

> I had always liked Neilly. He was a very nice guy and a great player in his day. I knew he would be a great trainer for the team and he certainly didn't let me down. We didn't have the science and heart monitors football clubs work with today, but he knew how to get the players' fitness to the highest possible level. We were one of the fittest teams in Europe and Neilly had a lot to do with that. He also was a great guy to have around the place, liked a laugh, and he was the kind of character who bounced off myself and Jock very well. We needed people like Neilly. It was the same with Willie Fernie, who came back later in the '60s to help me with the reserves and did a great job. He was another clever coach, a lovely man and a great friend. And the one thing about all of the people we had with us: they knew and loved the game.

But by 1965, that passion for football – and for Celtic – counted for little. So too did behind-the-scenes changes and pledges of better to come from promising youngsters. Supporters had heard it all before. The call ringing out was for meaningful change, and Fallon – fairly or otherwise – was perceived to represent more of the same. The team he had constructed would never be his and the manager's job would soon be offered elsewhere. But he had no cause to mourn. A bad cop par excellence was on his way and good times – the best of times – lay ahead.

Chapter 15
Laying Foundations

January 12, 1965. The Celtic directors make their way through the chilly midwinter morning to the heart of Glasgow, towards the North British Hotel in George Square. Their morning newspapers, once again, do not make for cheerful reading. "They are being left behind by provincial clubs with a fraction of their resources," is John Fairgrieve's take on Celtic in the *Scottish Daily Mail.* "They are being left so far behind Rangers that it is no longer a race."

The directors can only sigh. There is no arguing with Fairgrieve's analysis. Indeed, the city centre summit to which they are heading is a tacit acceptance of its accuracy. This is a meeting with a weighty purpose, and the minutes later reveal it to have been among the most significant in the club's history:

'After much discussion, all have agreed our desire to obtain the services of J. Stein as manager. Mr Kelly was to approach Stein with a view to offering him the position. Fallon was to be offered an increased salary with increased status if Stein was secured. McGrory was to continue as public relations officer.'

Life for Celtic, and for Fallon, would never be the same again. By the time the board reconvened two evenings later, the deal was done. Stein, after a little negotiation, had accepted. Fallon and Jimmy McGrory sat alongside the directors, having already been privately informed by Kelly of their new roles. Sean, in any case, had seen this coming. And while the chairman fretted that the Irishman would view the decision as a snub – or, worse, an act of betrayal – his worries were quickly allayed.

> I won't lie to you and say I didn't want the job. By that stage, being Celtic manager had become an ambition of mine. I had fulfilled a dream by playing for Celtic and captaining the club, and to have been made manager would have capped it all. And I believed in myself; believed that I could improve things and do a good job. But as soon as Jock went out to Dunfermline and did so well, I knew in myself what was going to happen. Even then, I knew he would be back. And, honestly, I wasn't too disappointed. After all, I knew Jock and I knew he'd do a good job. There was never any doubt in my mind that he'd be a success. The chairman was worried I would be annoyed. He thought I would feel that I had done my time in the background with Jimmy McGrory, and would think I was entitled to the job. Actually, I felt Jock was entitled to it. He had gone out into management and proved himself; I'd stayed with Celtic and things hadn't really improved. I wasn't annoyed: not at the club, not at Jock and especially not at Bob Kelly – because I would have made exactly the same decision had I been in his shoes. It was never about me anyway. All I wanted was for Celtic to be successful, and I could see Jock was the man the club needed.

Even for those accustomed to Fallon's humility and selflessness, this was a stunning reaction. "There has never been a more faithful, reliable Celtic servant both as a player and backroom man," was how a grateful Kelly would go on to describe him. And history would, of course, prove Fallon right. Stein was not only the best man for the job, but the best ever to hold the job. It was, however, only reluctantly, and belatedly, that Kelly entrusted it to him. "Everyone knew that Bob wanted Sean as manager," said Bertie Auld. "If Jock hadn't gone away and made such a great impact with Dunfermline and Hibs, I'm sure Sean would have got the job. But Jock made it hard for Celtic to appoint anyone else."

Even so, Kelly was not a man known for altering his course, however logical the change might be. He could, and likely would, have ignored Stein's successes had Celtic enjoyed a few of their own. That they did not was largely attributable to the chairman himself.

In the decade that followed Fallon's Scottish Cup-winning goal in 1954, the club reached the final on another four occasions. Each time, they began disadvantaged by a mystifying team selection from Kelly and, each time, they were beaten. The replacing of Jimmy Johnstone with Bobby Craig for the 1963 Scottish Cup final replay was perhaps the most infamous of all. Johnstone had excelled in the first match, a 1-1 draw, while Craig – out of form for months – proved predictably ineffectual as Rangers won the rematch 3-0.

Such changes were Kelly's hallmark. One journalist calculated that the forward line fielded in the replay was Celtic's 39th different permutation of the season. Bobby Murdoch described the selection as "a disgrace", while the supporters – taunted by chants of 'Easy! Easy!' from their rivals – provided an equally unequivocal verdict. As Jack Harkness wrote in the *Sunday Post*: "Thirty thousand fans, almost as if it had been organised, deliberately turned their backs on their team and stole quietly into the night. It was surely Hampden's most distressing sight ever. Celtic in a Scottish Cup final replay… half an hour still left for play. Then suddenly this mass exit from the Celtic end of the ground. A demonstration of resentment, proclaiming to the board that 'the Faithful' had lost faith in their team." Those who remained merely witnessed yet more humiliation, with Jim Baxter sitting on the ball and indulging in inimitable displays of keepy-uppy. Baxter, according to Murdoch, was a player who "scared" the Celtic team of the early '60s, and the Rangers star's record – just two defeats in 18 Old Firm derbies – gives an indication of why.

That Rangers side was one of the best they ever had. They had brought in some very good players, Baxter being an obvious example. He was a lovely lad, friendly with a lot of our players, and an excellent footballer too. Although he played for Rangers, you could appreciate he was a joy to watch. He had that bit of arrogance in his football that so many great players have. To have a chance of keeping him quiet and getting the upper hand on Rangers, we had to be at our best. And too often in that era we weren't. Going out with the wrong team didn't help of course. The players were already low on confidence in Old Firm matches, and decisions like dropping Jinky in the '63 cup final made them doubt themselves even more.

Addressing this inferiority complex was to become one of Stein's top priorities. Yet perhaps surprisingly, it was not Celtic's lack of managerial leadership and substandard training that separated them from their old rivals at this stage. In both respects, Rangers were similarly deficient. Bobby Watson, a long-serving defender, said of his first season in the Ibrox first team: "I was only 19 so I felt I needed some help, some advice. But I got nothing. You were really left on your own at Ibrox. Nobody said much which would help you to develop as a player." This was the picture across British football for much of the '60s. Even Scotland's national team was described by Paddy Crerand as "a bigger shambles [than Celtic]", with no team talks and tactical decisions left to senior players.

Rangers thrived because, unlike their main rivals, they kept their best players and invested in others. The Ibrox club still did things the traditional way, with a 2-3-5 formation and a McGrory-type manager in Scot Symon; they simply did them better. Stein, though, was something new and altogether different. He was not simply improving existing practices, but forging fresh schemes and employing pioneering methods. Along with Busby and Bill Shankly, he was in the process of completely redefining the manager's role. As Danny McGrain wrote in his second autobiography, *In Sunshine or in Shadow*: "[Stein] became so famous in the early '60s because he was like an inventor who noticed a gap in the market for a commodity he could provide. Nobody thought about the geometry of the game the way he did."

Kelly certainly did not. Seemingly unperturbed by successive failures, he pressed ahead with random variations on a familiar theme, further unsettling the club's already-demoralised youngsters. The self-doubt to which Fallon referred had become a crippling affliction, and was never more evident than when season 1963/64 began with three Old Firm defeats in the space of a month. It was at this time that a long-threatened uprising finally materialised. On August 17, 1963, after a 1-1 draw at home to Queen of the South, the entrance to Celtic Park was encircled by a 2000-strong mob. 'We want Kelly!' went up the cry. The chairman, as luck would have it, was at a reserve match that particular afternoon, but such resentment could not be dodged forever. There even followed a half-hearted takeover bid by one vociferous critic, the lawyer and councillor Baillie James Reilly, whose cause was championed by a Celtic fanzine of the time, *The Shamrock*. Reilly's failure, in hindsight, represented a lucky escape. Archie Macpherson remembers him as "a nefarious character", and was condemnatory of Baillie's subsequent involvement in Third Lanark, which ended with the Hi Hi's controversial demise.

Kelly was able to resist attempted coups and demonstrations, but he was not impervious to criticism. The stresses of Celtic's plight were impacting on his health and he could not fail to notice the worrying deterioration they were effecting in McGrory. Nor could he ignore an alarming drop in attendances. On January 4, just over a week before that fateful meeting in the North British Hotel, *The Scotsman's* John Rafferty highlighted the extent of the problem. "Celtic's support seems to have sunk to the solid corps of die-hard supporters," he wrote, "for it has stuck at about 14,000 for some weeks."

For what seemed like an age, Kelly had held firm, stoically enduring the abuse hurled towards the directors' box from the enclosure below. Panic buys were resisted, alternative plans dismissed and, towards the end of the 1963/64 season, it seemed that his obstinacy might even be rewarded. Less than eight months after fans had been baying for blood at the front doors, many of those same supporters could be heard demanding a lap of honour. Celtic had beaten MTK Budapest 3-0 in the first leg of the European Cup Winners' Cup semi-final and, to everyone present, a place in the final seemed all but assured. Basel, Dinamo Zagreb and Slovan Bratislava had been seen off in the preceding rounds, with a defensively flawless 1-0 win in Czechoslovakia having earned Celtic's place in the last four. Praise was heaped upon a side that seemed, not before time, to have added maturity and mental strength to their armoury. When Celtic travelled to Ibrox the weekend after returning from Bratislava, the players were applauded on to the field by their Rangers counterparts.

"It was some achievement when you think about it," said John Clark. "That was essentially a team of young boys, and there we were in a European semi-final. We weren't used to that kind of reaction, though." It might have made for a refreshing change, but all this adulation came accompanied by the very real danger of complacency. Talk at Celtic Park soon centred not on the second leg, but on the final, with club secretary Desmond White engaged in lobbying UEFA for a change of venue. John Divers, who had been carrying a slight injury, was omitted from the travelling party and told to concentrate on getting himself fit for the big one. Kelly, meanwhile, was becoming intoxicated by the all-too-rare acclaim his team had attracted for their adventurous European displays. This swashbuckling approach would continue in Budapest, he assured the media. It was, he said, Celtic's "duty" to entertain the Hungarian public by going for goals.

These public pronouncements set the tone for a notorious pre-match team talk. "Och, we beat them over there in Glasgow – we can beat them here as well," Kelly told the players. "Just go out and play." Combined with the return of MTK's brilliant talisman, Karoly Sandor – sorely missed in the first leg – this hopelessly naive approach spelled disaster. Celtic lost 4-0. There would be complaints about the Austrian referee and inferences naturally drawn when he arrived at the post-match banquet flanked by two pretty blondes. But Celtic's excuses – ill luck, poor officiating, inexperienced players – were wearing painfully thin.

It was a long flight back after we lost that match. I remember feeling sick for our supporters because they'd had so little to get excited about, and you could see how much the first leg meant to them. It hurt me a lot because I felt we were turning a bit of a corner and that some of the players were coming of age. But there was a cocky mood about the club in the build-up to the game in Hungary, and you saw that in the way the team was set up to play. But although the chairman made a mistake there, I think it ended up being a good lesson for everyone. Celtic were an attacking team with an attacking philosophy, but if you leave gaps against good European teams, they'll exploit them. Everyone always talks about that Dukla Prague semi-final in '67, when we played very negatively away from home to get through to Lisbon. It wasn't in our nature, and we never played so defensively again. But the way we played in Prague came from what had happened in '64. After Budapest, we knew – and so did Jock – that all that mattered in semi-finals was getting through to the final.

That triumph of pragmatism in Prague was less than three years away. However, at the time, Kelly was not interested in eyeing fresh European horizons. Indeed, he reacted to Celtic's defeat in Budapest by telling shareholders at the club's AGM in May 1964 that he did not see a future in continental competitions. "Surely a better tournament would be a British Cup," he said. Being badly wrong was a habit the Celtic chairman was struggling to shake. He did, however, make one shrewd decision around this time: he began to listen to Fallon on the issue of transfers. More specifically, he accepted the Irishman's recommendation that the Kelly Kids, decried even by McGrory for "lacking mental hardness", required an injection of experience and personality. What followed were two of the most significant signings in Celtic's history. Neither, though, was easily won.

Target number one was a goalkeeper who had been in the senior game three years longer than Fallon himself, having debuted for Queen's Park in 1945. He had enjoyed a sterling career, competing in the Olympics for Great Britain and winning FA Cups with Newcastle United, but it was a career drawing to a close. A fall-out with Stein, his then manager at Hibernian, had caused him to look at a life outside football, and he had even begun reporting on matches for a Sunday newspaper. "I wasn't drifting out of the game – I was galloping," wrote Ronnie Simpson in his autobiography, *Sure it's a Grand Old Team to Play For*. "I had chucked in the towel good and proper." The title of the next chapter, 'A phone call from Sean Fallon', gives a hint of what happened next. Yet at the time, it seemed ludicrous. Even Simpson was baffled by Celtic's interest. "Did they know my age?" he wrote, recalling his reaction. "Did they know I had pretty well lost interest in the game? Surely keepers weren't all that difficult to come by." Keepers were in plentiful supply. But not keepers like Simpson. Fallon realised that, even if the man himself did not.

> I remember the reaction I got when I suggested signing Ronnie. Everyone said, 'But he's finished. What are you thinking?' With him being the age he was, it was completely against the policy the club had at that time. The chairman went along with it in the end – probably because Ronnie was cheap. Jock wanted rid of him and I knew that, so I got the price down a bit. Jock was looking for £4000 but I told him we only wanted Ronnie for the reserves and bartered him down to £2000. What I said about the reserves

wasn't strictly true, but Jock forgave me for it. He had already given Ronnie permission to talk to Berwick Rangers about becoming their manager at that time. But I knew that he still had a lot to offer as a player.

I looked at our defence and saw that we needed someone like Ronnie because, although we had good defenders, they were lacking in the know-how that comes with years of experience in the game. They also had a habit of turning round and blaming the keeper every time we lost a goal and I knew Ronnie wouldn't stand for that. The thing about a good keeper is that he can give an entire defence confidence and make the players in front of him better. I knew that from my own career. Ronnie saw the game like a picture spread out in front of him and he would do our job on the field by organising the players in front of them, spotting mistakes before they even happened. He was outstanding, a 100-per-cent professional. I couldn't find a fault in him.

The Celtic supporters agreed. When they were polled for the club's greatest ever team in 2002, not even John Thomson – the beloved 'Prince of Goalkeepers' – could deny Simpson the No.1 shirt. The same keeper who had been choosing between journalism and Berwick Rangers had gone on to make almost 200 appearances for Celtic, winning Scotland's Player of the Year award in 1967 and making his international debut, aged 36, the same year. That phone call from Fallon had been life-changing, career-defining, and Simpson never forgot it. Just as 'Faither' was an undoubted favourite of Sean's, so the Irishman held a special place in the heart of Celtic's greatest goalie. "I was honoured at Celtic Park on several occasions to win cups and trophies, but the luckiest thing of all was meeting such a gentleman," he said in a speech at Sean's 80th birthday party in 2002.

By acquiring Simpson for £2000, Fallon had also proved himself a shrewd operator in the transfer market. He did, however, stretch Kelly's faith to its very limit with his next request. At first, it was met with a straight rebuttal. Bertie Auld was, after all, a player the chairman had been glad to rid himself of four years earlier. On that occasion, McGrory and Fallon had pleaded in vain for Auld to be kept on, with Kelly maintaining: "His attitude is all wrong. He's no use to Celtic." Little had happened to change his mind in the years since. Flashes of temper had followed Auld to Birmingham

City, where his most famous contribution came in delivering knockout punches to two Fulham players within seconds of each other. Fallon was acutely aware of this and realised that it would not be a well-received recommendation. But he firmly believed that Auld – both as a player and a personality – was desperately needed, and worth fighting for.

> I had to plead with the chairman before he finally agreed. At first, he was adamant about it. 'Once a player goes, Sean, they're gone,' he told me. But I kept at him because I knew Bertie would make all the difference. He was an older head; tough and cunning. And he could play – Bertie could take three players out of the game with a single pass. I knew he'd put his foot on the ball and slow things down for us because our football at that time was too fast and furious. Bertie knew how good he was – he fancied himself rotten – and we needed that kind of self-belief at the time. Other players you had to work hard to instil confidence in, to help them realise how good they could be, whereas Bertie just came in with that swagger of his, believing he was the best. And he was right to have belief in himself because he was a great player with an outstanding football brain. I was delighted to get him into the club, and he didn't let me down.

But wait. Didn't Stein sign Auld, or at least line him up in advance of being appointed? That, certainly, has become the received wisdom, and the player himself subscribes to this version of events. Auld explained in his autobiography, *A Bhoy Called Bertie*, that while there was no direct contact with Stein himself, it was a close friend of the then Hibs manager, Dougie Hepburn, who first sounded him out about a return. But there are significant problems with the theory that Stein orchestrated the deal. The first is that the dates simply do not tally. Hepburn's call was made on January 8; the following day, Auld met Fallon at Upton Park to arrange the transfer. It would be another 72 hours before Stein's potential return as manager was debated, and agreed, by the Celtic directors.

Brian Wilson, who enjoyed unprecedented access to board minutes in writing his club history, *Celtic: a Century with Honour*, is unequivocal. "It was he (Fallon) who persuaded McGrory and Kelly that he should travel south to bring Auld back from Birmingham City for an £11,000 transfer fee and, for the player himself, the deposit on a house in Glasgow," he wrote. Fallon was never in any doubt. He remembered the episode well and explained that, far from lobbying for Auld's return, Stein in fact counselled against bringing back this prodigal son.

> Jock and I had stayed in touch, and we still spoke often when he was at Dunfermline and Hibs. When I mentioned to him about trying to bring back Bertie, he wasn't a fan of the idea. I remember him saying to me: 'You're signing trouble there.' The whole thing had come about because of a conversation I had with Tommy Reilly, who was chairman of the Celtic Businessmen's Club at that time. He told me that Bertie wasn't too happy in England, and that was when I started making the case for bringing him back. The chairman felt the same as Jock – that Bertie could be trouble – but eventually he gave in. Bertie won everyone over in the end, of course, and Jock was very good that way – he kept an open mind about players. It was the same with Ronnie. Even though the two of them had fallen out at Hibs, Jock was fair about it and eventually gave him his chance. As for Bertie, he was never out of the team – he became one of Jock's favourites, and rightly so. It was clear from the moment he arrived back that he had matured into a magnificent player. He was such an important signing for that team.

To many, he was the most important. "The minute Bertie stepped back on to Celtic Park he made a difference," wrote Jimmy McGrory in *A Lifetime in Paradise*. "His return was almost as significant as that of Jock Stein a few months later." Willie Wallace, assessing the Lisbon Lions, described the midfielder as "our best player", adding: "He simply made the team tick. He was our general." Auld's impact was immediate, and Ken Gallacher of the *Daily Record* acknowledged it as such in his report of Celtic's 5-1 win at St Mirren on February 13. "Since Auld returned from England, this is a new-look Celtic… the team has added poise to the front line power they have always had. Auld has that ability to control a game, to coax his forward mates to better, more dangerous moves and also to place his passes with amazing accuracy to the weakest point in his opponents' defence."

Within a couple of weeks of the midfielder's return, Stein's appointment became public knowledge. But the new manager did not take up his position immediately, having asked to delay his arrival to pursue the championship with Hibs. With McGrory's move to the role of public relations officer effective immediately, that meant Fallon enjoyed a month-and-a-half as caretaker. It gave the Irishman a glimpse of the job he had missed out on, and everyone else a look at the kind of manager he might have made. In both respects, it made for pleasant viewing. By the time Stein took charge in mid-March, Fallon had led the team to six successive victories, securing a place in the Scottish Cup semi-finals and twice beating champions-elect Kilmarnock.

Such progress did not go unnoticed. "Jock Stein faces a most unusual problem," wrote the *Daily Record's* Hugh Taylor. "He has become the miracle man of Scottish soccer by going to clubs where all hope seemed to be lost – and, with a wave of his magic wand or, more correctly, his deep knowledge of football, turning them into champions. Now he joins Celtic on top of the world… They are playing with new depths of understanding, of intelligence, of strategy. And the spirit at Parkhead hasn't been so high since the days of their greatness away back when."

Auld's arrival had been hugely significant in sparking this revival, but Fallon's contribution did not go unnoticed by the players. "You only need to look at the latter stages, just before Jock took over, to see that Sean knew what he was doing," said Charlie Gallagher. "He left the big man with a lot to work with." Stein recognised this and publicly voiced his gratitude. "I am lucky to be starting again with Celtic when the club is getting results consistently, the atmosphere is good, and the supporters are in buoyant mood," he wrote in the programme for his first home match as Celtic manager on March 13. "Seeds have been sown and I hope to help them grow into powerful plants. One isolated success, one flash of glory, is not what I am aiming at. If it is in my power, Celtic are going to get consistent success that will take them into competition with the very best in Britain and Europe."

As a statement of intent, it was bold and hugely ambitious. Some wondered if Stein, in attempting to make European kings of Scottish also-rans, might have finally overreached. But these notes were, of course, to prove prophetic. Big Jock, with a little help from an old friend, would live up to every last word.

Chapter 16
The Return of Stein

If 1967 was Celtic's greatest year, 1965 was surely its most important. This club had arrived at a critical fork in the road and, as history proved, had chosen correctly. Stein's ranking on the list of football's all-time great managers can be debated, but his status as the best for Celtic at that time is beyond question. No-one else in the game could have effected such a spectacular and speedy resurgence.

But what if Celtic had taken the other road? Had Kelly stuck to his original plan and made Fallon manager, how would the club have fared? "Worse" was Sean's response and, while typically self-deprecating, it was also inescapably accurate. But, having accepted the impossibility of matching Stein's achievements, it is instructive to at least look at what might have been with the Irishman in charge.

Yet this leads to the first and, arguably, most important consideration: would he have been in charge? As Billy McNeill said: "I think things would have improved under Sean. If he'd been able to stand up to Bob Kelly and get sole control of the team, I'm sure they would." This, though, represents a big if. Kelly, after all, had initially continued to meddle in team affairs even after assuring Stein of full control and it seems highly unlikely that he would have handed over power to Fallon without a struggle. Would the Irishman have been up for that fight?

> I would have had to try. I would have sat down with Bob Kelly
> and told him that I wanted the freedom to make my own
> decisions because there's no point in being a manager if you can't
> manage. Whether I would have been successful in getting my
> way we'll never know. Jock had the benefit of having gone out and
> shown at Dunfermline and Hibs that he deserved the chance to
> be his own man. He had experience of having full control at those
> clubs, and had used it well. He had a stronger hand than I would
> have had. If it had come to it, I know I would have had to be clever
> to get my way with Bob; make ideas seem like they were his. Jock
> was brilliant at that. The best way, and Jock obviously realised
> this, was not to fight against the chairman but to work with him.
> The three of us would often sit for hours after matches, talking
> about the players and about football in general. The chairman was
> quite happy with that as he still felt part of things, and we were
> happy doing it as both Jock and myself had a great regard for him.
> By that stage, we were a good team and we worked well together.

It helped that every member of the trio was playing a defined role,
and playing it well. The manager managed, the assistant assisted
and the chairman focused exclusively – or almost exclusively –
on boardroom matters. All was as it should be. We will never
know, of course, whether Fallon would have been able to effect a
similar change and wrest away Kelly's control over team matters.
But assuming he had, would he have wielded it wisely? John
Gorman, who was coached by Sean in the reserves for much of the
1960s, saw the answer as being obvious. "Would Sean have made
a good manager? Of course he would," said the former Swindon
Town manager and England assistant. "I would have been totally
confident with him as Celtic manager. It was only loyalty to the
club and to Jock that kept him as an assistant because there's no
doubt he could have gone out and been successful as his own man."
There are plenty in Gorman's camp, all adamant that Celtic would
have been in safe hands. At the time, though, Fallon was widely
viewed as the continuity candidate; someone who would stick by
the flawed principles responsible for the club's stunted growth.

> People maybe saw me that way, but it wasn't the case at all. I don't

know if I would have been a good Celtic manager but I do know I would have changed things. I had done my coaching badges and I had my ideas about what I wanted to do if I got the job. There were massive changes needed and football was moving on. Celtic needed to modernise and it was important that we try some new things and, above all, get players playing in their right positions. But Jock knew all that and he made those changes brilliantly – better than I could have done. We were very much of the same mind on football in any case. I can't say I would have done as good a job as him, but I definitely think I would have improved things. Once you have good players, which we had by that stage, it's just a case of getting the most out of them. The main thing for me would have been instilling in them the same pride I always felt in pulling on that green and white shirt. I would have died for Celtic and I always wanted our players to feel the same way.

Fallon was rightly confident in his own abilities. But he was also intelligent enough to realise that, however many grand ideas he had, the perception that he represented more of the same was a barrier in itself. To usher in a new era, Celtic needed a new man.

Jock being a fresh face definitely helped. I do think the club needed that, someone coming in from outside, to make it seem like a proper fresh start. Right from the beginning, the players had confidence in him. They saw what he had done at Dunfermline and Hibs, and they looked up to him and wanted to impress him. They felt he would make them better players, and they were right. Confidence in your manager means a lot when you go out on the field, and that was one of the most important aspects of Jock being able to come in and have the impact he did.

There were, of course, other areas in which Stein – as one of the game's truly great managers – had the edge on Fallon. He was a superior communicator, for example, and decades ahead of his time as a strategist. John Clark, who has worked with innumerable Celtic managers in his various roles at the club, described him as "the best I've ever seen with a tactics board", adding: "You came out of the dressing room with more or less a video inside your head."

Stein was also the personification of a character trait that his assistant neither possessed nor desired: ruthlessness. Even among his biggest admirers, there are some who believe that Fallon was simply too principled, genuine and kind-hearted to have excelled as a manager. Others are simply relieved the theory was never put to the test. "To be honest, I'm glad he never got the job," said Danny McGrain. "But that's for selfish reasons, not because I don't think he could have done it. I just love Sean as the man I know and the man he was at Celtic, and I'm not sure he could have been that man if he was the boss. I think he would have needed to become harder. For him to change his approach to life and his basic kindness of spirit is something I wouldn't have wanted to see." Yet McGrain need not have worried. Just as being involved with Celtic was more important to Fallon than becoming a manager, so remaining true to himself was of greater value than any professional objective.

> You can't change your personality. If I'd tried to become like Jock and manage that way, the players would have seen through it straight away. I've seen a few people try to do that and it never works. You have to be yourself and, if I'd got the job, I would have done it in my own way. Not everyone manages like Jock; back then, you had people like Matt Busby, who took a slightly different approach. I'm not saying I could have been as good as Busby but that's the kind of personality I was closer to. I wouldn't have tried to be harder than I was. I respected Jock for his approach, though, and I saw that it worked. He was definitely tougher on the players than I was and that was exactly what they needed at that stage. Too many of them had been wasting their talent, and Mr McGrory and myself hadn't been hard enough on them. It's important to strike a balance because you need to keep that whip behind your back. It can't all be niceness. There has to be a bit of carrot and stick, and Jock was better at wielding the stick than I was. He had a presence that no-one could ignore.

It remains, however, overly simplistic to suggest that Fallon was simply 'too nice' to have succeeded as Celtic manager. The implication is that he was a man incapable of making tough decisions or instilling discipline, and that is a portrayal consistently rejected by Stein's players. "Sean didn't suffer fools," said Bobby Lennox. "He could be as tough as Jock when he wanted to be; there's no way he was just the nice guy. There was no such thing of:

'It's only Sean who's in charge today.' Everyone knew he wouldn't accept any messing about."

Others agree, and insist that if Fallon lacked a crucial managerial ingredient, it was not the strength of his character but the size of his ego. He was someone to whom arrogance and self-centredness were alien. While that made him a fine man, it did not always equip him well in a profession in which egotistical and fiercely driven personalities invariably reign.

> A bit of ego is a good thing when you're a manager. Jock was a prime example of that, and I don't mean that as a criticism. It helps as a manager to have real belief and conviction in yourself, and Jock not only believed completely in himself but expected others to believe in him too. He never doubted himself for a second. He struck the right balance though, because he wasn't arrogant in terms of not listening to other people or seeing things only one way. He took notice of other people's opinions – at least in people he respected – and would change his mind if you could convince him. But once his mind was made up, heaven nor earth could move him. It was a pleasure working with him though, and I honestly never really thought about what would have happened if I'd been manager. It was never a regret of mine, especially when things turned out the way they did. They were great years we had, and Jock and myself were a great team.

Scottish football has never seen its like again. "You're talking about Celtic's greatest manager and greatest assistant manager together," said Davie Hay. "Both had their own qualities but they complemented each other brilliantly and I always admired Sean for the way he played his role. He was a vital cog in the machine during those great years for Celtic but the fact he didn't get much recognition didn't seem to bother him. He was humble enough to accept that Jock was the man in the spotlight. What I've learned in football is that some guys are cut out to be managers, some are cut out to be assistants and some are cut out to be neither. You need to be a certain kind of character to be a good assistant and Sean was absolutely perfect for it."

Hay cuts to the heart of the issue here. Opinions can be offered on whether Fallon's knowledge, personality and talent-spotting ability would have made him a successful Celtic manager, but opinions are all they will ever be. What can be stated with certainty is that he was an outstanding assistant. Kelly, though, had grander ambitions for him than the rank of No.2 – even after agreeing with the board that Stein was needed. It has been well documented that the chairman's negotiations with the Hibernian manager began with a stunning proposal: that he return to Celtic as Sean's deputy. The offer was naturally doomed to failure and was all the more remarkable as Kelly knew that Wolverhampton Wanderers – still a formidable top flight team – had approached Stein about taking charge at Molineux.

Yet, still he dithered. His first plan having been rejected, Kelly returned with the suggestion that the former team-mates could work together as co-managers. While the ideas did not appeal to Stein – "no three-legged race for a man who was the supreme individualist," wrote Archie Macpherson – he nonetheless hesitated, refusing only after being advised to hold out for full control by club secretary Desmond White. Kelly, as always, meant well and was doubtless attempting to honour this unwritten, unspoken arrangement that Fallon would succeed McGrory. But a quiet word with Sean would have revealed that this potentially costly bargaining was entirely unnecessary.

> The joint-manager idea was never discussed with me beforehand and, if it had been, I would have told the chairman to forget it. A manager has to be able to lead and it's important to have one voice calling the shots. I found out about it later, when Bob came to tell me about Jock getting the job and explained that this co-manager idea was what he had wanted. He said it as a kind of apology because I think he was very worried about hurting me. I think his idea was that one of us would be in charge of the team and the other would manage the administrative side of things. But I told him, 'Look, I'm quite happy. I appreciate what you were trying to do but that wouldn't have worked. This way will be better for Celtic'. I was honest enough to admit that they had made the right decision. I had my own qualities, and I still like to think I could have done the job well. But I've no shame in admitting it: Jock was a better manager than I would ever have been.

Relieved and elated by this response, Kelly suggested to Fallon that he meet Stein to discuss their future working relationship. With

Sean having already arranged to take in a reserve game at Easter Road, it was a get-together swiftly co-ordinated, with the pair sitting down over a pot of tea in Stein's office.

I could see Jock was nervous about it. He must have thought that I'd see it as him stealing 'my job' because, right away, he tried to reassure me about things. 'I know you'll be disappointed,' he said. But I just told him: 'Not working with you, Jock, I'm not. With someone else then, yes, maybe I would be. But I know the club's in good hands. Celtic right now needs a fresh face, and you're it.' I could see how relieved he was. That was when he told me that he wanted me to be his assistant. 'There aren't many people in football I trust, Sean,' he told me. 'But I know I can trust you completely.' That was nice to hear, and that trust was reciprocated. Everything we did together was based on it. I remember Jock saying how he was glad, too, for the chance to repay me for making him my deputy all those years before. 'This is just an old partnership being renewed,' he said. And he was right. We were a good partnership, and we became great friends – even closer than we had been when we had been playing together. I always felt we'd work well together, but it was even better than I could have hoped for.

And just as Celtic could not have picked a more accomplished manager, Stein could not have chosen a better assistant. There are, though, doubts over whether the decision was his. The minutes from that meeting at the North British Hotel make clear the board's determination to retain and promote Fallon, and Kelly would have considered it unthinkable to add to the injury of missing out on the manager's job with the insult of dismissal. There have been suggestions, therefore, that Stein was presented with a fait accompli, and that his assistant was effectively foisted upon him.

It is a theory his son, George, is able to effortlessly debunk. He said: "There were a whole load of issues to be sorted out before my dad agreed to come back, the main one being Bob Kelly's interference in team selection. But there were also discussions on the staff and there's no doubt that Sir Robert wanted Jimmy McGrory kept on as a figurehead, and for Sean to be my dad's assistant. But those things wouldn't have happened unless my dad agreed. At that stage, he held all the cards and, if he felt that something wasn't going to work, he would have forced the issue – especially on something as important as his No.2. As it was, he was happy to work with Sean from day one because he knew him, he liked him and, most importantly, he trusted him. He wanted people around he could trust because that had been an issue for him at Dunfermline just before he left. He had wanted certain people to be there and others to go and find their own way in the game, but he wasn't being supported on that by the club's directors. It was totally different at Celtic. My dad valued Sean. He couldn't have done it all on his own and he had a real respect for all the unseen things that Sean did, and did very well."

The tone for their harmonious and hugely productive partnership was set at that initial Easter Road summit. An accord having been reached, the two men had strolled out to the main stand to watch Hibs reserves, where talk turned to the promising youngsters on Fallon's radar. When the name of Davie Hay was mentioned, Stein provided a priceless nugget of information.

> We had been trying to get Davie from Paisley Boys Guild but, although he'd been training with us, nothing had been signed. As luck would have it, Tommy Docherty had been in seeing Jock that day, telling him he was about to meet Davie and his father at the North British Hotel to try to sign him for Chelsea. Davie was only 16 at the time but I knew he was a player we didn't want to lose, so I left the reserve game before half-time and went straight back to get there first. Sure enough, Davie and his father were at the hotel waiting for Tommy. Needless to say, he ended up coming to Celtic.
>
> People say I signed him for the price of two footballs; actually, the footballs weren't even needed. I just gave them to the boys' guild team as a thank you for their work in developing Davie, and the two priests who ran the team, Father Matthews and Father Heffernan, were absolutely delighted. For us, it was such a small price to pay. Davie turned out to be a brilliant all-round footballer; one of those players you could rely on in any situation. He was fearless and very tough – I saw a bit of myself in him. But he was a better player than me. I spent a lot of time with him in that great reserve team we had and he was a pleasure to work with.

That feeling was mutual. "Big Jock got all the accolades, but Sean was instrumental in the team's success," said Hay. "I had total respect for him, and that respect grew even more later in life when I realised the importance of what he had done for us. He was a real father figure. There was no mollycoddling with Sean – that wasn't his style. But he was always there if you needed support, and he instilled in us the right values in football and in life. Sean taught us how to play the Celtic way and how to become footballers worthy of that shirt."

Hay is one of several players who believe that, far from feeling restricted by the job of assistant manager, Fallon revelled in it. As John Clark said: "When Jock came back, Sean could get on with doing what he was best at. Before, he was doing a bit of scouting, a bit of coaching and also a bit of managing, but also trying to be the middle man. Under Jock, he knew exactly what his role was."

It was a role that entailed a wide range of responsibilities and, if anything, increased Fallon's influence at club. Stein might have been a man for whom control was everything, but he also recognised talent in others and fully utilised the Irishman's evident abilities. Evan Williams, another of Sean's signings, remembers being struck by the extent of his involvement. "I worked with a lot of assistant managers, and was lucky that Wolves had a guy called Gerry Summers who was very good," he said. "But Sean was a different type, more involved in everything that was going on, and it seemed to me that he had a lot more input than assistants normally do. Everyone talks about all the great signings he made, and it was obvious Jock trusted him on that front. But I think Sean's greatest contribution to that team was on the training ground. Training was fantastic and Sean was always in amongst things, game for a laugh but keeping everything at a high intensity. He also seemed to have this knack for knowing what kind of mood a player was in and what he and Big Jock needed to do to get him focused and playing to his best. That made him a very important figure."

Within the club, he was recognised as such. To the wider football world, though, Fallon was – and remained until his death – either under-appreciated or, more often than not, entirely unknown. Not for him the honours, plaudits and profile bestowed on other assistants such as Jimmy Murphy and Peter Taylor. That remains a source of irritation to John Gorman, who is himself best known for his role as deputy to Glenn Hoddle with Chelsea and England. He said: "I think an image has developed, particularly since he passed away, that Jock did it all by himself at Celtic. Part of that has been the diminishing of Sean's role and that really annoys me because he was a lot more than just Jock's helper. I know what it's like though. I was in a pub last night and all everyone was asking me was: 'How's Glenn doing? What's he up to now?' And I'm telling them: 'I don't know. I've not worked with Glenn for years.' But that's the way it is for an assistant, particularly when you're assistant to a high-profile manager. You almost cease to become a person in your own right. You're just so-and-so's sidekick."

However, Gorman's frustrations failed to strike a chord with Fallon, even though he had spent the best part of five decades fielding questions on Stein. For all that Big Jock cast a lengthy shadow, assuming that his assistant would have craved some of that limelight was to misunderstand his entire outlook on life.

John Gorman was always a nice lad and a very good player, and I can see what he means there. But it never bothered me one bit. I expect to be asked questions about Jock and I'm always happy to sing his praises – because he deserves it. I knew at the time that a lot of my work was going unnoticed by most people, but I wasn't in the job for recognition. I was there to do my best for Celtic and to do what I thought would help make the club successful. Assistant manager is a tough job. It's difficult sometimes to find the right balance. But I think I had the right attitude for it. I never felt frustrated I wasn't the manager and, looking back, I think assistant probably was the right job for me, certainly with Jock there.

I had a few offers over the years to become manager at other clubs but Jock stopped me from going and said he needed me at Celtic. And I never wanted to leave the club anyway. As long as Celtic were successful and I felt I was playing my part, I was always more than happy to stay and work away as Jock's No.2. That might not have been the case if someone else was in charge. I don't think you could do the job of assistant if you didn't believe completely in the person you were working with. But I was fortunate to work with one of the greats; someone who knew the game inside-out but also respected my opinion.

Fallon's attitude towards such matters might seem almost too good, too unassuming, to be true. Yet there was no question of him projecting an image. Every conversation with a friend or former colleague led to the same conclusion about his selfless acceptance of Stein's pre-eminence. As Sir Alex Ferguson, who was close to both men, recalled: "He was never bitchy about Jock getting the job. Never. Sean just looked at what was best for Celtic. He had a tremendous attitude and was always positive, and that's why I think he was one of life's wonders; a truly great guy. He was a rock of a man."

This rock would be one of the central foundations on which Stein would build his empire. And while 1965 had begun with the dashing of Fallon's managerial ambitions, it would be the year in which his dreams for Celtic began to come true.

Chapter 17
The Double Act

"A job is easy if you're working with people you can depend on. I was very fortunate in that respect." This was Jock Stein in reflective mood, looking back on his and Celtic's glory years. He was, like his assistant, unduly modest. Managing Celtic was never easy, and behind every one of his stylish successes were innumerable hours of tireless toil. But Stein was right to acknowledge his good fortune in having fine men like Fallon and Neilly Mochan at his side; men who, if unable to make the job easy, at least ensured it was a great deal easier. Stressing the importance of co-operation and mutual dependence became a habit during Stein's title-strewn tenure. "Our success comes from the feeling of everyone working with each other, everyone helping each other," he said shortly after Lisbon. This was echoed by Bill Shankly, who marvelled at the way in which Celtic functioned, describing it as "a form of socialism".

But Stein hadn't always worked in this collective, inclusive way. Tommy Callaghan, who had the unique distinction of playing under him at both Dunfermline and Celtic, remembers being struck by the different way in which he approached both jobs. "At Dunfermline, Jock did it all on his own," he said. "It was much more of a team effort at Celtic, and it was obvious the trust he had in the likes of Sean and Neilly. It was all kept very close-knit though. You think about Celtic these days and it's a cast of hundreds running the club. Back then, it was Jock, Sean, Jim Kennedy [supporters' liaison officer], and a secretary, Audrey Douglas, who worked at Celtic Park – that was who kept the club going. It's fantastic when you think about it."

But whether on the training ground or in the office, Stein's "form of socialism" did not equate to an alliance of equals. Though respectful of his colleagues' talents and grateful for their input, he ensured that everyone was aware of his position as the undisputed kingpin. It was a strategy of which Fallon wholeheartedly approved.

> Leadership is very, very important at a football club, and Jock was a born leader. He was a great manager. A master. People talk about the greatest managers of all time and I still believe that Jock is at least on a par with the best of them. Alex [Ferguson] is up there with him these days and I like Mourinho, even though I know he rubs a lot of people up the wrong way. I'm also pleased to see Davie Moyes doing so well as he was a young lad we had at Celtic.
>
> There are so many things that go towards making a great manager and, to me, Jock had them all. His reading of a game was second to none and he could pick up on the smallest details quicker than anyone I ever saw. What always impressed me was his knowledge of the game and the way he could communicate that knowledge to the players. Whenever he criticised someone, and he wasn't shy in doing that, he would explain why. That's so important, especially for younger players. Everything had a point with Jock. He was also very strong on discipline. People asked what changed between 1965, when he came in, and 1967, and I think the main thing was the discipline he instilled and the confidence he brought to the place. It turned good players into great players.

Fallon, of course, wasn't alone in appreciating Stein's attributes. Jock Wallace, with whom the Celtic boss fought a fierce battle for supremacy during the 1970s, described his old rival as "the greatest manager ever to draw breath". "As a football man, there was no-one who came anywhere close to him," added the former Rangers boss. "He eclipsed Shankly, Busby and all the other legends in the game. He was in a class of his own." Even Ferguson has consistently contradicted the admirers who ascribe him the title of 'greatest ever', insisting that it will forever belong to his old mentor. "I would have happily remained big Jock's assistant for the rest of my days," was a remarkable and revelatory comment from the former Manchester United manager.

Yet pre-eminence should not be mistaken for perfection. Stein, like any manager, made mistakes, and came perilously close to making several more. It was on these occasions that he needed an assistant willing to confront as well as concur, and Fallon never disappointed. "Jock being the strong person he was, he needed a strong character beside him," said Bertie Auld. "Sean was ideal in that respect because, if there was one thing he wasn't, it was a yes man. He was one of the few people brave enough to tell Jock exactly what he thought. There was always a united front in front of the players, but I know they disagreed on a few things."

One of the most notable examples arrived early in Stein's tenure. Those early months were not entirely unproblematic, for although history credits Celtic's greatest manager with an instant impact, results initially worsened after his appointment, with April bringing a humiliating 6-2 defeat at Falkirk. The Scottish Cup final beckoned but rumours were rife of an impending clearout, and Stein did nothing to dispel them. "Our staff of players have had their chance," he said after the defeat at Brockville. "There can be no justified complaint if we seek to strengthen the team and that is going to be done irrespective of what happens within the next week or two."

Twelve days later, Stein sat down with the board to discuss plans for the following season. He arrived armed with two sheets of paper: one carrying the names of players he wished to buy; the other with those he wanted sold. Featuring on the latter list were John Hughes and Charlie Gallagher. So, too, incredible as it might now seem, was Jimmy Johnstone. The board discussed the manager's recommendations and, ultimately, gave the green light. It was only the absence of suitable bids that prevented Celtic from offloading two outstanding servants and ridding themselves of the club's greatest ever player.

Stein, of course, came to love Johnstone like a wayward son. But he was a late convert. "For a long time I honestly didn't think he liked me," was the player's seemingly accurate assessment. That impression dated back to the early '60s, when Stein had drawn unflattering comparisons between Johnstone and Dunfermline's young winger, Alex Edwards. The doubts were hardly assuaged when, shortly after his 1965 appointment, the Celtic manager took on a part-time role managing Scotland. Johnstone, who had forced his way into the international team the year before, did not feature in any of Stein's seven matches in charge, with Rangers' Willie Henderson consistently preferred. Though dispirited, Johnstone could live with that snub; even convince himself that the SFA selection committee were to blame. But when he was dropped from the Celtic team for the club's biggest matches of the season, there was only one possible explanation. "The worst moment for him, outside of leaving the club, was when Big Jock didn't pick him for the Scottish Cup final of 1965," said friend and team-mate John Clark in *Jinky, The Biography of Jimmy Johnstone*. "He was devastated… just inconsolable."

According to Archie Macpherson, who has written books profiling Johnstone and Stein, the manager's position was clear: "He thought that Jimmy was not cut out to be in the new Celtic." Motherwell and Tottenham Hotspur both registered an interest and were not discouraged. The player himself, meanwhile, was to be found in tears, telling friends: "They're going to let me go." If ever Johnstone required an influential ally, it was now. Stein's need for a strong dissenting voice was equally pressing. Fortunately, Fallon supplied both.

> It took Jock a while to realise how good some of our players were when he first came in. I had to try to talk him round on a few of them, Jinky included. He was one I would have hated to see leave. I had known him since he came on the ground-staff and I just loved watching him play. As soon as I saw Jinky, I knew he was the kind of winger I would have hated to play against. He'd take the ball right up to you, almost on your toe, and before you knew it he'd be away from you. And he was so brave. You couldn't keep him quiet by hitting him early; he'd just keep coming back at you. He could infuriate you at times but what I loved about him was that, whether it was training, matches or a kick-about on the street, you knew he'd play exactly the same way. He was a joy to watch, and you could see how much pleasure he took from playing the game. And, like myself, he just loved playing for Celtic.
>
> The fans got it right when they voted him the club's best ever player. Jock wasn't convinced at first – he thought Jinky was

too much of an individual, not a team player – but he ended up loving him. It just took him a while. Everyone can make mistakes though, even the best managers in the game. And one thing I always liked about Jock was that, when he did get things wrong, he would be honest enough to admit it. If I'd told him beforehand, he'd be the first to say, 'You were right, Sean. I should have done it your way'. But in this case, I think it was Jinky himself and the way he played, more than anything I said, that changed Jock's mind. I could say what I wanted but the wee man needed to show Jock what he could do. Once he started doing that, there was no chance of us letting him go.

The episode had, though, reignited an old debate between manager and assistant on the point at which a supreme individualist becomes a self-indulgent luxury. Stein had held firm on Charlie Tully. On Johnstone, he allowed himself to be persuaded. And just as well. Within a couple of years, the winger was the poster boy of Celtic's European champions; a player so world-renowned that he came third in the voting for the 1968 Ballon d'Or.

Johnstone always remembered, however, how close he had come to being sold during that fraught summer of 1965 and he had an inkling of who would have been fighting his corner. "I always thought Sean had a wee soft spot for me," he said in 2002. "Myself and the boss had our differences, to put it mildly, and if I was ever looking for a wee bit of comfort, you could be sure that Sean would take me to the side and give me a bit of insight. He'd say: 'Just you do what you can do out there and everything will be alright.' He was a cracking guy around the place, he really was. I loved him. He was such a great asset to the club, and a hell of a lot of people had so much respect for him."

This esteem was not restricted to the players. Stein was quick to spot that the qualities he had admired in Fallon the player – candour, dedication, integrity – had not only been preserved in the intervening years, but enhanced. "Sean was exactly the right man to be my dad's assistant," said Stein's daughter, Ray, in *Jock Stein, the Authorised Biography*. "He provided the perfect balance and my dad knew he could rely on him. You need the right mix in management and their partnership definitely worked." Such phrases – "perfect balance", "right mix" – crop up frequently among those who worked under Stein and Fallon. "Their personalities complemented each other so well and, to me at least, they seemed to go everywhere together," said Tommy Callaghan. "I used to think they were like Morecambe and Wise, they were that much of a double act." The image was matched by reality. Celtic's manager and assistant were just the kind of indivisible duo Fallon always hoped they would be.

> When you're a manager, you need your No.2 to be close to you, and I don't think there have been many closer than I was to Jock. We were great pals and had a lot of time for each other as football men and away from the game too. That undoubtedly helped when it came to working side by side, day in, day out. You need to be close because I always think that a good assistant should become like an extension of the manager. You should be able to read each other's minds, and I would certainly know what Jock was thinking in most situations without him saying anything. We were quite different personalities in some respects but that seemed to work well. The fact we enjoyed each other's company and had the same basic views on football was a good start. We had a lot of great times together. There was a tremendous feeling about the club in general back then.

Players, too, highlight this harmonious atmosphere, and give Fallon much of the credit for maintaining it. And while this may seem a fairly unremarkable accomplishment, Celtic's current chief executive believes that it eclipses even the achievements for which the Irishman is best known. "Everyone knows Sean for the great signings he made, and rightly so," said Peter Lawwell. "But I've always felt, and I've seen this during my own time at the club, that establishing the right chemistry is the most important thing an assistant can achieve. And from what I know of Sean, no-one did that better than him."

Providing a foil requires different things from different assistants. For Fallon, it entailed tempering the harsher excesses of Stein's uncompromising approach. "Managing by fear" was how that approach was described by Ally Hunter, who said of his former manager in *The Head Bhoys*: "He was not a likeable person; I wouldn't expect anybody would actually like him as a person." Fallon did, and he rejected this portrayal as one-dimensional, insisting that while Stein "did not mess about", there was a great deal more to his approach than mere intimidation. It was, all the same, with a sense of incredulity that he and the players heard Stein say of himself in a 1972 interview: "I'm supposed to be hard, but I'm softer than most of them."

"Jock was a tough man, very often hard to deal with, and I think most of the players were frightened of him," said Stevie Chalmers. "At that time, Sean was always in the background and he was a fatherly figure to us. We always felt we could approach him when we couldn't approach Jock. That way, Sean played a massive part in our team and in our success." Stein, of course, may well have moderated his abrasive approach had Fallon not been around to smooth over disputes. He had, after all, succeeded without the Irishman's peacemaking abilities at Dunfermline and Hibs. Yet Billy McNeill is one of several players who insist that Fallon's presence wasn't so much beneficial, as essential. "Quite honestly," he said, "Jock – for all his qualities – needed Sean. He was able to supply all the things the big man wasn't particularly good at."

Nor was it merely Fallon's kind-heartedness that enabled him to play the role to perfection. Joe McBride recalled thinking that Stein's deputy had "a sixth sense" for spotting demoralised and disgruntled players and, to his children, this was no surprise. Fallon's son, Sean Jnr, remembers him as "a great student of human nature", while Marie Therese – the eldest of five daughters – believes that assistant manager wasn't the only role for which her father was tailor-made. "I always felt dad would have made a great psychologist," she said. "He had this amazing knack of always knowing the right thing to say, and so much empathy and emotional intelligence in reading people." Fallon, naturally, was too modest to acknowledge in himself these attributes. But he did admit to feeling that his influence at Celtic benefited both Stein and the club.

> Jock was a magnificent manager but he was hard and the players didn't find him easy to talk to. If you were unlucky and caught him on a bad day, he could be very intimidating. He would also deliberately hurt players sometimes if he thought it would get the best out them. That's when I would come in to try to soften the blow. If he had really angered someone and I thought they were

going to react badly, I would look to calm the storm. I enjoyed that role. If I saw a man with his head down, feeling he wasn't doing enough, I enjoyed trying to pick him up and give him a bit of confidence again. It's like what I was saying about the carrot and stick – Jock and myself had a good way of working to make sure the players had plenty of both. We each had our roles to play and Jock was quite happy for the players to be a bit scared of him. He had a bad temper anyway, but a lot of the big explosions were done for effect. They worked, too. But I knew him and I could see when he was genuinely angry and when he was just looking for a reaction. Sometimes he would even give me a wink and let me know what was coming before he started on the players. We'd laugh about it later.

This bears out a view expressed by Sir Alex Ferguson on the way in which Stein and Fallon interacted. He said: "Don't think for one second that Jock didn't realise what Sean was doing in the background, ironing out little issues and giving the players a bit of faith in themselves. As a manager, you know that players will often go to the assistant rather than speak to you, and that's why Jock picked someone he would have trusted with his life. He knew that he never had to worry about being undermined because, if there's one thing Sean guaranteed you, it was loyalty."

According to Danny McGrain, this was an issue on which Fallon was passionate and entirely inflexible. "There was never a hint of disunity from Sean," recalled the right-back. "Mr Stein would often say to him in the dressing room, 'Sean, what do you think?' And he would always take up the same themes that Mr Stein had been stressing, maybe press them home further to emphasise the point. There were never mixed messages. If Mr Stein decided the team had to jump off the Erskine Bridge at eight o'clock, Sean would tell the players to make sure and be there for 7.55." Fallon, said McGrain, was "loyalty personified". Few descriptions pleased the Irishman more.

If there is a secret to being a good assistant, it's loyalty. Even if I disagreed with Jock on something, I would never go against him in front of the players. Once you start doing that, it's all over. You have to be unified. I would disagree with Jock on a few things, but always privately. We would talk things over, he'd make his points and I'd make mine. Sometimes I would win him round and other times I wouldn't. But once a decision was made, it was our decision as far as I was concerned.

I respected that he had the ultimate say and that my job was to back him up. If he stood firm, I would always say: 'Right Jock, let's give it a go'. It didn't mean agreeing with everything he did, but it meant being loyal. And, anyway, what would it have achieved if I undermined Jock? No-one would have benefited from that, and certainly not Celtic. That's why it's so important as a manager to have people around you that you trust. Because there are always going to be tough times, and what you don't need is people saying behind your back, 'Well, I told him not to do that'. I always hated that kind of thing. It eats away at the confidence in the manager and the unity at the club if you have someone doing that, especially when things are going badly.

Difficult periods were in limited supply during Stein's record-breaking reign, but those awkward early results – home defeats by St Johnstone, Hibs and Partick Thistle, and that 6-2 thrashing at Falkirk – could have sown seeds of doubt. Unity, though, was maintained and, just 10 days after that thumping at Brockville, it was rewarded. The 1965 Scottish Cup final has taken on a mythical status in the decades since, with Stein himself labelling it the key victory of his tenure, and a turning point in the history of the club. Until the day he left the club, in fact, two of the three photographs adorning his office wall were of the team that beat Dunfermline 3-2.

The stakes were reflected on the eve of the match when Brian Meek of the *Scottish Daily Express*, assessing Stein's position, wrote: "He has to win. If he doesn't, Celtic will once more be excluded from the rich pasture lands of Europe. And, if that happens, the importance of Celtic in Scottish football will be equal to St Johnstone, or Falkirk, or Partick Thistle." Three days later, the same newspaper was reporting on Billy McNeill's headed winner, not merely as a goal, but as "the official seal on a return to greatness". Early as it was to be making such a bold declaration, it proved to be accurate.

There's no doubt that winning that game was the most important thing that happened in turning the tide. The players had got so used to losing finals that it had become a mental issue as much as anything. But Jock coming in gave them confidence and, once we beat Dunfermline, I knew there would be more trophies to come. It was a fantastic match, a great spectacle for the neutrals, but the only thing that mattered for us was winning and giving our supporters something to cheer. Jock had done a good job in the build-up to that game in relaxing the players and giving them confidence. He had the ability to make the players think they could take on anyone and beat them and, even when we went behind that day, no-one panicked. That change in mentality was vital. If you have ability and you can get things right in the old brain up there, chances are you will be a success. The 1965 cup final showed our players what could happen when they focused their minds and really believed in themselves.

Yet significant as ending the trophy drought was, the Celtic players still had another substantial psychological barrier to overcome. It loomed in the imposing form of Rangers or, more accurately, the inferiority complex that Rangers effected in them. The numbers alone indicated the magnitude of the problem, with Stein taking over a team that had won fewer than a quarter of the Old Firm derbies in the preceding 17 seasons. Such was the ensuing transformation that, by the mid-70s, it was Rangers who were facing up to this same, miserable success rate. The extent of the power-shift in the intervening years had been nothing short of astounding, and many consider it an achievement every bit as momentous as Lisbon or nine-in-a-row.

I think Jock probably felt that way himself. Going after Rangers was a big thing for him. He would tell the press that an Old Firm game was just the same as the rest and offered the same number of points but, behind the scenes, it was a totally different story. He wanted desperately to beat them. There were other teams capable of winning the league back then but Jock knew that if we could get the upper hand on Rangers, it would be half the battle. He had enjoyed some success against them with Hibs and always felt that all we needed to do was make the players physically and mentally tougher in Old Firm games. Jock felt they needed to believe in themselves more, and he was a master at giving players confidence. He had this aura of being successful in anything he did and players admired him because of that. He could be tough on them, but a bit of praise and they would go out there feeling 10 feet tall, ready to take on anyone. He also gave the players freedom to be more physical than they had been before, and told them not to let themselves be pushed around in these games. He wanted them to give as good as they got.

For the Celtic players, previously held to a higher ethical code by Bob Kelly, the effect was liberating. In *Dreams and Songs to Sing*, Tom Campbell and Pat Woods recount the story of Kelly visiting the dressing room before one particular derby to impress upon the players the need for sportsmanship and good behaviour. "The manager listened in respectful silence, as did the players; he then ushered Sir Robert to the door and closed it. Turning to his players, he growled, 'Well, you can forget about all that for a start...'"

The League Cup final of 1965 was Stein's first Old Firm derby as manager, the acid test of his new approach, and the tone was set inside the first minute by a ferocious early tackle from Ian Young on Rangers' Willie Johnston. The match duly descended into what the *Glasgow Herald* described as "an orgy of crudeness", and yet Celtic not only survived this almighty battle, but emerged triumphant. A point had been proved. When the teams next met, on January 3, 1966, they were level on points and an early Rangers goal suggested the continuation of a tired and familiar theme. This was the kind of blow that would have sent previous Celtic sides reeling, but Stein's players rallied and ultimately ran out 5-1 winners. It was the club's first Ne'erday win since the double-winning season of 1953/54, and its wider significance was acknowledged by *The Scotman's* John Rafferty, who wrote: "Celtic, romping on the way up, passed them (Rangers) on the way down."

By the end of that season, the Bhoys were champions for the first time in 12 years and their manager had been named the best in Britain. But instead of a warm glow of satisfaction, Stein experienced only a burning desire for more achievements, greater than those already secured. Speaking in May 1966, he said: "It is up to us, to everyone at Celtic Park now, to build our own legends. We don't want to live with history, to be compared with legends of the past; we must make new legends." The championship, he said, "was merely the first step towards doing that". And he left little doubt about what the next phase would be, remarking:

"The greatness of a club in modern football will be judged on performances in Europe."

The gauntlet had been thrown down. It would not be easy but, with the help of those around him – the people on whom he could depend – Stein believed the European Cup was within his grasp. Lisbon glistened on the horizon, and immortality beckoned.

Chapter 18
Lisbon

The Spanish call it *La Orejona* (big ears). To everyone else, it is simply the most coveted and instantly recognisable trophy in club football. And the first man to hold aloft the current European Cup was Billy McNeill.

For Celtic fans old enough to witness it, this was their JFK moment. All can remember exactly where they were on May 25, 1967, when they watched their conquering captain, his green-and-white kit illuminated against a backdrop of dark suits, present this prize to the world. Fallon was never likely to forget. "I had the best view in the house," he reflected with a smile. It was a vantage point well earned. With the Celtic players holed up in their dressing room, stripped of their shirts, shorts and boots by delirious supporters now blocking the route to the podium, the job of reaching the trophy seemed impossible. But Stein felt otherwise. He considered the chaotic scenes above, looked around the dressing room for someone capable of thrusting through the throng, and found just the man. An Iron Man.

Yet before explaining how Fallon went about reaching the European Cup, we should first look at how Celtic found themselves in the final. It was not so long, after all, since that ambition would have seemed preposterous. But Stein's side had come close to reaching the same stage of the Cup Winners' Cup just a year earlier. That final was held at Hampden and the feeling was that Celtic – essentially on home turf – would never have a better chance of lifting a European trophy. They were, however, edged out by Liverpool 2-1 on aggregate in a semi-final remembered for the offside decision that wrongly denied Bobby Lennox a late goal in the second leg which would have put Celtic into the final. It was of little consolation that the Belgian referee, Josef Hannet, admitted to his mistake afterwards.

> We were very unlucky at Anfield and I think that experience, knowing how close we'd been, gave the players a belief that they could match anyone at that level. It hurt at the time though, and Jock was as angry as I'd ever seen him about that referee. He even had a few cross words with Bill Shankly afterwards, and Shankly was a great friend of his. But in the longer term, it didn't do us any harm. It kept everyone hungry and, because we had been the better side over the two legs, the players started the next season feeling very confident in themselves.

It had been an eventful European run in more ways than one and, while the Liverpool matches were undoubtedly memorable, the quarter-final against Dynamo Kiev proved to be of even greater long-term significance. Fallon had good reason to remember the away leg in particular because, by this stage, his remit extended to the formulating of Celtic's European travel plans. It was a thankless task at the best of times, but on this occasion he was caught in the middle of an impasse between Bob Kelly and the Soviet authorities. The chairman was a match for even the most intransigent Politburo official and proved immovable when the Soviets – on the basis that they had no diplomatic ties with Ireland – objected to the club's decision to fly with Aer Lingus.

> I felt like I was working in the diplomatic service by the end of that one. We couldn't play the game in Kiev because the city was under 10 feet of snow, so everything had to be switched to Tblisi in Georgia. But Tblisi was a ballistics centre for the Soviets and they seemed to be worried about us spying, so they wanted us to transfer on to one of their own planes in Moscow. Bob Kelly would have none of that. We wouldn't budge and, eventually, UEFA became involved, we got our way and were able to use our own aircraft.

That, however, turned out to be more of a curse than a blessing. The Aer Lingus plane was beset by problems almost from the moment it left Glasgow, with a mechanical fault quickly necessitating an unscheduled stop in Copenhagen. But it was on the return journey, the morning after Celtic had secured a 4-1 aggregate win, that the real drama began to unfold. It got off to a bad start when their pilot, who had arrived drunk at the players' post-match party, and left considerably drunker, turned up late at the airport and in no fit state to fly. "They couldn't get him sobered up," said Tommy Gemmell in his autobiography, *Lion Heart*. "You could see the steam coming out of Jock's ears."

A lengthy delay in Tblisi was followed by five hours on a Moscow runway, where scowling, rifle-wielding guards and increasingly heavy snow made for an unnerving combination. The plane eventually spluttered along the treacherous runway before struggling into the air, but worsening weather convinced the hungover pilot that another diversion was required. So it was that Stockholm became the fourth capital city on this increasingly tiresome trip, with an overnight stay required before another attempt could be made at returning to Glasgow. By now, the clock was ticking down to a 3pm kick-off at Tynecastle the following day, and there was no sign of an end to the technical troubles.

> The engines had iced up. I don't think Aer Lingus were used to flying to countries like Russia in those days and the plane was struggling. We were on board, off, then back on again. Each time they would try to take off and something would go wrong. I wasn't one of the most nervous fliers in that group, but it was quite frightening. This was only a few years after the Munich air disaster, so that was uppermost in everyone's minds. Eventually, when we were climbing up the stairs for another take-off attempt, Bob Kelly shouted out, 'Stop! Get everyone off. And get another plane out here!'

Demanding an alternative aircraft was entirely reasonable given the circumstances, but it did have one significant downside. By the time a replacement had been rerouted from Brussels and returned the weary Celtic party to Glasgow, the match with Hearts was just 16 hours away. Worried relatives had congregated at the airport, but family reunions were brief, with Stein insisting on a late-night training session under the floodlights. Unsurprisingly, that loosening-up exercise, combined with a few snatched hours of sleep, proved insufficient preparation. Hearts won 3-2, and the player who did most to torment the sluggish visiting defence was a striker by the name of Willie Wallace. His contribution did not go unnoticed.

But more important than Wallace, or indeed European progression and dropped points, was the role played by the Dynamo Kiev and Hearts matches in ending Kelly's influence on team selection. The pivotal moment arose after Jim Craig, harshly sent off in the former match, refused to apologise to the chairman for his perceived indiscipline. Kelly's anger at this show of obstinacy led to the right-back being omitted at Tynecastle in favour of John Cushley, who endured a particularly torrid afternoon. Years later, Stein told Craig of how club secretary Desmond White, furious at the chairman's intervention, demanded a meeting at which the issue was finally settled. "Jock told me that was the turning point," said Craig. "From then on, he made all the decisions."

There would be plenty of shrewd calls in the years ahead, and some of Stein's most inspired, on and off the park, were made during the following pre-season. Celtic's five-week summer tour of North America has become legendary, with Bobby Lennox describing it simply as "the greatest trip ever". Its itinerary was staggering, with Celtic's players whisked to Bermuda, New York, San Francisco, Los Angeles and Vancouver, and treated to the delights of Malibu Beach, Broadway, Disneyland, Hollywood and Niagara Falls. There was also an unexpected treat for their assistant manager.

> While we were in Bermuda, we got chatty with Bruce Forsyth, who was there on holiday. He was looking for a game of golf one day but wasn't booked on, so we managed to get him a space. I was going fishing, though, and he asked me, 'Would you mind taking my girlfriend along with you?' 'No problem,' I replied. It turned out that his girlfriend was Miss World! So, of course, I reluctantly accepted. It was better than looking at Jock across the boat.

It might have seemed like a jolly, but this unusually long and extraordinarily extravagant pre-season tour did have a legitimate purpose. As Tommy Gemmell said: "Jock had captained the 1954 double-winning side and they were pretty much one big happy family... That was what he wanted for us." Room-sharing arrangements were rotated to avoid cliques developing, and community singing became a nightly routine. Each player and member of staff had his party piece, with Stein specialising in the mawkish 'Auld Scots mother mine'. Fallon? He had a homesick ballad of his own to bring tears to expatriate eyes and, according to the players, it earned the Iron Man a new nickname: 'The Sligo Thrush.'

> It was always 'I'll take you home again Kathleen' for me. I enjoyed it and, well, let's just say I wasn't one of the worst. Nor was Jock. He had a fine voice. The best, though, was wee Jinky – he was outstanding in those sing-songs. Everyone joined in and we all had a great time. That whole tour was tremendous. We were away for a long time but it just brought everyone together. The players will tell you that it made them friends for life. Spirits were very high and we gave the players a bit of freedom on the understanding they weren't to let the club down. Any minor things that happened, we dealt with them quietly, kept everything under wraps. But it wasn't just a holiday. We worked the players hard and a lot of important things were achieved.

The most significant, besides the building of togetherness, was a subtle tactical switch that turned out to be a masterstroke. Stein, on taking charge, had initially stuck to the traditional 2-3-5 formula and fielded Bertie Auld in his accustomed position on the left wing. But the game was evolving, and in this, the same summer in which England's 'wingless wonders' lifted the World Cup, Stein plotted a change of his own. So it was that Celtic lined up for the first time with Auld and Bobby Murdoch, together in central midfield, at the beating heart of a beautifully balanced 4-2-4.

> That was an important change. The move to that formation gave us an advantage over a lot of teams who were still using the old system and Jock picked exactly the right men to implement it. Bob Kelly had never fancied Bobby Murdoch as a midfielder, or

wing-half as they were called in the 2-3-5 days. He always wanted him played at inside-right and he made that clear when we started to play him in the midfield. But Jock knew what he was doing and he held his ground. He always respected the chairman but he knew that, although he loved the game, some of his views on football weren't always right. For us, it was obvious that Bobby was a midfielder. He was a magnificent passer, could read situations brilliantly, and he didn't mind the physical side of the game. And Bertie was the perfect partner for him. He brought his personality to that position, dictated games and, like Bobby, he could take three or four players out of the game with a single pass. When you put the two of them together, they were one of the best midfields in the game.

Their impact was immediate. In between the singing and sightseeing, Celtic played 11 matches, facing opponents such as Bayern Munich, Bologna and Tottenham Hotspur, and emerged unbeaten. Pre-season ended with a dominant 4-1 win over a star-studded Manchester United side and their domestic campaign began with an equally impressive 4-0 win away to Rangers. By the time Christmas arrived, 30 competitive matches had been negotiated and Celtic had yet to taste defeat.

Underpinning this unblemished run had been the astounding goalscoring form of Joe McBride. His status was emphasised in late November, when Celtic, having comfortably disposed of Zurich in the first round, travelled to face French champions Nantes. "When we arrived, the press wanted to meet only one man: Joe McBride," recalled Ronnie Simpson. "He had already scored 33 goals and was the obvious danger to the Frenchmen. They took one look at him and promptly named him 'football's Marlon Brando'." McBride went on to justify his billing by scoring the opener in a 3-1 Celtic win, but 'Brando' had very nearly fluffed his lines. With kick-off approaching, he realised that he had left his boots in the hotel and it was only after a mad dash accompanied by Fallon that he retrieved them with minutes to spare.

Stevie Chalmers and Bobby Lennox were also on target that night and, with Johnstone at his brilliant best, Celtic looked to have a near-flawless frontline. Stein, though, had his doubts about Chalmers and, within a week of returning from Nantes, he made Wallace his only major purchase of the season. It was a signing that thrilled and excited the Celtic manager. Billy McNeill recalled being told by Stein: "I think Wallace and Joe McBride could become the greatest striking partnership in the history of the Scottish game, maybe in Europe too." This belief would only have been strengthened when the pair marked their first appearance together by combining for three goals. Fate dictated, though, that this was to be one of only two occasions on which Stein saw his dream duo in action.

Joe's knee injury around Christmas time meant he didn't play for the rest of the season. I felt so sorry for him and Jock was very disappointed too, because there is no doubt he saw Joe and Willie being his first-choice centre-forwards. And I'm sure they would have made a great pairing because both were outstanding in their own ways. I'm glad, though, that it didn't happen at the expense of Stevie because he deserved his role in all that great success we had, especially having stayed loyal through all the lean years.

Chalmers' reward was on its way. By the time Celtic arrived in Lisbon, having secured a domestic clean sweep and seen off Vojvodina and Dukla Prague, he and Wallace were in sparkling form. But lying in wait were a side that had won the European Cup twice in the previous three seasons and beaten holders Real Madrid en route to the final. *World Soccer* magazine previewed the final as a foregone conclusion, with Roger MacDonald writing: "Soccer is said to be unpredictable but Inter, with their ruthless, relentless tactical system, have reduced uncertainty to a complete insignificance. When Inter win the final..."

MacDonald's misplaced conviction appears foolish in retrospect, but such predictions were not restricted to ill-informed pundits. Jim Craig remembers being "floored" by his father telling him that he did not want to go to Lisbon. "He was quite honest about it," said the full-back. "He said he thought that Inter Milan would be too strong for us and he did not want to go over there and see us beaten." Fallon wasn't nearly so pessimistic. In a newspaper column in the build-up to the final, he confidently forecast a Celtic victory. He was even bold enough to predict the scoreline.

I said it then: Celtic will win 2-1. I could have made a fortune if I'd stuck a bet on. That column got me into trouble though. Jock was raging about it at first. He said I was tempting fate by saying we'd win. He was worried about the players getting cocky, but with everyone out there saying that Inter would have it easy, I didn't see any chance of that. I felt confident and thought it was important that we inject some of that into the players. But Jock and I didn't fall out for long. The preparations were actually very smooth. As soon as we knew Joe wouldn't make it, there weren't any big debates or discussions about the team. By that stage, it almost picked itself. As the game got nearer, I could see Jock becoming more and more confident. He knew we were as ready as we would ever be.

What Stein and Fallon could not prepare or legislate for was the driver of the team coach taking them in the opposite direction from the stadium. But while there was a suspicion that this mistake might not have been entirely honest, Celtic's late arrival at the Estadio Nacional seemed, if anything, to work in their favour.

I'm sure that helped us. The players had been singing Celtic songs at the back of the bus on the way to the stadium to keep themselves relaxed and, by the time they got ready in the dressing room, there was no time to be nervous. What I remember more than anything is the first sight of the stadium, which was beautiful, and then hearing the fans. They said we had three times as many supporters as Inter that day, and they seemed to make 10 times as much noise. Jock used that. He sent out the players ahead of Inter so that they could see that we had the crowd behind us.

Bertie Auld remembers this focus on the fans being central to Fallon's own pre-match involvement. He said: "The boss gave quite a short speech, just saying: 'You've made history. Now go out there and play to your capabilities.' But after it was finished you knew that Sean would come round and give everyone little individual pep talks. He would know how each player reacted and, with me, he would say things like, 'How many are you going to score today, Bertie?' Just things to get you going, get the blood pumping. But I always remember in Lisbon, he said to me: 'Did you see all those people? Did you hear those songs? Go out and do those supporters proud.'"

And Fallon's psychological work was not yet done. In his

autobiography, *Hail Cesar*, Billy McNeill recalled looking on as Helenio Herrera, Inter's revered manager, attempted to snatch Celtic's pre-assigned bench ahead of kick-off in a brazen display of gamesmanship. "Herrera was in for a shock," wrote McNeill. "Jock marched up and growled, 'You'll have to find another place', and Herrera was forced to walk a hundred yards with his tail between his legs. I also recall Sean Fallon threatening to 'set about' Herrera if he didn't shift – and Sean was not a man to be messed with… It was a perfect example of confidence-building."

McNeill and his team-mates had to draw on these reserves of self-assurance as early as the seventh minute, when Sandro Mazzola put Inter in front from the penalty spot. Celtic fans might not have appreciated it at the time, but there was a poignancy to this moment. It had, after all, been in this same Lisbon arena that Mazzola's father, Valentino, played his final match before boarding the flight on which he and his Torino team-mates perished. Sandro, who had been six at the time, could have provided this final's fairy tale ending. As it was, that honour belonged to Stein's team of humble, home-grown heroes, famously drawn from within a 30-mile radius of Celtic Park. So accomplished was their performance that, even at half-time – 1-0 down to the heavy favourites, a team built for counter-attacking – Fallon felt sure of success.

> I always thought we would win. So did Jock. Inter's goalkeeper [Giuliano Sarti] was having the game of his life – we were shaking our heads at some of the saves he was making – but he was the only man keeping them in it. At half-time, Jock said to the players that they were doing the right things and playing well, and that chances would come. You try to seem as calm and as confident as possible in those situations, but it was a tense day. Extremely tense. It was very warm, but I remember shaking like a leaf on the bench.
>
> It's amazing the way tension can get to you. It's easy for the players – once they're out on the field, the nerves disappear. I always found that during my own career. But sitting at the side, I couldn't stop myself from shaking. Jock was nervous too; I remember seeing him grinding his fist into his palm. But we knew the plan was working. By dragging players out of position with good movement, which our forwards had, we were creating space for players that Inter weren't so worried about. And we had people all over the park who could score goals.

The source of Celtic's equaliser – set up by one full-back, scored by another – confirmed the wisdom in that strategy. From the moment Tommy Gemmell's shot flew in, and with any remaining neutrals in the stadium now firmly behind the Scots, there was only ever going to be one outcome. Even Inter sensed the futility of their struggle. Tarcisio Burgnich, one of four players in that team who went on to represent Italy in the 1970 World Cup final, vividly recalls the extent to which they became demoralised. He said: "I remember [Armando] Picchi turned to Sarti and said: 'Giuliano, let it go, just let it go. It's pointless. Sooner or later they'll get the winner.' I never imagined my captain would tell our keeper to throw in the towel. But that only shows how destroyed we were." Burgnich's memory of this stunning exchange chimes with the impression formed by Stevie Chalmers, scorer of Celtic's 84th-minute winner. "When my goal went in," Chalmers wrote in his autobiography, *The Winning Touch*, "it was almost as though the Inter players were relieved that it would soon be all over."

The point at which the inevitable became official – the final whistle – was captured in a memorable photograph of the Celtic bench. Bob Rooney is leading the charge, but front and centre – springing forward, fist raised in triumph – is Fallon. "I love that photo," said John Fallon, Celtic's substitute on the day. "I'd been sitting beside Sean the whole game and, by the end, he was just ecstatic. I remember him running round all the players, giving each of them a huge hug." The first man he reached was Auld. "I still watch the game from time to time and it's great when you get to the end because you can see Sean charging on, grabbing everyone for a cuddle," said the midfielder. "And even from a distance, you can see that smile of his." Conspicuous by his absence, both in the photograph and the footage, is Stein. The last shot of the manager, as the match neared its conclusion, shows him heading towards the dressing rooms, seemingly unable to watch. Yet his assistant saw immediately that it was not the tension of the situation Stein found unbearable. It was the emotion.

> Jock wasn't nervous; he was just so proud by that point that he had started to get tearful, and he was embarrassed. He didn't want the players to see him like that so he just got up and walked away. While everyone was celebrating, he was down in the tunnel

composing himself. I always knew there was another side to Jock but that was something to see, even for me, because he wasn't an emotional man in normal circumstances. I was always very soft-hearted compared to him in that respect – I'll start crying watching the telly if something sad comes on. But that day, it all hit him. He was so proud of that team that he was almost bursting.

It had been a performance well worthy of Stein's tears. The manager's pre-match pledge – "we want to make neutrals glad we've won it, glad to remember how we did it" – had been fulfilled in style. As Francois Thebaud, of French magazine *Miroir du Football*, wrote: "Surely, never in the history of world sport has a team created as many new fans as Celtic, never has a victory been more warmly welcomed, nor a winning goal been greeted with such an explosion of joy throughout the continent." The result was viewed not just as a triumph for Celtic, but as a victory for the beautiful game. Even the supposedly neutral UEFA general secretary, Hans Bangerter, described it as "the best thing that could have happened to football". "If Inter Milan had won with their defensive style of play, it would have put the game back 10 years," he said. "Celtic showed everyone that attacking football is successful and I hope their method of play will revolutionise the game." The transformation from national laughing stocks to continental revolutionaries had been little short of miraculous and, at this moment of moments, Fallon's thoughts found a familiar focus.

> I just remember looking around the stadium, feeling so happy for the supporters. They were the best around, the Celtic fans, and we hadn't always repaid them as we should have. For that reason, I actually think the part of the European Cup win I enjoyed the most wasn't Lisbon, but bringing the cup home to Glasgow and seeing the joy it had brought to so many people. That journey back to Celtic Park, with the streets packed and the stadium overflowing, will stay with me forever.

But before the trophy could be returned to Glasgow, it had to be collected. Easier said than done. Initially, Stein provided Fallon with a fellow bodyguard by asking Ronnie Simpson to help usher

McNeill through the crowds. "When we got outside the dressing room, it was pandemonium," Simpson wrote in his autobiography. "I soon lost contact with Billy and when a fan shouted, 'Hey Ronnie, don't come out again – you'll never make it', I took his advice. I fought my way back to the comparative safety of the dressing room."

McNeill, exhausted and overwhelmed, was tempted to do the same. "I had no idea where I was going," he said. "But Sean had his wits about him and he just pushed me through. You couldn't have had a better man to muscle you through a crowd than Sean. I still don't know how he managed it." Nor does Myra Fallon, who remembers the anxiety with which she watched from the stand as her husband and McNeill began their long journey. "I thought, 'My God, they'll never make it.'" Sean, too, had his doubts.

> I remember when Jock asked me to take Billy up, thinking, 'How am I going to manage this?' We had to push through a bit at first – some folk nearly pulled the ribs off me, trying to get my blazer off. But, before long, the Celtic supporters had crowded round us and were helping us get there. I don't think I've ever shaken so many hands or been patted on the back so often. And it was tremendous to be up there with Billy, so close to him as he lifted the cup. It was the first time they had used that trophy and I remember thinking it was magnificent. That was the big one for us; the ultimate success. It's one of those moments you know you'll never forget.

Looking past the gleaming silver of the new European Cup, across an expanse of green covered by cavorting Celtic supporters, he only wished that Stein and the rest were there to share it. The best view in the house of the greatest moment in Celtic's history. This, Fallon knew, would take some beating.

Chapter 19
Uncle Jock

"John, you're immortal now."

This greeting, from Shankly to Stein, one kindred spirit to another, has itself proved imperishable. It was, as Fallon said, "classic Shanks". Who else could provide the most memorable sound bite from a match in which he had no part?

That the Liverpool manager's words are still remembered and celebrated is testament not only to his flair for the theatrical, but to their accuracy. Stein's legend, his achievements, have lived on and will continue to endure. But, as time passes, he has also come to be viewed as a mythical, almost superhuman figure. Though everyone is familiar with Stein the manager – fearsome motivator, cunning strategist, master manipulator – few can claim to know a great deal about Stein the man. This is true even among those who worked with him. To most who encountered the Celtic boss in their daily lives, he was not so much immortal as inscrutable.

"Few people ever got really close to him," Billy McNeill wrote in his autobiography. "Jock kept people at arm's length and dictated the depth of his relationships." This was an assessment endorsed by Stein's daughter, Ray, who acknowledged that her father "didn't make close friends easily". Naturally wary, Stein spurned quantity in favour of quality, letting down his guard only amid the tightest circle of confidants. Fallon was at the very heart of that circle.

When Archie Macpherson, in his biography of Stein, described the Irishman as "virtually a constant companion", he did so without a hint of hyperbole.

Work alone ensured that the bulk of the duo's week was spent together. In Fallon's foreword for *An Alphabet of the Celts*, he wrote: "Celtic was not just a football club to me, it was my home. I spent more time there than I did at my own house." John Clark, who joined the coaching staff in 1973, saw first-hand that this was no exaggeration. "I had a lot of respect for Jock and Sean already, but I respected them all the more after working with them in that context, seeing what went into their jobs. What I saw right away was that the two of them worked themselves into the ground for Celtic. Every day, they'd arrive together at 8.30 in the morning and wouldn't leave until after 6.30. Sundays too. And then they'd both go to watch the same game in the evening, driving across the country and down to England. They never seemed to be apart. I used to wonder how they didn't get sick of each other."

It certainly would have been reasonable to expect that, after long hours cooped up together in the car and their cramped office, Stein and Fallon would have been glad to end the working day by going their separate ways. Not so. "My memories of them aren't as a manager and assistant, but just as two great friends who would come home from training and then be straight in the car again, out to the golf course," explained Siobhan Connolly, one of Sean's five daughters. "Looking back, I can't imagine how they managed to spend the amount of time together that they did, or how they got away with it, with Jean [Stein's wife] and my mum. Even when they had time off on a Sunday, we'd all get packed up, head round to Uncle Jock's, and the families would go out to Largs for the day."

Uncle Jock. The title alone indicates the intimacy that existed between the two men and their respective families. These days of joint outings and get-togethers are remembered with evident fondness by George Stein, who spoke of calling Fallon not Uncle Sean, but a name that conveyed their common passion. "I used to say Sean wasn't my godfather – he was my golf-father," he said. "Sean and I were much keener on golf than my dad was, and if he was going for a game and there was a spare place, he would always take me along. I was just a boy at that time so it shows how close he and my dad were, and how well the families got on, that he made the effort to do that. I tutored Sean's girls in maths around that time and I was glad to be able to help because Sean was always a really great guy with me, and had a lovely family."

This affection was reciprocated. Fallon's son, Sean Jnr, recalled that it was Uncle Jock who taught him his first Celtic songs, while his sister, Louise, reminisced about the mirth and mischief that permeated the friendship. "Jock was full of fun," she said. "He had a wicked sense of humour and he and dad used to kid each other on constantly. I remember, every year, him coming round to our house the day before we went on holiday to help pack the car. There would be a great atmosphere in the house and Jock would be at the heart of the fun, laughing at all the luggage my dad was trying to squeeze in."

The two families would, in fact, have holidayed together had it not been for Fallon's insistence on making his annual pilgrimage to Sligo. "Jock and Jean Stein really were great friends of ours and they loved the kids," said Myra Fallon. "They were always wanting us to join them when they went abroad during the summer, but we couldn't miss Sligo. There wasn't a single year that we didn't make it over there as a family." Those weeks on Ireland's west coast represented the only portion of the year that Fallon spent apart from his great friend and colleague. Stein even insisted that the duo room together on pre-season tours and European trips, invariably keeping his assistant up to the small hours with conversations on an unchanging subject.

Football. That was all we ever talked about, which was fine by me. Even when we were out for dinner with our wives on a Saturday, it was still football. It's really a wonder they didn't leave us. Football was Jock's only real interest in life along with his family and a wee bet on the ponies. I used to try to get him to stop talking and let me get some rest when we'd be away on those foreign trips, but he always was a terrible sleeper. He arranged for us to room together so there was someone he could talk about this player and that player, what this manager was up to, that kind of thing.

Neither of us took a drink, so we didn't go out to pubs or anything like that. Even after Lisbon, we just sat up together going through pots and pots of tea, talking over the match. We had the trophy with us in the room for most of the time and just sat up, looking across at it and talking over every little detail of the game.

Jock loved doing that. He respected football men – people who loved the game and dedicated themselves to it. Right from when we first met, that was the key to our friendship. And Jock was a good friend to me. He was a straight man, very much down the line, and we were close for years, even after we both left Celtic. We lived for the game. It helped that our wives got on very well too. Every Saturday night, we'd all go for a meal to the Vesuvio or the Beechwood, and that was when Jock would loosen up. He could be quiet in company sometimes and he was always wary of what he was saying when he was around strangers or people he didn't know well. But he really did relax when it was just him and myself with Myra and Jean. You saw the real Jock then, and he could be great company when he was like that. When the restaurant was closing, he wouldn't want to go home. He'd have talked through the night if they'd have let him. We had some great nights together, the four of us.

It was during one of these evenings in the Beechwood that Stein and Fallon noticed they were attracting the attention of a fellow diner. "I was earwigging on their conversations," the young man in question would later admit. "Eventually they just gave up and invited me over." Alex Ferguson, already with ambitions to become a manager, could hardly believe his luck. It was there that his friendship with both men took root, with Ferguson struck from the outset by the rapport that existed between two very distinct characters. "The fact that they socialised with each other all the time just shows you what a good relationship they had," said the former Manchester United manager. "There was an obvious closeness there, and it was unusual. I mean, I have never socialised with my assistants. It's not that I haven't got on with them; it's just that the little time I've had, I've tended to go to a wee quiet hotel to spend some time with my wife. Sean and Jock, though, were out together all the time."

So close were the men and their families that, when the Fallons moved to Menock Road in King's Park, the Steins decided there was only one thing for it. When a house 50 yards along the street came on the market, they immediately snapped it up. That proximity helped in the mornings, when Celtic's manager would help his assistant with the daily school run. For Sean's eldest daughter, Marie Therese, this led to some surreal experiences. She said: "It

The chairman: Sir Robert Kelly presents a radiogram to Fallon on behalf of the Celtic Supporters Association at a CSA rally at the old Odeon cinema in Glasgow

Club business: Sean takes a call in the manager's office at Celtic Park with a picture of the 1965 Scottish Cup winners behind him on the wall

Festive fun: Sean played the role of Santa, though not always entirely convincingly, at the Celtic staff and players' family Christmas parties

Silver service: Billy McNeill holds the European Cup with Fallon in the background (centre), the only other member of the Celtic party present at the historic moment

Moment of triumph: Sean, in the foreground, springs from the bench at the final whistle in Lisbon. Joining him in rushing on to the pitch are (from left) Bob Rooney, John Fallon and Neilly Mochan

The ultimate prize: The brand new European Cup trophy, adorned with green-and-white ribbons, is clutched by Fallon on its return to Celtic Park

Lions celebrate: The newly crowned European champions celebrate with the trophy at a post-match banquet in Lisbon, with a beaming Fallon (third from left)

Happy homecoming: A smiling Fallon (second from left) waves to the capacity crowd as the heroes of '67 are given a rousing reception at Celtic Park on the day of their return from Lisbon

Backroom Bhoys: (from left) Bob Rooney, Jock Stein, Fallon and Neilly Mochan pose with the league championship trophy at Celtic Park

The double act: Stein and Fallon, the greatest managerial duo in Celtic's history, stand together in a familiar shoulder-to-shoulder pose

Friends and rivals: Bowls was one of several sports in which Fallon and Jock Stein competed, often fiercely. "The money would be down on the table and that was it: friendship suspended," said Sean

Generation game: Some of the heroes of 1967 are flanked by youthful members of the Quality Street Gang including the boyish trio of Kenny Dalglish, Lou Macari and Danny McGrain (front row), with Fallon in the back row (second from right)

Glory days: Celtic's greatest team arguably at the peak of its powers, celebrating in the Hampden dressing room having beaten Rangers 4-0 in the 1969 Scottish Cup final. Sean (second from left) has his arm round the injured Ronnie Simpson

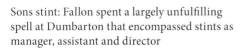

Sons stint: Fallon spent a largely unfulfilling spell at Dumbarton that encompassed stints as manager, assistant and director

Friends reunited: Old pals and former signings were among those who toasted Fallon at a supporter-organised testimonial dinner on October 31 1993. Top row (from left): Packie Bonner, Jim Brogan, Stevie Chalmers, Tommy Burns, Jackie McNamara Snr. Bottom row: Danny McGrain, Sean, Jimmy Johnstone, Bertie Peacock

Introducing a friend: Sean directs Sir Alex Ferguson to a portrait of his father, John – a former mayor of the town – during a visit to Sligo's Town Hall with the then chairman of Sligo County Council, Tony McLoughlin, in 2002

Son of Sligo: Sean at his beloved Rosses Point, with Sligo's iconic Benbulben Mountain to his left and the North Atlantic stretching out behind him

Birthday Bhoy: Fallon is front and centre at a surprise 90th birthday party thrown by the Lisbon Lions at Celtic Park. (From left) Jim Craig, Bobby Lennox, Billy McNeill, Sean, Bertie Auld, John Clark, John Hughes and John Fallon

Accepting the acclaim: Arms outstretched, Sean acknowledges the crowd's cheers after unfurling the league championship flag on August 4, 2012. Joining the ovation (from left) are Celtic players Paddy McCourt, Scott Brown, Celtic chairman Ian Bankier and SPL chief executive Neil Doncaster

Fans' tribute: The Celtic supporters unveil a banner before the 4-1 win over Hearts on January 20, 2013, two days after Sean's death

Proud father: Sean with wife Myra and the couple's six children at the wedding of their youngest daughter, Sinead, in 2003. (From left) Colette, Sean Jnr, Louise, Sinead, Sean, Myra, Marie Therese, Siobhan

Nana and Papa: A proud Myra and Sean Fallon surrounded by 19 of their 20 grandchildren. Sean Anthony (inset) was born less than four months after his Papa's passing (family)

Photographs supplied by: The Fallon family, Scottish News & Sport, Mirrorpix, Press Association, Getty Images, Express Newspapers, the Connaught Rangers Association.
Cover image: Mirrorpix

was always Jock and dad who would drop us into school in the morning and, if for some reason dad was away doing something else, Jock would come and take us himself. I remember the two of them coming to collect me quite soon after Lisbon and the car being swamped by boys in my school. It was literally covered; they were even on the roof, all with little bits of paper looking for autographs. You would have thought the Beatles had arrived."

They were not quite Lennon and McCartney but, at that time, Stein and Fallon were proving to be a combination every bit as potent. "They were incomparable as a management team, in my view," said the former Clyde winger Norrie Innes, who became friendly with both men. "They were a real double act and that was the case socially as well as in a work environment. I can still hear them now, singing away together. They both loved a song. The two of them were great company and I was fortunate on a few occasions to go with them to the boxing, which they both loved. I remember going to see Muhammad Ali together, and Jim Watt too. And Sean and Jock always got the best seats because the people at the boxing loved them." Though football was and remained their shared obsession, these trips to fight nights were representative of Fallon and Stein's wider appreciation of sport. And as two born competitors, they were never likely to stick to merely spectating.

> We used to play each other at billiards, snooker, darts, golf, bowls, table tennis… you name it. There were always some good competitive games between the two of us. The money would be down on the table and that was it: friendship suspended. We were pretty evenly-matched in most of them. Jock had played billiards growing up, but I don't think he realised that I'd also played the game in Ireland. I was probably slightly the better at billiards, whereas he had the edge at snooker. One thing about Jock was that he always played to win. Whatever the sport, he would be out to beat whoever he was playing against. No mercy. He was also a terrible cheat.
>
> In the sports where I was better than him, like table tennis and billiards, he was so competitive and desperate to win that he would always sneak in little cheats here and there. I'd call him for it too, and he would deny it completely. Most of the time we'd end up laughing about it though. The two of us had our own little passions. He got me playing bowls and I introduced him to golf.

Jock would win at bowls, but I always knew that I had it over him at the golf. We played up at Bonnyton in Eaglesham in those days and all I can say is that he was a better manager than he was a golfer. But he kept on cheating anyway. He used to enjoy the walk round more than anything else, slipping in his sneaky moves when he thought I wasn't looking.

It was always with the heartiest of laughs that Fallon would refer to his old friend's dishonesty, and John Clark was similarly amused when he heard of these allegations. "I saw the two of them at golf and all I can say is that, when it comes to cheats, it took one to know one. They were as bad as each other. Neither of them wanted to lose and, in the end, it probably came down to who was the more successful cheat of the two. I think that was part of the fun they had."

But it wasn't all singing, socialising and swindling. Though mutual friends recall the laughter that ensued whenever the two men were together, there was another, less ebullient side to Stein. Hugh McIlvanney, who knew the Celtic manager well, spoke of his "passages of great melancholy", during which he would dwell on regrets and perceived personal failings. Fallon, too, remembers a man who, away from the public gaze, suffered greatly from the intense demands he placed on himself.

You always knew that Jock's mood could change from one extreme to the other very quickly. That old mind of his was always going and he would worry himself sick about certain things. He put himself under a lot of stress and strain, and I always felt that played a big part in his health problems. I would try to cheer him up, reassure him, and the fact we were so close meant that I was able to do that sometimes. I'd imagine he was closer to me than anyone but his wife at that time, and I often worried about him. He was a terrible sleeper – that was the case even before his car accident – and he would get into dark moods if things were getting on top of him. I was more fortunate in that I could stay quite positive no matter what was going on. The results would affect me, of course, and I could get down about things like anyone else. But I think I managed to keep my problems away from home, from the kids and Myra, most of the time. Jock couldn't let go though, and he would allow things to get to him. He would take setbacks very badly.

People didn't realise how stressed he was behind the scenes. I saw it because I was always with him at such close quarters and could read him. Sometimes I could see the pressure building up inside. The thing about Jock and myself you have to remember is that it wasn't just a job for us – it was Celtic. Jock might not have grown up a Celtic fan but he became as big a Celt as anyone, and we both wanted so much for the club to be successful and to bring a bit of happiness to the supporters. When you have a big responsibility like that, it helps to be able to get away from it for an hour or two. But Jock found that difficult. The only time he unwound was watching the horses. He would get really into that and forget about football for a little while.

Everyone has their different releases. Mine was to go out to the golf course and smack that little white ball about for a couple of hours. I tried to get Jock to relax out there, too, but he never really got into it. I can hear him now: 'Ah, Sean, I can hardly hit the ball at all.' And I'd tell him: 'It's because you're not concentrating.' He gave golf a go but it never became a passion. It was always the horses for Jock.

Fallon felt the same way about horseracing as Stein did about golf. But though he was neither especially passionate about the sport nor an avid gambler, indulging his friend's hobby was no chore. Enjoyable days would be spent together at Ayr races, while John Clark remembers the pair holing themselves up in a room with Neilly Mochan and Bob Rooney to watch the meetings at Cheltenham and Aintree. "The four of them were a great team," said Clark. "They would normally have their wee meetings in the treatment room and when you saw the door shutting, you knew they could be in there all day. But whenever there was a big race on, it was along to what they called Lady Kelly's room. Then it was a case of 'do not disturb'."

Mochan's son, Neil Jnr, saw the quartet at close quarters every second Saturday, and his memory is of a group bound tightly by common factors. "They all trusted and respected each other and they all lived for their football," he said. "They were pals, simple as that. The way they would act and talk in those situations, when they were really relaxed around each other, was very different to the way they would if an outsider came in. They could switch it on and off. There was one face for the press and the public and another behind closed doors." Jimmy Steele, who worked unpaid as Celtic's masseur for almost half-a-century, was the honorary fifth member of that backroom team. His view was that it was the energy and toil of his colleagues which earned Stein's esteem and affection. "I think the secret at Parkhead is that he wants fellows around him who are dedicated to the job," Steele said of the manager in *Playing for Celtic*. "Everybody has a job of work to do or he doesn't want to know them."

The result of these efforts, not to mention the skills and personalities of the individuals concerned, created an intense yet enjoyable atmosphere in which the players thrived. "I used to wake up in the morning and look forward to it all," Joe McBride said of training. "I'd jump in the car and head for Barrowfield with the same expectations as going to play in a vital cup tie." And it was not merely the players who approached their working day with such enthusiasm.

> I enjoyed coming into the park every single day. It was a great place to work, and the four of us – Jock, Neilly, Bob and myself – were all pretty close. Jock was the boss and he was a good man to work with; a great leader. But no football club gets success without an awful lot of people doing their jobs well, and Jock would have been the first to tell you that myself, Neilly and a lot of other people played our parts. We didn't let anyone down. With Jock, trust was so important and he liked to be surrounded by folk he knew well. He was naturally suspicious of people and, if he didn't like you – and there were plenty he didn't like – you knew all about it. He was close to myself and Bob Kelly at Celtic, got on well with Neilly, and had some friends outside the game, but not many. What Jock really loved was to be among 'football men' as we called them, talking about the game, going into detail. You didn't get his respect or his trust easily but, once you had it, he would trust you with a lot.

This willingness to delegate to those he valued is reflected in Fallon's wide range of responsibilities. As George Stein said: "There was definite respect there for the things Sean did, and did well. A lot of his work went unseen by the fans and the players, but my dad always appreciated it. For example, my dad would never have claimed to be a great administrator, so Sean took care of a lot of the admin side of the manager's job. Again, it came down to trust. My dad knew he could leave jobs in Sean hands and be completely confident they were being done well." Those tasks were often of the unrewarding variety, from arranging Celtic's foreign travel to organising the players' ticket allocation. Yet Fallon handled them with the fastidiousness one would expect of a man so devoted to his club. Celtic were invariably the beneficiaries.

> It was all work that people didn't see, but it was important all the same. For instance, there was one occasion when I was checking through all the contracts, making sure everyone was signed up. You had to have players signed up by a certain date at that time, otherwise they were considered free agents. Anyway, I'm looking through our list, checking everyone, even all the young boys, and I notice that there's a player who hasn't been signed up. Kenny Dalglish! I nearly had a heart attack. When I went through to tell Jock, he went as white as a ghost. This was in the early 70s, so Kenny was already establishing himself, and losing a player like that in those circumstances would have been a disaster. Can you imagine it? I think we only had a day to get it sorted and Jock felt I would be the best man to speak to Kenny about it, so he sent me round straight away to get it sorted. I had a good relationship with Kenny, and he signed the form right away. But what an embarrassment that could have been for the club if it hadn't been caught in time.

Though not an office worker by nature, Fallon readily and without complaint applied himself to his administrative responsibilities. And while Jim Craig sympathised in *A Lion Looks Back*, remarking that the role of Stein's assistant must have been "hard on the nerves", with responsibility for tickets "a nightmare" in itself, the Irishman would insist otherwise. There was, though, one job he genuinely dreaded. Even decades later, with his 90th birthday approaching, Fallon would choke back the tears as he remembered the individual stories involved.

> Jock gave me the responsibility of releasing players who didn't make it, and it was by far the worst job I ever had to do. I would never sleep a wink the night before I had to do it. I'd be lying there awake thinking, 'What am I going to say to them?' And

what could you say? These boys just wanted to play football, exactly as I had. The days when I had to speak to those players were some of the worst of my life. How do you tell someone: 'You're just not quite good enough.' And most of the time, that was the honest truth. You've got to have that something extra to make it at a club like Celtic and you would have boys who would get so far and then God almighty couldn't push them any further. It used to break my heart. I always thought back to how happy I was when my dream was realised, and now here I was dashing theirs. I'd tell them: 'Listen, son, we could be wrong. I hope you prove us wrong.' But it was no real use. I doubt they even took it in.

So many of them didn't recover from the disappointment and never made it elsewhere, even though plenty of them had the talent to make it at other clubs. I always kept an eye out for those boys though and, if I could help them, I would. I tried to find out if they had exams coming up so as not to tell them at the worst time, throw things off for them there. But you knew that, whenever you did it, you were going to break their hearts. It was hard not to think of yourself as being responsible.

Fallon need not have felt this way. It has forever been the harsh reality of professional football, particularly at bigger clubs, that more hearts will be broken than dreams realised. But it was typical of the man that these youngsters were not mere statistics to him. Someone who came to learn of Fallon's paternal outlook was his friend, Norrie Innes, who by the 1970s had become a high-ranking figure with the civil engineering company RJ McLeod. He said: "Sean put Celtic before anything and anyone. But he was also a very caring man and if there were any boys who weren't quite going to make the grade, I knew he would be straight on the phone asking if I could help find them some work. I can't imagine too many other managers or assistants managers in the game going to the lengths he went to, certainly not at a club as big as Celtic."

Few would have applied these same sentiments to the man he assisted. Though rightly revered as one of the greatest managers the game has produced, Stein was not a beloved figure among his players. John Fallon's opinion of him as "hard-hearted" is far from uncommon. Similarly blunt language is used in an account by Tom Campbell and David Potter in *Jock Stein, the Celtic Years*: "Some of his players hated him. One famous ex-Celt, walking towards a supporters' function, expressed his frustration: 'How could we ever tell these people (the supporters) what a bastard he was?'" Fallon was well aware that such opinions existed. Yet he believed, both at the time and years later, that they were symptomatic not of Stein's character, but of the way in which he purposefully projected himself.

> Jock showed only a certain side of himself to the players. I could understand why some of them didn't like him because he could be very hard on them at times. As a manager, he was ruthless and not the kind of man who was easy to approach at all. But he felt he had to be that way – not show any weakness – and even if some of the players didn't like him, he still got the most out of them. As far as he was concerned, that was his job and the only thing that mattered. He wasn't there to be liked. But I was in a different situation to the players. I did like Jock. He was a great friend of mine for many, many years and we spent so much time together that I still find myself missing him sometimes. It took a long time to get used to the fact that he was gone. But I look back on all that time together with a lot of happy memories. I feel very fortunate to have known him.

Stein had been dead over 27 years by the time he was joined by his old friend in the great dugout in the sky. But Fallon's words reaffirmed that Shankly had been right. It also showed that immortality is not only secured by continued recognition of remarkable achievements. There is another famous and poignant phrase from Celtic's history that expresses it better. It can be seen on the tombstone of John Thomson, and applies to Stein – and indeed Fallon – every bit as much as the tragic Prince of Goalkeepers.

'They never die who live in the hearts they leave behind.'

Chapter 20
Opportunities Missed

Bill Shankly had not been the only man to congratulate Stein in the bowels of the Estadio Nacional. Jimmy Gordon, who had been filming his *Celtic Story* documentary, remembers enthusing to the manager, "What a season!" "Aye," came Stein's muted reply. "But what do I do next year?"

Perhaps this simply encapsulated the mindset of a football manager, for whom triumphs are all too briefly savoured and challenges always loom large. Yet the tone of Stein's remark is revealing because, on the face of it, Celtic's future had never looked brighter. The team's performance in Lisbon; its average age of 26; the competition provided by Fallon's outstanding young reserve side: all these factors and more pointed to this European Cup not being his last.

Stein's Celtic, for a few glorious months, were the talk of the football world. For Jimmy Johnstone and Tommy Gemmell, that meant being ranked among the game's top six players in the Ballon d'Or, with Franz Beckenbauer, Eusebio and George Best among those left to gaze upwards at Celtic's red-haired winger. Fallon, too, was caught up in the avalanche of accolades. The most rapturous of welcomes awaited him in Sligo, where a civic reception had been organised to hail the town's homecoming hero.

Flags and bunting lined the streets, crowds gathered in

anticipation, while local dignitaries competed over who could pay the grandest tribute. "The name of Sean Fallon," said one speaker, "will shine and shine forever like the morning star in the sky." The man himself, blushing at such immoderate praise, said that recognition should instead be given to his parents and the volunteers running Sligo's sports clubs. "These people," he said, "have been responsible for everything I have achieved." There was also praise for Celtic, who received a particularly glowing commendation from Sligo's mayor, Sidney Gallagher. "It is universally recognised," he said, "that they are the greatest team of all time."

Real Madrid, with six European Cups already to their name, might have queried Gallagher's logic. But Celtic had just returned from beating the Spaniards in Alfredo Di Stefano's testimonial and, while perhaps not the greatest of all time, were undoubtedly the team of the moment. Still, Stein saw trouble ahead. "For some of you, football will never be the same again," was his message to the players when they returned from their summer break. "I think he wanted to provoke us into proving him wrong," said Bobby Murdoch. "But he turned out to be right."

Celtic, of course, remained a formidable and often irresistible force for years to come. Nonetheless, the innocent harmony that characterised the pre-Lisbon era quickly dissipated, and was never fully regained. As for the source of discord, it was nothing if not predictable, with a pattern emerging as early as that blissful summer of '67. That was when Tommy Gemmell discovered, through dating Stein's secretary, that Billy McNeill was earning £50-a-week to his team-mates' £40. Having confronted the manager and lobbied unsuccessfully for an equivalent rise, Gemmell relayed the divisive information to an unhappy dressing room. And so it began.

> Money became a big issue after Lisbon and got bigger and bigger as the gap grew between what Celtic and the clubs down south were paying. Celtic never paid high wages, and that went for Jock and myself as much as it did the players. The bonuses kept the players going but if you ever found yourself out of the team, you were in trouble. I felt, with the Lions, it would have been easy enough to sort though. I could never understand why the club didn't play a big game after Lisbon, a kind of testimonial

for that team, and clear up any money issues once and for all. It would have been the easiest thing to do, there would have been a tremendous crowd, and it would have generated a lot of money to be shared around.

As it was, the players ended 1967 not with a bonus, but facing a hefty £250 fine. That substantial penalty, which equated to more than a month's wages, came about after the most notorious encounter of Celtic's history. It was a match that could have seen them crowned world champions, but which succeeded only in tarnishing a hard-earned image that, after Lisbon, had gleamed like never before.

Few teams, though, would have withstood the provocation to which Stein's side were subjected. Racing Club of Argentina were the champions of South America, with the toughness and technical ability befitting that title. But their coach, Juan Jose Pizzuti, had watched Celtic dismantle Inter and arrived at a conclusion: his team could not win the Intercontinental Cup by fair means alone. Years later, Racing's goalkeeper, Augustin Cejas, told Soccer Monthly that the players' orders were to "take whatever measures necessary to stop Celtic from winning by provoking our rivals beyond endurance". The beautiful game it was not. But in a sport in which the end almost always justifies the means, Pizzuti considered himself vindicated.

> "I couldn't have looked myself in the mirror if Celtic had played like that. I honestly thought I'd seen it all by then, but I was really shocked by Racing. To see those kind of players – internationals most of them – going out with the intention of putting their opponents out of the game, it was very sad. I felt the same when we played Atletico Madrid a few years later and they played in a similar way. It angers you to see talented footballers – and there's no question that Racing and Atletico could play – wasting their ability by playing like hooligans. But it showed how worried the Racing coach was about us that he sent his team to play that way. Those games were a crime against football more than anything else because football should be a great game, and this was meant to be the best against the best. But all they wanted to do was spit and punch and kick."

It was not, though, mindless violence. Racing's brutality was, as

Cejas explained, carried out with the clear and defined purpose of knocking Stein's players off their stride. It worked. Celtic did win the first leg at Hampden on October 18 by a solitary McNeill goal, but a disjointed performance betrayed the extent to which they were taken aback by the South Americans' cynicism.

Yet Racing's display in Glasgow was merely a trailer for the feature-length show of savagery that would follow a fortnight later. Celtic had good reason to withdraw even before a ball was kicked in Buenos Aires, and must have wished they had, after Ronnie Simpson was struck by a missile that left blood gushing from his head. Instead, John Fallon was drafted in and performed heroically in a frenzied, foreboding atmosphere. "I am not a man who is easily scared," remarked Stein. "But I am not ashamed to admit I was terrified at that game." Bob Kelly later reflected that it was the one occasion on which he was grateful for a Celtic defeat. "I think there is no doubt that had we won or drawn the game and thereby won the world title, there would have been such serious trouble as would have shaken the very foundations of world football," he wrote. "How our players would have fared at the hands of players and spectators who would not have stopped at anything, I shudder to imagine."

Having been beaten 2-1, Celtic found themselves in limbo. The away goals rule, which would have handed them victory, had not yet been introduced in this competition, and tournament regulations stipulated the need for a decisive third match on neutral ground. Kelly's inclination was to walk away, return to Scotland, bruised but with dignity intact and somehow free of serious injury. Stein, ever the competitor, saw a trophy still up for grabs and an eminently winnable match in Montevideo. "We were, I thought, bound to get fairer treatment in a neutral country," he would ruefully reflect. Backed by club secretary Desmond White and the majority of his players, Stein was relentless. It wasn't long before Kelly, while still muttering "against my better judgement", submitted.

> We should have listened to the chairman on that one. He could be very far-seeing sometimes and, on that occasion, he read the situation better than anyone. I had supported Jock on it at the time as I wanted to be loyal but I did feel – and I told him so –

that playing the third match was a mistake. We had already done well enough and, with the way Racing had gone about things, we would have gone home with a moral victory if nothing else. But Jock didn't want to be seen by anyone to be running away, and I could understand his position. He knew that, if we were allowed to play football, we would win. Unfortunately, that was never going to be allowed to happen, and Bob Kelly obviously saw that. It was the only time I saw him and Jock have a major disagreement about anything, and Jock admitted later that the chairman had been right.

Stein was aware of his players' smouldering anger, and gave them licence to, within reason, fight fire with fire. "The time for politeness is over," he told the press. But those players, just as Pizzuti planned, had been 'provoked beyond their endurance'. "We went out like avenging angels," recalled Billy McNeill. And while Racing's viciousness three days earlier had been calculated and cunning, Celtic – in the words of Jim Craig – simply "lost the plot". Of six players sent off in a brutal, farcical match immortalised as 'The Battle of Montevideo', four were Scots. One member of that dismissed quartet, Bertie Auld, simply refused to leave the field and played on under the gaze of an impotent and hapless Paraguayan referee. Celtic's reputation paid the price. Viewed out of context, the statistics and snippets from this notorious play-off suggested that the villains had been clad in green-and-white. When images of Racing's 1-0 win were beamed around the world, they showed John Hughes delivering a boot to a grounded goalkeeper, and Tommy Gemmell kicking an unsuspecting rival in the nether regions. "I was livid," Stein said of the latter incident. "So livid, so outraged that I leapt from my seat, got past the steel-helmeted police and raced across the pitch to tell Gemmell exactly what I thought of him." The manager knew that, at best, it would appear that he had failed to contain his players; at worst, that he had sent them out to exact retribution. The personal cost to Stein would be significant. In 2007, papers released under the Freedom of Information Act revealed that he was removed from the 1968 New Year's Honours list and denied a knighthood "because of the unfortunate events in South America".

That wasn't fair on Jock. He had sent the players out to play fairly – 'hard but fair' was always the message – and couldn't be blamed for what happened. But I think the knighthood, even if he'd known about it, wouldn't have bothered him much. What he cared about more than anything was Celtic's reputation, and he knew that the game had shown the club in the worst possible light. Jock had always been very strong on discipline and representing the club well, so the Racing Club thing hurt him very badly. He was down about it for a long time, as were we all. It was amazing to think that we could all be so low a few months after winning the European Cup, but that was what those games did to us.

Reports that Racing's players had each received £2000 and a complimentary car would not have improved the mood. Nor did the BBC coverage, which painted Celtic as the instigators. But the heaviest blow was inflicted from within Celtic Park, with Bob Kelly telling a press conference: "For our reputation and the reputation of British football, the players must suffer for their conduct." Indignation followed. The players' anger stemmed not from being punished, which was inevitable, but from the severity of the fine and the fact that every squad member – from the most glaring offenders to the guiltless – faced the same penalty. "I always thought that was a really despicable punishment," reflected Jim Craig, one of several in the latter camp. "I was quite bitter about it."

He was not alone, and this lingering resentment chipped away at the morale and unity that had been so crucial to Stein's early successes. Celtic became the first European Cup holders to exit the tournament in the opening round, having gone down 3-2 on aggregate to Dynamo Kiev in October 1967. By February 1968, Celtic were two points behind Rangers and had no Old Firm derbies remaining in which to narrow the gap. Stein, advised by Fallon and Mochan on the depths of disillusionment, called a team meeting and, by adopting an unusually conciliatory tone, pacified his players. It was to prove the turning point in a season which ended with the club's third successive championship.

But other concerns remained. Stein and Fallon viewed with disquiet the effect that their new-found fame was having on some of the players. "With one or two, it went to their heads," Sean reflected. "That happens. Some of them started to believe their own publicity." Tommy Gemmell, by his own admission, was the most conspicuous example. Always an extrovert, the full-back's lifestyle became increasingly lavish, with the purchase of a white S-type Jaguar an act of unashamed symbolism. "I went on an ego trip when I got that," Gemmell admitted in his autobiography. "My head was swollen with our success at Celtic and I felt that the S-type would fit right in with my image as a flair player."

Stein was unimpressed. He remained mindful of Gemmell's role against Racing, and when the same player was sent off for Scotland in October 1969 after a similarly wild kick at Helmut Haller of West Germany, Celtic's manager took the chance to cut him down to size. The following Saturday, Gemmell arrived at Hampden for the League Cup final against St Johnstone, smiling and laughing, and was taking off his coat in the dressing room when he received a tap on the shoulder. "Jim Kennedy, who was working on the club's staff as a liaison officer, said, 'There is your ticket for the stand'," Gemmell recalled. "Jock Stein walked past me and never said a word; he did not even acknowledge that I was there."

Humiliated in front of his team-mates, Gemmell stormed in to Celtic Park the following morning to submit a transfer request. He was met by a manager he described as "fantastic at flannelling, a master at taking the heat off himself", who on this occasion intimated that he had been leaned on by Kelly to make the call. It was, Gemmell thought, an entirely unconvincing explanation, and Fallon is in no doubt that the player's scepticism was warranted.

The chairman had no part in dropping Tommy. That was Jock's decision and Jock's alone. Knowing Bob Kelly and his views on discipline, I'm sure he would have approved. But there is no way that Jock would have had anyone make his decisions for him, certainly not by that stage. Jock was the master of everything by then. With Tommy, we spent a lot of time talking about how to deal with him because, although he was a great talent, he wasn't always the easiest player to handle. Some players, like Bobby Lennox and Bobby Murdoch, never gave you a minute's bother from the day they arrived until the day they left. But some you needed to keep a close eye on, and Tommy was one of those.

Gemmell would be on the transfer list for the remainder of his Celtic career, and would find himself on collision course with Fallon before he departed. Yet it was on the recommendation of the Irishman, who had been impressed by the full-back's reserve showings, that he was recalled on November 12 for a European Cup tie against two-time winners Benfica. Gemmell responded with a magnificent long-range goal, his trademark, as Celtic won 3-0, although a Eusebio-inspired comeback in Lisbon left them requiring a coin-toss to go through. For the supporters, this stroke of luck could mean only one thing: Celtic's name was on the trophy. A comprehensive victory over Fiorentina in the last eight the following March merely heightened that sense of expectation.

And then there was Leeds United. Don Revie, Stein and Fallon's latest adversary, was regarded by both men as an old friend. The summer before, Celtic's manager and assistant had been guests at Revie's Lancashire home, with all three attending The Open golf championship at Royal Lytham and St Anne's. It was mooted then, as they watched Tony Jacklin become the first Brit to win that title since 1951, that an all-UK European Cup final between their respective teams would be worth aiming for. Meeting in the last four represented the next-best thing.

> Those Leeds matches were amazing – two of the best. It was an interesting test for Jock and myself because we both knew Don Revie well and he knew all about us too. I liked Don. He could rub people up the wrong way, but he was a nice big guy and the kind of man you always hope will go on to do well in football because he lived and breathed the game. And he did exceptionally well with Leeds, making them an excellent side. The English media didn't give us a hope in hell, I seem to remember. Scottish football was much stronger back then but they wouldn't give us any credit at all.

The tone of the coverage was encapsulated in an article by Alan Smith, who wrote that Celtic's five successive championships "merely established them as the biggest fish in surely the smallest pond ever dug". Revie himself was no stranger to sly digs at Scottish football; in 1965, he predicted the game north of the border would be "dead" in five years.

Don might have said that but, by the time of those games, I know he respected Celtic. You could see he was worried in the build-up; I remember talking to Jock about how you could see it in his face. The first leg was at Elland Road and Don had said that Leeds would wear a different colour of socks because of the colour clash. But when we got there, he insisted that he had made no such agreement. We had to wear socks from one of Leeds' change strips and there were two options: blue or orange. I think he probably thought it would cause a bit of consternation in our dressing room and unsettle everyone. But we just laughed it off. To us, it showed he was worried and it just gave Jock, myself and the players even more confidence.

What he maybe didn't realise is how mentally strong that Celtic squad was. Those players had been there and done it by then and were ready for anything. They were tremendous in that tie. We won 1-0 down there with George Connelly scoring an early goal, and it could have been a lot more. And, of course, the second leg was even better. The game was played at Hampden and you could have reached out and touched the atmosphere – that's how electric it was. The pressure on the players was immense, and Billy Bremner scored a great goal to level things up quite early in the match. But as I say, that team were very mentally strong. They came back and won brilliantly. Jock and myself were so proud. I remember he had to leave the dressing room because it was like Lisbon all over again: he was worried he was going to cry in front of them. I don't think I've ever seen him happier though. That was one of the great Celtic nights.

Some consider it the greatest. Goals from John Hughes and Bobby Murdoch, both early in the second half, had put Celtic in the European Cup final. "That was Celtic's finest ever hour-and-a-half – and I'm not forgetting Lisbon," wrote Danny McGrain in *Celtic: My Team*. It had been watched by a colossal crowd of 136,505, a European record which stands to this day. Revie, to his credit, was nothing if not gracious in defeat. The Celtic fans, the referee and Stein's players all came in for praise, with the outstanding Jimmy Johnstone lauded as "better than George Best". "Celtic were great at Elland Road," said Revie. "But they were out of this world before their own fans."

The mood in Scotland was euphoric. Feyenoord lay in wait at the San Siro but, for many, the hard work had already been done.

"There is no doubt in my mind that we climbed our mountain against Leeds," said Jim Craig, an unused substitute in both ties. "We lulled ourselves into thinking that Feyenoord represented the other side of the peak, and that we were coasting downhill." Debate since has centred on the degree of responsibility that Stein – and, to a lesser extent, Fallon – should carry for this mindset, and for the subsequent, thoroughly deserved 2-1 defeat.

McGrain insisted that it was "totally wrong" to blame the management, stressing that every training session included warnings about the threat posed by Feyenoord and their likely dangermen. Johnstone was equally adamant. "Nobody can say a word about Jock on this game," he said. "We just didn't play well." Others, though, remember Stein's team-talk, in which the elegant Wim van Hanegem was dismissed as "a slower Jim Baxter, with a right foot just for standing on". Wim Jansen, the players were told, "could only play for 20 minutes before disappearing, and wouldn't be seen again". "Jock was right enough about that," said Bertie Auld. "I never did see Jansen after that. He got faster as we seemed to get slower."

Stevie Chalmers, who had missed out on a place in the team, saw another glimpse of this misplaced confidence. As he wrote in his autobiography, *The Winning Touch*: "I remember the lads running out on to the field and me being left with the manager in the dressing room, and then saying, conversationally: 'What do you think, boss? Do you think we can get a result?' He turned to me and said: 'If we play at all, we'll take six off of them.'"

But what of Fallon's role in all of this? Some players, though not all, have implicated Stein's assistant in establishing a mood of complacency. However, as Eugene MacBride wrote in *Alphabet of the Celts*: "Sean was the one Celt to speak out like a Cassandra amid the euphoria of April 1970." Fallon had, as always, accompanied Stein on his pre-match scouting mission, and he returned from Rotterdam full of effusive praise for Celtic's opponents. "A first-rate team in every way," was his assessment in the *Evening Times*. "'We couldn't spot any weaknesses." Something, therefore, did not add up, and amid such a dizzying variety of contrasting accounts and opinions, it was left to Fallon to sort fact from fiction.

Truthfully, I think everyone underestimated Feyenoord. Even the

Dutch journalists thought we would win. I had been impressed by them but I can't have been telling the truth in that interview because we had seen weaknesses. Every team has weaknesses. But they were a great side and, on that night, they played tremendously well. We met our match, and there's no shame in admitting that because Feyenoord's coach put together a team with the right players, the right balance – they were a pleasure to watch. I had nothing but admiration for the way they went about playing football. Every game has a winner and a loser, and sometimes the winner deserves more credit than the loser does blame. I always felt that Feyenoord, like ourselves in '67, deserved all the praise in the world for the way they went about their business that night in Milan. And I'm sure they would have gone on to achieve even more success had it not been for the magnificent Ajax team that came along at the same time and won three European Cups in a row.

But it's also true that we were very poor, and I always felt a lot of that was down to the Leeds games. They killed us for the final. I don't think we had the energy left to match Feyenoord on the kind of form they were in. People have thrown up the things Jock said before the game, but that was all psychological. Jock was no mug – he knew Feyenoord's players were very useful. He just wanted our players going out with plenty of confidence. In the end, maybe he misread the mood and gave them too much confidence. But both of us felt at the time that the biggest mistake he had made was in the way the team was set up. That was something he regretted more than anything that was said.

In this, there was no room for interpretation. In dropping George Connelly and abandoning the 4-3-3 formation that had functioned so flawlessly against Leeds, Stein simply made a rare and uncharacteristic error. Davie Hay described the decision as "unfathomable". Midfield was the area in which Feyenoord were strongest and, with Stein's 4-2-4 handing them a numerical advantage to supplement their technical superiority, the Dutch dominated.

Even with his initial mistake seemingly apparent, Stein proved abnormally slow to adjust. "We've not started to play yet; we'll get going now," were his words at half-time, having watched Gemmell's ill-deserved opener quickly cancelled out by Rinus Israel. But no alterations were made to effect such a change, and

Feyenoord merely tightened their stranglehold. Celtic survived until extra-time but Ove Kindvall's 116th-minute winner ensured that, in Milan, as in Lisbon, justice was belatedly done. Those on the bench remember Fallon pressing for a change in approach during the second half, and for the utilising of substitutes that included Connelly and Lou Macari. Still, Stein had hesitated. Even when Connelly was belatedly introduced, with 13 minutes of the 90 remaining and Celtic hanging on grimly to a 1-1 draw, it was essentially a cosmetic change. While the personnel altered, the failing system remained in place. "Celtic took off Bertie Auld and put me on, instead of taking off an attacker and tightening up the midfield," Connelly explained in *Celtic's Lost Legend*. "Looking back on it, it was kind of screaming out for that."

> Jock had his reasons for playing that team. He loved his wingers, as did I, and he felt that stretching Feyenoord would be important if we were going to get the better of them. But it was a mistake not playing George. He would have helped the balance of the team, and he would have relished the occasion because he was a big-time player. The better the players he was up against, the better George would play. He had been absolutely tremendous against Leeds, and did a lot to help Bobby Murdoch and Bertie Auld. So, yes, Jock got that one wrong, and he knew it later. But it was an honest mistake, and what manager hasn't made mistakes? Feyenoord stands out for people because it was one of the only times Jock got it wrong, and that shows how often he was right.

Stein, in truth, attracted only modest criticism. The bulk of opprobrium was heaped on his players, who took the ill-considered step of holding a press conference the following day to announce a commercial syndicate. Bob Kelly later wrote that this had "rubbed salt in the wounds of the many supporters who had travelled to see the final", adding that he believed Celtic "lost the match before it even began". The insensitivity of the players' timing stunned Fallon and yet he understood their anger at the way in which the final was subsequently reported. It had, after all, been a collective failure, and yet Stein's post-match comments – "I was surprised, not by Feyenoord, but by my own team" – seemed to deflect blame from the dugout to the dressing room.

An uneasy summer lay in store for Fallon and Celtic, while

Stein was again left to ask, for very different reasons: "What do I do next year?" Only this time there was an additional question to ponder. "Should I stay, or should I go?"

Chapter 21
Dilemmas and Disaster

By the summer of 1970, the harsh reality was that Celtic's greatest years were behind them. Domestic dominance was maintained, but the European Cup final in Milan would be their last. Worryingly, it seemed that Stein, too, had peaked. "Jock should have left after the final in 1970 and become manager of Scotland," is the assessment of his captain, Billy McNeill. "He wilted visibly after our defeat in Milan and was never again the same vibrant personality."

Fallon, at least for a while, was able to buck this downward trend. In the wake of Feyenoord, amid disagreements, despondency and the first signs of decline, Stein's assistant was at the peak of his powers. And he needed to be. No longer was it sufficient simply to preserve, protect and, where possible, enhance what the manager had so brilliantly established. Now, with the Lisbon Lions having lost a little of their lustre and Stein a degree of his enthusiasm, the challenge was to renew and to revitalise. Fortunately, it was a job for which Fallon came well prepared. As the evolution of the team would illustrate, Celtic's unobtrusive No.2 had been keeping himself busy.

Though assessing assistants is never as straightforward as evaluating managers, the reserves was one area on which Fallon could be judged almost exclusively on his own merits. Certainly, no other aspect of his job so adequately showcased those attributes to their full, impressive extent. His reserve team had been dubbed the Quality Street Gang by the tabloids, and the moniker would stick. But that side, undoubtedly the greatest second string in Celtic's history, were also known by another name. "We were Sean's boys," said George Connelly, one of the side's first high-profile graduates. "There was myself, Dalglish, McGrain, Macari, Hay, Paul Wilson and a few others who could have been just as good, so you can see what a great team it was to be a part of. Sean did wonders for us all. That was him in his element, I thought: working with young players, making brilliant signings and taking the pressure off Jock Stein. I always felt he didn't get anywhere near the credit he deserved."

The household names rhymed off by Connelly – all signed and managed by Fallon – underline the scale of the Irishman's achievement. Between them, 'Sean's boys' would go on to win over 200 caps and earn Celtic a series of record-breaking transfer fees. "If anything, they had more natural ability and talent [than the Lisbon Lions]," said McNeill. "Can I pay them a higher compliment than that?"

So formidable were the Quality Street Gang that, in 1968, Celtic sought permission to enter them in Scotland's second tier. The proposal was met by fierce opposition. As Scottish football historian Bob Crampsey wrote: "Apart from the danger of creating a precedent, there was every possibility that the Celtic reserve side of that time could have won the Second Division championship, which, even if they were ineligible for promotion, would have been embarrassing for all concerned."

Denied that opportunity, they simply won whatever was on offer. In 1970/71, that equated to a clean sweep of Reserve League, Reserve League Cup and Second XI Cup titles, scoring 157 goals in the process. More important, though, was the invigorating impact they were having on the first team. Hay and Connelly had emerged as key men en route to Milan, Dalglish was beginning to dazzle, and Macari ended the 1970/71 season with a goal in the Scottish Cup final win over Rangers. It should have been a time that Fallon remembered with immense fondness and pride and, in some respects, he did. Yet this success-laden period had also been punctuated by two of his darkest days.

Ibrox would be the venue for the second and, for all his innumerable visits to the home of Celtic's great rivals, it was this one that would never – could never – be forgotten. The first, though, had befallen him in a more unexpected location. America, at that stage, held only happy memories, not merely from the blissful pre-season of 1966, but from two equally memorable tours in the early 1950s. Yet the 1970 version was never likely to be a carefree repeat. Celtic's first match, in Toronto, took place just five days after the misery of Milan, and was the first of seven within the space of two weeks. What had been intended as a triumphant, money-spinning addendum to the club's second European Cup win became an excruciating ordeal.

And while Celtic did not bring with them the trophy everyone had expected, they did arrive accompanied by plenty of baggage. There was undisguised resentment among the players at the way in which Stein had allowed them to be portrayed, and anger too that Jimmy Johnstone – because of his fear of flying – had been excused a trip inflicted on the rest of them. Add in end-of-season fatigue, uncomfortably humid conditions, rutted pitches and poor crowds, and it was no wonder that McNeill declared it "the unhappiest trip the club ever undertook". What happened next, according to the Celtic captain, was "an accident waiting to happen".

The details remain contested, but whatever offence was committed by Bertie Auld and Tommy Gemmell at a New Jersey supporters' function, it prompted an official complaint. Fallon was the man to whom the organisers' grievance was brought and, ordinarily, he would have dealt with the matter quietly and, if possible, privately. As an unnamed "prominent player", speaking in confidence in *Jock Stein, the Celtic Years*, said: "Sean would be prepared to cover up for you... but later on he would speak to you and you knew very well what would be expected of you in future. He made you want to behave in order to maintain Celtic's good name, and you knew that he would never divulge what you had done as a daft wee boy."

The same book concludes: "Fallon was a man of honour and principle: minor infractions could be overlooked, but he was not a man to shirk the hard decisions when the reputation of the club was at stake." Sadly for Auld, Gemmell and, indeed, Sean himself, the incident in New Jersey was deemed worthy of one such decision. These Celtic legends, both of whom he had brought to the club, were summoned to a meeting, spoken to at length, given $50 expenses, and handed tickets for the next flight home.

> That was one of the worst moments I had at Celtic. I had a sleepless night afterwards and felt low about it for days. I had wanted to keep the whole thing quiet and I had asked the press men to agree to that. But one of them broke ranks and splashed the story all over the front pages, which was embarrassing to the players and the club. Sending those boys home was the last thing I wanted to do. Tommy and Bertie had been outstanding servants, and were two of my signings. But I felt I had no option. I would cover for people and try to keep things under wraps if I could, and the players knew that. They were a good bunch and, if it was a one-off, I'd let them off and keep it a secret from Jock. But they also knew where the line was drawn.
>
> I wanted them all to be good professionals, to care about representing Celtic well, and I was very conscious – especially because I worked with the reserves – of how important it was to show the right kind of example to the young players. We had a lot of young lads on that tour like Macari and Kenny Dalglish, and although they were quiet then and didn't say much, they were watching everything the senior players did. I couldn't have them thinking that bad behaviour would be tolerated. But, all the same, I hated having to send Bertie and Tommy home. And it never changed my opinion that they had been two of the greatest players Celtic ever had.

It is reasonable to wonder at this stage why the decision was Fallon's to make. Stein would later quibble with his assistant's approach in a conversation with Alex Ferguson, saying: "Why make enemies for yourself? By the time they got home, the families of the players would have had no time for Sean. Why give yourself that problem?" Stein, Ferguson was told, would have done things differently; trodden more carefully. But Stein wasn't there.

A couple of days earlier, midway through the second half of a tempestuous 2-2 draw with Bari, the Celtic manager turned to his assistant and said simply: "I'm away home." Within seconds, he had disappeared up the tunnel and was heading for the airport. Fallon was stunned. Celtic still had four matches of the tour to negotiate and he was left with players, staff and journalists pressing him for answers that, having been deserted without warning, he did not have. Eventually, Stein released a statement claiming that he had returned to handle a backlog of paperwork and receive treatment on his troublesome ankle. The truth, his wife Jean later revealed, was that "he didn't have his heart in it".

There was an additional factor. Celtic's first opponents on the tour had been Manchester United and it was while in Canada for that fixture that Stein began tentative discussions about moving to Old Trafford. It was the beginning of a saga that would take most of the season to resolve and, for once, the manager chose to keep his principal confidant largely in the dark.

> Jock was very cagey about the whole thing. He told me later that he was thinking about moving, but I think he knew I was annoyed with him over upping and leaving like that in America. That was one time I wasn't entirely happy with Jock. The uncertainty about the Man United thing wasn't helpful to anyone and I felt he could have been more up front about it all. But you just get on with it. There wasn't a big fall-out or anything like that; I just let him know what I thought. I wanted it sorted out one way or the other.

For weeks, months even, it seemed likely that Stein would leave. By February 1971, patience was wearing thin, with the minutes of a crisis board meeting revealing a hardening of attitudes towards the club's vacillating manager. "It was agreed to put out to the manager that he was being paid a very high salary, that 'loyalty to the club should play a very important part' in his thinking and that 'we were not prepared to enter into an auction'," the minutes read. Billy McNeill, in *Hail Cesar*, remembered driving to Stein's house to confront him on the persistent, unsettling rumours. "Jock was up front with me," wrote McNeill. "'I've been offered the Manchester United job, Billy, and I think I'm going to take it', he said."

Busby, having made his initial approaches through Pat Crerand, met the Celtic boss at a motorway service station near Haydock on April 14, 1971. Terms were discussed and, seemingly, agreed. But within 48 hours, the deal was off. As Crerand explained: "Later that week, Matt said to me: 'That's some pal you've got. He took the job and then phoned me this morning to say he's not taking it after all.' I was surprised because I knew Jock definitely fancied coming to United, although I knew Jean didn't want to leave Glasgow. It was a shame because Jock would have been ideal for United at that time. To have had him and Sean come down, it would have been the perfect set-up. There's no doubt that he'd have brought Sean along, and I would imagine Neilly Mochan would have come too."

Plenty would have made the same assumption, although George Stein suggested that this was in fact a critical issue on which Busby and his father did not see eye-to-eye. "Initially I was sure that he was ready to accept," he said in *Jock Stein, the Authorised Biography*. "Gradually, though, the more he talked, the more the doubts filtered through. Not about my mum's feelings, because he knew that she was reluctant to move, but about the job itself... He was insisting that he wanted to bring in his own backroom staff so that he had his own people round about him. But Sir Matt had his own loyalties." Yet if this is indeed the case, and Stein was fighting for Fallon's place in the Old Trafford hierarchy, it was a needless battle.

> There's no way I would have gone with him to Manchester United. Jock never spoke to me about joining him there, but it wouldn't have interested me if he did. I wouldn't have left Celtic unless they wanted me out. Why would I walk out on a club I'd always dreamt of being part of? Manchester United is a great club as everyone knows, but it's not my club. So, honestly, I wouldn't even have been tempted. Jock and I had great years together and were very close, but my main loyalty was always to Celtic and he knew that. I actually don't think he would have asked me to come with him and, if he did, he would have expected me to say no.

Given Fallon's adamance on the issue, one wonders what would have happened to him, and to Celtic, had it not been for Stein's late change of heart. Might Sean, six years on, have been offered the job snatched away from him in 1965? The health of Bob Kelly, now Sir Robert, was failing, but Fallon had grown in stature, strengthened his reputation as a talent-spotter, and offered a measure of continuity. At worst, he would surely have been a strong contender; at best, Stein's natural heir.

I'm not too sure about that. I didn't always see eye-to-eye with the people who were becoming more influential on the board at that time, and nor did Jock. I certainly didn't have my eye on Jock's job and I always hoped he would stay. At the time, I felt he should stay. I could understand it was a big decision for him and I could see why he was tempted because he would have had more money to spend at Manchester United, and would have been paid a lot more himself. But, back then, Celtic were still a team with lots of possibilities. We were certainly a stronger football side than United at that stage. I didn't see it being a step up for him.

As it happened, Fallon and Stein were at Old Trafford the following year, though merely to provide the opposition for Bobby Charlton's testimonial. But as Celtic's players trotted out for their warm-up, disturbing news reached the club's assistant manager. An enormous box of chocolates had, he was told, just been delivered to Old Trafford for his wife, who had travelled down for the match with Jean Stein. This was disconcerting because Fallon had ordered no such gift, and realised that Myra would know that only too well.

It turned out Sean Connery had sent them. I know – the last man you would want sending chocolates to your wife! He was a good friend of ours at that time and would often come for dinner at our house in King's Park when he was over for games. I used to pick him up at the airport and he never wanted to go to a hotel or anywhere fancy. He always preferred to come up to our house. He was a lovely man. He'd be telling Myra, 'Now, please don't be going to any bother for me'. As you can imagine, she wasn't exactly put out by him being there. That was during his James Bond days, so he was the biggest heartthrob around.

I remember once, when we were going to Celtic Park with him in the car, we stopped by the Steins' house to pick up Jean. She didn't know that he was with us, so we got him to go to the door and shout up in that great voice of his, 'Jean, are you ready to go?' All we heard was her screaming 'Oh my God!' He was always up for a laugh like that. He was just a very down-to-earth guy who liked his football and happened to be almost as handsome as me. I nearly had a heart attack that night at Old Trafford. But I must give him his due because, although he always had a soft spot for Myra, he never tried to steal her away from me. That was just a

thank you for having him up for dinner again because he knew
we'd be in Manchester that night. It said a lot about him to do
that, and he was a pal of ours for quite a few years.

The increasing infrequency of Connery's visits to Scotland meant
that the two men eventually lost touch. For a period, though, he
was Celtic's unofficial mascot. He would even visit the team at
their Seamill retreat and, with Stein's blessing, chat to the players
in the dressing room before big matches. After the first leg against
Racing Club in 1967, Connery made his way down from the
main stand at Hampden to vow that he would tell the world of
the Argentinians' underhand tactics. Earlier the same year, he had
told an interviewer that Celtic's success in Lisbon meant as much
to him "as all the Bond movies combined". Yet it was at Ibrox that
Scotland's most famous actor was most recently seen, prompting
talk of a change of allegiances. Sean was unconvinced. "I think he
got on with David Murray at that time but I'd bet you anything
that, deep down, he's still a Celtic man at heart."

In the early '70s, Connery and Celtic faced a similar dilemma.
Just as the former had earned global stardom on the back of his
role as 007, so the club owed its fame and renown to the Lisbon
Lions. But Stein saw that this magnificent side, like the Ian Fleming
adaptations of that era, was beginning to look a little tired. The
time had come to move on; take a new direction. In 1971, the same
year Connery hung up his tuxedo after *Diamonds are Forever,* the
Celtic manager moved swiftly and ruthlessly to dismantle Celtic's
greatest team. It was all done within the space of seven short
months, by the end of which Auld, Clark, Chalmers, Wallace,
Hughes and Gemmell had either been released or sold. Most left
reluctantly, hurt by the indifferent way in which they were treated
in their final days. As Stevie Chalmers wrote: "Lisbon Lions would
be summoned to the manager's office and within hours would
be departing Celtic Park with their belongings, entirely without
ceremony."

Stein, though, was nothing if not resolute. The defeat by
Feyenoord had told him that a revolution was required, and losing
successive League Cup finals to Rangers and Partick Thistle merely
increased the sense of urgency. "The biggest blow we ever had as
a club," was how he described the latter result, although of greater

concern to the Celtic boss was "the fact that a lot of our players thought defeat was impossible". "It was a sign to us that things had to change," he added. "We needed players who were hungry, we needed to get going again, to believe that teams could beat us and that when we stepped over that white line we had to make things happen." That meant a call, almost en masse, to the Quality Street Gang. And while Fallon felt sympathy for the all-time greats suddenly deemed surplus to requirements, he backed Stein's faith in the club's extraordinary group of youngsters.

> We discussed it all at the time and I told him that I thought he was doing the right thing. The club had gone a bit stale, a few of the older players didn't get on with Jock any more, and we had more than enough talent in the reserves to freshen things up. We were very fortunate at that time to have young players of great potential and Jock, to his credit, realised that they had to be given their chance to become the backbone of the team. If we hadn't promoted them at that stage, we would just have been holding them back and they'd have ended up losing confidence in their own ability. These boys were natural footballers, everyone could see that. Jock and myself talked a lot together about how to bring them in – when to promote them, when to rest them – and I think we got the balance right in most cases.
>
> It was a shame for the senior players who were let go, especially as there were a few of them who still had a bit to offer. But Jock felt the place needed freshening up and, by and large, I agreed with him. By moving on someone like Willie Wallace, for example, it gave Lou Macari and Kenny Dalglish more opportunities. I sympathised with the Lions because I knew most of them felt the same way about Celtic as I did, and hated to leave. There were a few tears shed, I know. But that's football. You could only try to help them realise that it wasn't the end of the world.

For Fallon, retaining a sense of perspective had never come easier than in that particular season. The summer before, he had felt utterly despondent about banishing Gemmell and Auld. A few months later, he realised just how trivial the whole episode had been. That became clear on January 2, 1971; in Fallon's words, "the worst day of my life". It was an afternoon on which 66 men and boys lost their lives in the Ibrox Disaster, crushed to death as they attempted to leave an Old Firm derby. The victims, the youngest of whom was just nine, included five school-friends from the same Fife village, and Fallon was there to witness the appalling aftermath. Standing at his side was an old friend, Willie Waddell, and the then Rangers manager's recollection of the scene still sends a shudder down the spine. Waddell said: "When I first went to the top of the steps and looked down on the pile of bodies, my initial thought was of Belsen, because the corpses were entangled as they had been in the pictures which came out of the concentration camps. My God, it was hellish. There were bodies in the dressing rooms, in the gymnasium, and even in the laundry room. My own training staff and the Celtic training staff were working at the job of resuscitation, and we were all trying everything possible to bring breath back to those crushed limbs."

As a trained lifesaver from his days patrolling Sligo's beaches, Fallon was especially busy in those frantic moments. Tragically, most of those he attended to were beyond saving and, though instinct kicked in at the time, he returned home to the full, devastating realisation of what he had witnessed. "That was a dreadful night," remembered his wife, Myra. "Sean's father and his brother Padraig had come over for the game and it was hours before he got home. I remember he just sat there, sobbing. We couldn't get anything out of him. All he kept saying was that these poor boys had been lying there without a mark on them." To the day he died, those terrible, haunting images remained painfully vivid.

> That was the worst day of my life, seeing all those kids lying there and having to carry their bodies. I'll never forget it. For a young boy to go to watch his team and never come home, it should never have been allowed to happen. It was just heart-breaking. I shed more than a few tears that night and I'm not ashamed to admit that I still get emotional thinking about it. What happened that day was more important than all the football in the world. At a time like that, you'd gladly forget about trophies and winning Old Firm matches if those people could be back with their families. It made you think about your own kids, what you would feel like, and that's what broke your heart as much as anything. I think everyone who had been there that day would have gone home and just thanked God their own family was safe. Jock and myself went along to a lot of

the funerals, and it was a terrible time for everyone. We'd done our best to save who we could. But in most cases there was nothing you could do.

Most, but fortunately not all. Though Fallon had never spoken of it publicly, it has been verified – first through one of his daughters, then through an unrelated third party – that it was to Celtic's assistant manager that one youngster, seemingly left for dead, owed his life. The boy in question had stopped breathing and, with paramedics overwhelmed and focusing on those with the best chance of survival, his frantic father pleaded with Sean to do what he could.

I was trained to give the kiss of life so, naturally, I tried my best to save him. After a while, we thought we could see some movement. So we kept at it and eventually, thank God, the lad started breathing again. He survived, I know that. That was one good story to come out of that day; I just wish there had been more like it. All I know is that it wasn't for the lack of trying, and it wasn't just me. Bob Rooney and the Rangers physio – anyone who knew what they were doing, in fact – were going round, looking to help whoever they could. But there was no hope of getting most of them back. It broke your heart.

Fallon would return to work the following Monday, though Billy McNeill recalls that the Celtic backroom staff "bore the look of haunted men". Amid the desolation, hope emerged that the Ibrox Disaster would not only be a watershed in stadium safety, but in relations between Glasgow's warring football tribes. "This terrible tragedy must help to curb the bigotry and bitterness of Old Firm matches," was the wish expressed by Stein in the *Celtic View*. "When human life is at stake, this kind of hatred seems sordid and little."

For a while, these words seemed to resonate. Celtic Park stood in solemn, flawless silence to honour the victims the following Saturday, and packed memorial services were held on both sides of the religious divide. Yet, before long, it was business as usual. For the fans, that meant returning to the trading of insults and the same old songs. For the men in charge, it meant attempting to give those same supporters something to cheer.

Fallon was to be kept busy.

Chapter 22
Sean's Boys

"You have to see this, son."

A proud, beaming smile illuminates Fallon's craggy features as he looks at the box resting on his coffee table. Opened gingerly, lovingly, it reveals an international cap. The lion rampant reveals that it is not one of the Irishman's. "Danny McGrain's first," he says, still grinning. Then there is the dedication, eloquent in its simplicity:

'To Sean. Thanks for making it all happen.'

"Lovely thing to do, wasn't it?" he says, leaning back in his favourite chair. Here is yet another window into Fallon's inimitable character. He is showing me the gift, not to indicate his significance to McGrain's career, but to illustrate a point he loved making: what a fine man the Celtic coach had become. That I knew already. The message itself, though, is of genuine significance and, in the process of interviewing Fallon's former reserve players, I would hear countless similar tributes.

Kenny Dalglish, for example, said: "There are a hell of a lot of people in football, myself included, who are eternally grateful to Sean. He was a huge influence on my career. Really, it was him who started it all off."

Had Fallon done nothing else in his career but sign Dalglish and McGrain, he could have retired a proud and happy man.

Others have dined out on less. But 'making it all happen'? It could be argued that, in acquiring two world-class footballers, Sean's success was merely in getting there first. Surely, had it not been him, another scout or manager would soon have enjoyed the same good fortune? Perhaps McGrain's dedication was simply an indulgent stretching of the truth, carried out in the name of kindness.

"Not at all," insisted the player himself. "I owe Sean everything. If he hadn't signed me, I don't know where I would be today. He was the one who saw me, believed in me and took the bull by the horns. Before then, I'd never seen myself becoming a footballer. I didn't really believe that people like me, boys from Drumchapel, could become stars like the ones I saw on telly on a Saturday night."

Dalglish tells a similar story. He might be revered throughout football as 'King Kenny' – the man voted Liverpool's greatest player and Britain's best post-war forward – but the youngster Fallon signed was, in his own words, "a wee fat No. 4". So, when Dalglish was asked by *FourFourTwo* to pinpoint his biggest achievement and proudest moment in football, he did not name his Scotland caps record, nor the English player of the year awards or his three European Cups. "Signing as a professional for Celtic," he said. "It all starts from there. I might have been an apprentice joiner, so for me to sign for Celtic was wonderful." In another interview with *The Telegraph*, he described this same, seminal moment as "my happiest memory", adding that he had gone into pre-season training "thinking I had joined the best team in the world".

Having been signed in May 1967, Dalglish was not far wrong. Celtic were weeks away from winning the European Cup with a team that, unbeknown to him, had been largely recruited by the same man chasing his signature. Fallon, not content with assembling the bulk of one great Celtic side, was now busying himself gathering together another. Indeed, long before the Lions even dreamt of Lisbon, the Quality Street Gang were already in the making.

First to arrive, in July 1964, was George Connelly. He was just 15 when Fallon first watched him in a Junior Cup tie in Kincardine and, unlike Dalglish, Connelly was no ugly duckling waiting to become a swan. "He was magnificent even then," Sean recalled. "There should have been a queue half-a-mile long to sign him." As it was, the Irishman found himself in competition with a solitary fellow suitor. "Jock Stein wanted to sign me for Dunfermline, so Sean got one over on him there," explained Connelly. "As soon as he took me through to Celtic Park with my dad, there was only one place I was going. Sean was a household name in my family anyway because my brothers had watched him as a player and used to come home singing songs about him. So for me, there was respect and admiration for the man from day one." Connelly would, in time, become one of Fallon's greatest sources of regret but, back in '64, he saw only boundless possibilities.

> George was slightly built as a young lad but you could see even at that stage that he was something special. I tended never to say, 'This one's going to be a great player', because you never know how young lads will develop. But with him I made an exception. He had everything a professional footballer could want: great balance, tremendous skill and the ability to read a game. People compared him to Beckenbauer and it wasn't over the top to do that because the boy had so much class, and his touch on the ball was magnificent. Others achieved more, but I can honestly say that Connelly was the most gifted all-round player I ever worked with.

Perhaps it was the memory of having this outstanding talent snatched from his Fife doorstep that convinced Stein to defer to Fallon on player recruitment. "There's no doubt my dad trusted Sean when it came to signings," said George Stein. "Even with the likes of Willie Wallace, who was obviously my dad's choice, he would seek Sean's opinion because it was an opinion he respected. With other players though, young players especially, he would know he could leave Sean to go out and do the groundwork, spot the right player, speak to the parents, and get it done." From any manager, this would have been a compliment. From Stein, whose natural inclination was to control and command, the freedom afforded to Fallon was the ultimate accolade.

> If I liked a player, Jock trusted me enough to let me get on with it. He didn't come to have a look himself because he knew I wouldn't recommend anyone I didn't think was up to the job. People say I had an eye for a player and, without being too immodest, I do think that was a strength I had. My record was pretty good. I did

always believe that I had an idea of the kind of player who could do a good job for Celtic, and that's not just about having talent. I was conscious of looking for something extra in a player and looking at their character too. Most importantly, I always kept my ear to the ground and I worked hard. Any chance I got, I would be out watching matches, even if it was just a schoolboy game somewhere. I had lots of people who would let me know if they thought a player was worth watching, and I would always go and check out any recommendation. Some were better than others, but the worst thing you could do was not to make the effort.

Fallon's network of informers grew to gargantuan proportions. His former team-mate John Higgins, who from 1967 worked alongside him as chief scout, remarked in an interview with *Playing for Celtic* that the club had just nine scouts covering the length and breadth of Scotland and Ireland. "Unofficially, we have 9000," he added. Fallon's signings were a testament to this. It was, after all, a bookie who tipped him off about Lou Macari, while McGrain, Davie Hay and Tommy Burns came recommended by a publican, a priest and a car dealer respectively.

Naturally, not every nugget thrust in his direction was solid gold, and for every future legend there were another hundred not worth pursuing. For Joe Coyle, who played under Fallon at Celtic and Dumbarton, the Irishman's strength lay in consistently being able to spot the difference. "People might think spotting a good player is easy, but there are countless boys out there with ability, who look good in their own environment," he said. "It takes someone like Sean to see them and think, 'Aye, you'll do a job' or 'No, you're not quite good enough'. Guys who can make those judgments, and get them right nine times out of 10, are worth their weight in gold."

This same ability is highlighted in *One Afternoon in Lisbon*, in which Kevin McCarra and Pat Woods provide an insightful analysis of what made the Stein-Fallon partnership so successful. "It must be said that Stein's interventions in the transfer market were erratic," they wrote. "For every McBride or Wallace there was a host of quickly forgotten signings. His greatest gift lay not in discovering players but in working with them and kitting them out with the best tactics... Sean Fallon played a great part in providing that raw material... Fallon stresses that the players had to be brought to his attention by others. All the same, Celtic receive countless recommendations and Fallon was clearly masterful in separating the wheat from the chaff."

Sean's daughter, Louise, recalled that there was recognition of these complementary roles even at the time. "I remember people saying, 'Sean picks them and Jock places them', and I think that was quite accurate," she said. "Dad had an obvious gift for spotting talent, while Jock was unrivalled when it came to organising and motivating. What was important was that they both appreciated those talents in each other, and saw where the other was superior."

There was another area in which Stein astutely recognised his assistant to be without equal. "When it came to going out to a player's house and talking to the parents, there was no-one better," said McGrain. "Sean's blarney, his whole relaxed, reassuring demeanour, would put anyone at ease. I'm sure he charmed 100 players and their parents like he did with me and my mum and dad because he was just someone you immediately trusted and warmed to. Everyone could see the kindness in Sean."

Dalglish also perceived this to be one of Fallon's most significant and underrated talents. "That kind of thing might not seem all that important, but being able to deal with people is one of the most vital aspects in being successful in football – and Sean could deal with anyone," he said. "He was just great with people and that all came from him being a genuinely nice man. Everyone loved being in Sean's company, hearing his great stories. I seem to remember some of his stories lasting longer than our training sessions."

There was certainly a tale behind every one of Fallon's signings and none was more famous than that of Dalglish himself. It had all started, not with a priest or a publican on this occasion, but with a letter from Mrs Davidson, imploring Celtic's assistant manager to scout her son, Victor. Such correspondence was not uncommon and Fallon – having learned that mothers do not make the most objective judges – was pessimistic about finding anything worthwhile. Still, diligent as ever, he made his way to a red ash pitch in Cambuslang to watch the 15-year-old play for Glasgow United, and was pleasantly surprised. Young Victor, he quickly saw, was a fine player, and he had a team-mate – strong, determined, beautifully balanced – who also caught the eye.

Strangely, though, the offer of training at Celtic Park left Davidson's shy, slightly surly friend evidently underwhelmed. It was only later that Fallon understood why. The youngster, he learned, had been waiting, praying, for a call from the team he followed loyally and fervently – and that team did not play in green and white. Dalglish's bedroom overlooked Rangers' training ground and, even after signing for Celtic, he initially maintained his practice of travelling on a supporters' bus to cheer on his employer's great rivals. But his adoration was not reciprocated. Rangers had been given plenty of opportunities to at least take him on trial – he had even played at Ibrox for a schoolboy select – yet seemed not to like what they saw. "The folk at Rangers thought he was too slow," recalled Fallon. "A few people felt that way about Kenny at the start. But I saw that he was fast in the head."

So impressed was Fallon by those early glimpses that, despite the youngster's apparent indifference, he resolved to persevere. The next opportunity he had, Celtic's assistant manager drove to the Dalglish family flat in Ibrox and, a few hours later, emerged with a prized and hard-earned signature. But it nearly came at a heavy cost. There was, after all, a reason he always remembered May 4, 1967, the date on which this signing was made, and it had nothing to do with his esteem for King Kenny.

It was my wedding anniversary that day, so we were meant to be going out to the coast. Myra and three of my girls had been in the car the whole time I was up in the flat – two hours at least – so signing Kenny nearly got me a divorce. It was a lovely, sunny day, and Myra had said, 'Why don't we all go out to Seamill, do something nice for our anniversary?' 'No problem,' I said. 'But do you mind if I stop off somewhere first? It won't take long.' When I got into the flat, though, I felt the atmosphere was a bit tense, so I spent an hour chatting about nothing really, just trying to put them at ease.

The family made me feel very welcome but I got the impression that Kenny's dad wanted him to become a joiner rather than a footballer because he was worried he might not make it. I think it took a good hour-and-a-half for me to get round to talking to them about bringing the lad to Celtic and, by then, I'd completely forgotten about Myra and the kids down in the car. It was only when I was coming down the stairs, having got Kenny and his father to agree to sign, that I remembered. And I'll tell you, I wasn't popular. Myra was going mad. She told me to forget about Seamill – that the day was ruined – and to just drive home. I don't think she spoke to me for the rest of the week.

Fortunately, 46 years on, their marriage still intact, Myra was able to look back and laugh. "I could have killed him that day though," she said. "I remember saying to him, 'Whoever this boy is, he better have been worth it'. Just as well for Sean he was."

Dalglish, meanwhile – blissfully unaware of the domestic dispute he had caused – felt a sudden and unexpected surge of elation at having signed for Celtic, and relief that a potential catastrophe had been averted. In *Dalglish: My Autobiography*, he wrote: "[After it had been agreed I would go to Celtic], my mum had decided to show Sean around the flat. I panicked. My bedroom wall was covered with pictures of Rangers players and Celtic's assistant manager was about to see my room. Fortunately, I managed to get most of them down before Sean saw them." According to Fallon, he need not have bothered.

I hadn't even noticed but, even if I had, I wouldn't have cared one bit. I'd seen from other players – and from Jock – that even if you don't start out as a Celtic fan, becoming part of the club makes you one. Kenny's allegiances didn't worry me in the least. If anything, it was quite nice to know that we had brought in this great player right from under Rangers' noses. Even then, I was pretty confident he would make it. He wasn't an obvious standout at that stage, but he had great spirit and bravery about him, and obviously loved playing the game. And, right from the start, he had that great balance and ability to shield the ball. I always felt he had the necessary potential.

Remarkable as it might now seem, not everyone agreed. Rangers' scouts were far from alone in highlighting Dalglish's lack of pace as a barrier to professional success. Even Stein, who would in time become a wholehearted convert, took some convincing. In his biography of Dalglish, Stephen F. Kelly twice refers to the Celtic manager's initial scepticism, writing: "[Stein] wondered if Dalglish was not too slow and wasn't so sure that he would make the grade." This is an account verified by Fallon, who also revealed that, having lobbied on behalf of Dalglish and Jimmy Johnstone, he later had to do the same for another Celtic great.

> I thought the world of Jock, and I'll say again: he was a much better manager than I ever would have been. But if there was one quality I had that he lacked, it was patience. He wanted things to happen right away and made judgments about players very quickly. I remember him saying: 'They're either good players or they're not.' And a lot of times he was right. But some boys develop more slowly than others. Often I would see something in a player that made me think that they were worth persevering with. Tommy Burns was an example of that because he was another one Jock wasn't sure about at first. I remember saying, 'Just wait. He'll turn out a good player'. That was another situation where Jock was more than happy to be proved wrong. Later, he was as big a fan as anyone of Tommy, who became a tremendous player for the club. And of course, he absolutely loved Kenny.

Stein's initial doubts may seem extraordinary in hindsight but, in his early days at the club, Dalglish was widely seen as the runt of the Quality Street litter. In 1968/69, a season in which Connelly, Hay, Macari, John Gorman and Jimmy Quinn all took their first steps in the first team, he managed just one goal in 13 reserve outings. And even when Dalglish did begin showing signs of improvement, he found that it was his old Glasgow United team-mate who was being touted as Celtic's most promising youngster.

> Vic Davidson was a great prospect at that stage. He was one of the ones you wonder if you could have done more with because he had all the talent in the world. What he lacked, though, was the single-mindedness that Kenny had in abundance. Kenny hadn't started off as the most promising in that team but he dedicated himself completely to the game and, over time, developed a real confidence about himself that helped him immensely when he went up to the first team. He had a real competitive spirit and, off the park, he was an example to a lot of our senior players because he stayed away from the drink and was always focused on his football. You think how many goals he scored in his career, and yet the funny thing is that he wasn't a very good finisher at first. Every afternoon, we used to send him out with a bag of balls to practise, and he would never complain. Gradually, you started to

see an improvement. And in the end, well, everyone knows what a magnificent player he became.

Dalglish was a source of pride to Fallon, but it was pride that emanated almost solely from having spotted and stuck by him when he was not so widely admired. When it came to the development of this celebrated former pupil, he sought little credit. "There's one person Kenny owes for the career he's had, and it's Kenny himself," Fallon would say. This, though, is a version of events with which Dalglish takes issue. He said: "Every player has people they look back on as having been really important to their development, and that's definitely the case for me with Sean. He was a hugely important part of the football club at that time and I'm sure there wasn't a single player who didn't benefit from him being there. The encouragement I got from him is what stands out, but he was also someone who would give you into trouble if the occasion demanded and drum the right habits into you, encourage you to do things properly. The lessons you're taught at that age stay with you, and I don't think it's an accident that so many players in that reserve team went on to have the careers that they did."

Dalglish remembers, too, that the practical education he received did not begin and end with a bag of balls and an empty goal. Though results were not discounted in the reserves – "you must get used to being expected to win," Fallon would tell the young Celts – the central focus was on developing well-rounded, first team-ready footballers. With the Quality Street Gang, that entailed a far-sighted selection policy in which every outfield player would be tested in a variety of roles. "It was way ahead of its time and we all benefited," said McGrain. "I played every position bar centre-forward and, by playing at outside-left for example, I learned how a player in that position thinks and how I could makes things difficult if I was playing against him. I do the same myself these days with the development team, even with the goalkeepers and centre-forwards, because it's a great way of seeing things through another player's eyes."

Connelly also praised the careful, considered way in which youngsters were introduced to the first team. In his autobiography, *Celtic's Lost Legend*, he referred to Michael Owen and Norman Whiteside as players damaged irrevocably by being played too often, too early. "They should have been given the benefit of my upbringing," he wrote. "That's why Celtic were so good – these guys [the Quality Street Gang] played here and there in the first team and then were back out again so that, when they came into the side again for real, they were men."

Like Dalglish and McGrain, Connelly's recollection of life in the reserves is of good habits being taught early and then continually reinforced. One mantra in particular still resonates. "Sean gave us a great education and something he used to tell us, which has always stuck with me, was the importance of 'starting in top gear'. When you won a throw-in, he would want you running to try to take it quickly. If we got a corner, he'd want everyone ready to get it in the box as soon as possible. He always said: 'Start at a slow pace and you'll find it very hard to lift it later in the game.' I've remembered that all my life because he was so right. I always think back to when Celtic lost the league on the final day of Martin O'Neill's last season. I was shouting at the telly because they were walking up to take shies, taking their time over corners – there was no tempo, no pace to what they were doing. And when things started to go wrong, they couldn't pick it up." The lesson mentioned is, on the face of it, simplicity itself, and for Fallon that was no bad thing. 'Starting fast', in fact, was a perfect example of the uncomplicated wisdom on which he based his entire coaching philosophy.

> All I wanted from my players was that they played as a unit, helped their team-mates if they were in trouble and took a pride in representing Celtic. I focused on their strengths, praised them when they deserved it and told them in no uncertain terms when they had let the team down. A lot of the time it was important to be critical to stop a player making the same mistake again, but you could combine it with a compliment to show it wouldn't take much to get it right. It would be things like, 'That was great build-up play from you, so why ruin it all at the end by being greedy?' Nothing revolutionary, but little things like that tend to get through to young players. It was also very important to me to consider what would help them as people as well as footballers.
>
> When young lads came in, I'd try to look after them like a second father. I knew that they would have fears and doubts, and I felt that if they could feel at home at the club, they would settle down and be able to play their best football. It was important

to get the mental side of things right, and so much of that was making players feel comfortable and instilling confidence in them. Lou Macari, for example, lacked a bit of self-belief initially but once we made him realise how good he could be, he was one of the most confident players at the club. That was as important as any technical coaching. You had to iron out little faults in their game, but what's important – and I still see managers getting this wrong – is to do that without knocking players' confidence or taking away their basic enjoyment of the game. Once those things are gone, you might as well forget it.

The evidence of his charges' glittering careers suggests that, as coach and psychologist, Fallon struck the perfect balance. Yet it is as a man rather than as a manager that he made the most indelible impression on those reserve players. McGrain, for example, will tell of the long weeks he spent in hospital after fracturing his skull, when his wife Laraine – unable to drive – would be ferried to visit every day by the club's assistant manager. Another example of Sean's compassion was provided by Tommy Burns, a man whose life and career would be marked by the same humanity, integrity and devotion to Celtic. He said: "I was 15 when I started working at Celtic Park, and Sean had obviously noticed I was coming in without a coat in the cold weather. One day he called me over and said: 'Son, have you not got yourself something you can wear to keep yourself warm?' 'Not really, Mr Fallon,' I said. Five minutes later he came back with £10, which was serious money then, and told me to go and buy myself a heavy coat or a warm jumper. That kind of thing you don't easily forget."

The result of such gestures, and many more small, unseen kindnesses besides, is the enduring affection Fallon inspires in his former players. As John Gorman said: "Sean was respected by the boys in that team but, more than that, he was loved." McGrain employed the same verb, adding: "I actually don't understand how anyone couldn't love the guy." As for Dalglish, asked to single out Fallon's greatest contribution to Celtic, he replied instantly: "Just being Sean."

We can analyse his signings and his methods, but to these players the Irishman was a great deal more than the sum of his professional parts. Fallon would maintain until his dying day that McGrain had been excessively generous, and that he had not 'made it all happen' for anyone in the Quality Street Gang. But little in football pleased him more than knowing that these players – "the finest group of lads I ever managed" – felt he had made a difference. "That," said Sean, "was all I ever wanted to do."

Chapter 23
The Beginning of the End

"Never make predictions, especially about the future." There cannot be a sports journalist who, at one stage or another, did not wish they had heeded Yogi Berra's famous advice. For Brian Scovell, a Fleet Street veteran of four decades, his moment of weakness arrived on April 16, 1970. Celtic, he boldly predicted, were "surely destined to become Europe's soccer supremos of the 1970s".

Halfway through that same decade, Scovell must already have been cringing. By then, the idea of Celtic as a dominant '70s equivalent of Puskas and Di Stefano's Real Madrid would have seemed absurd. While Ajax had just won three successive European Cups and Bayern Munich were in the process of doing likewise, the once-mighty Celts were – in European terms at least – a busted flush.

But examine the context in which Scovell made his forecast and it is easy to see why he envisaged such a bright future. Celtic had just beaten Leeds United home and away and, in almost every respect, looked an improved version of the team that had lit up Lisbon. The heroes of '67 had been retained and, as well as adding experience to its existing enthusiasm, Stein's squad now had strength in depth thanks to Fallon and his Quality Street Gang. With Hay and Connelly established regulars and the transition from one great side to another already well under way, there was every reason to believe that Celtic's greatest days lay ahead. Indeed, the question posed by reassessing Scovell's prediction is not 'what was he thinking', but 'why wasn't he proved right?'

Much debate has surrounded the moment at which Celtic began their steady slide towards mediocrity. For many, Hay's departure was a defining moment; for others, the point of no return arrived years earlier, with defeat by Feyenoord. Fallon, though, pinpointed another date: September 21, 1971. That was the day Bob Kelly died and so, too, according to Celtic's then assistant manager, did his beloved club's hopes of scaling new heights.

> There's no doubt that Celtic went downhill after we lost Bob Kelly. It was never the same again and I know Jock felt that way too. Desmond White took over as chairman and, although he wasn't a bad guy, money was more important to him than football. With Bob, it had always been the other way round. Jock and myself never felt as happy without him and the relationship with the board got gradually worse. The three of us – Jock, Bob and myself – had shared a great bond because we all had a real love of the club and its traditions, and a great affection for the supporters. Everyone talks about Jock's Lanarkshire background, the mining and so on, and Bob Kelly was a man who saw the world the same way. He loved working men – the attitude they had to life – and there was a working-class philosophy around the whole club at that time, and a charitable one too. That was all lost once Bob passed away.

Stein, according to his son, George, also viewed Kelly's death as "the beginning of the end". It was, in the view of both manager and assistant, the key moment in the '70s becoming defined not by success, but the selling of prize assets. Sir Robert had not been without his faults. As Fallon readily acknowledged, he was a divisive and, at times, destructive figure. But in the years following Stein's appointment, he played a vital role in maintaining Celtic's upwards trajectory – and did so by changing the habit of the club's lifetime.

After all, while the '70s tends to be seen as the decade in which Celtic 'became a selling club', this was hardly a new phenomenon. If anything, it was a return to form. The team Fallon joined was still smarting from the loss of Jimmy Delaney to Manchester United, and Kelly himself had readily accepted bids for fans' favourites Bobby Collins and Willie Fernie. Even the great Jimmy McGrory would have been offloaded to Arsenal, this at the peak of his peerless powers, had it not been for his stubborn refusal to leave. That was Celtic. Selling star players was simply what they did; what they had always done.

Where Kelly never received ample credit was in not only halting that practice, but in doing so at a time when Celtic's players had never been so sought-after. Though most bids were kept quiet, it is common knowledge that AC Milan came in for Jimmy Johnstone, that Arsenal bid a British-record fee for Bobby Lennox and that Boca Juniors offered a small fortune for Bobby Murdoch. All were flatly rejected and, according to Fallon, they represented the tip of a substantial iceberg.

> I always remember that, right after Lisbon, we beat Real Madrid 1-0 in a testimonial for Di Stefano. Wee Jinky was absolutely brilliant that night and the reception he got from the crowd was just unbelievable. At that time, we could have sold him for a fortune to Real or to any big club in Europe. It wasn't just Jinky either; we could have sold any of our top players, and for serious money too. But we spoke about it – Jock, Bob Kelly and myself – and we all said that we wanted to keep Celtic at the top; that success was more important than money. Jock would have told you what a great chairman Bob was in that respect. There was never any pressure put on Jock to sell a player while Bob Kelly was there.

The result was a team that, by 1971/72, was once again ready to take on Europe. It was a side that fused the most electrifying elements of the Lisbon Lions and the Quality Street Gang, and left supporters sensing history in the making. "That 1972 team was the one you really felt could emulate the Lions," said Jimmy Payne, a regular contributor to the fanzine *Not the View*. "The young players coming in looked fantastic and seemed to give everyone a lift, and you still had Jinky, big Billy, Bobby Murdoch and Bobby Lennox all playing, and playing well. It was a great team to watch."

Not for supporters of Rangers, who would win the European Cup Winners' Cup that season and still finish 16 points adrift in the race for the title. Just two defeats had been suffered by Celtic en route to an unprecedented seventh successive championship, while the double was secured by a record-equalling 6-1 Scottish Cup final win over Hibernian. Suddenly, Stein had a spring in his step again. Reinvigorating him was the emergence of players such as Dalglish, Macari and McGrain, all of whom excelled in a 2-1 win at Ujpest Dozsa lauded by the manager as "our best European display since Lisbon". Two goalless semi-finals against Inter and a cruel defeat on penalties followed, but this Celtic team – young, hungry and richly talented – seemed destined for greatness.

Then came 1973. A year that had promised so much instead began with the sale of Macari, and ended with Hay and Connelly going out on strike. These were equally ominous events, and both stemmed from the same increasingly thorny issue of Celtic's wage structure. Macari had hoped to sign a new contract, yet soon founded himself requesting a transfer when Celtic's best offer amounted to an increase of £5-a-week. Within weeks, he was off to Old Trafford, quadrupling his salary in the process. The £200,000 transfer fee – a record for a Scottish player – ensured no resistance from White, while Stein was concerned less by the untimely departure than Macari's chosen destination.

> Jock had wanted Lou to go to Liverpool. He was big pals with Shankly and they had arranged it between themselves. I drove Lou down to Anfield myself to get the deal done but, as it happened, Manchester United got wind of what was happening and ended up convincing him to go there. Jock wasn't happy at all about that, but he wasn't particularly upset about losing Lou. If you look back, he didn't play all that often for Jock except for that one season (71/72), when he did exceptionally well. Lou was a boy I was very fond of and I felt should have had more of a chance because, as he showed at United, he was a great little player. If it had been up to me, I would have done more to keep him. But Jock saw that we had Kenny, Dixie Deans and Harry Hood and, although he would have preferred to keep Louie, he felt we could get by without him.

Had Macari been the only player sold, the only player unhappy, Stein might well have been right. But the little forward was merely the thin end of a substantial wedge. Next to knock on the manager's door was Davie Hay, who was genuinely indispensable. Many, in fact, saw this dynamic and versatile player as the heartbeat of that early '70s side. Hay had also become a Scotland regular and learned while on international duty that he was earning several times less than his colleagues south of the border. He had also discovered the hard way that Celtic's bonus-heavy wage structure made no allowances for bad luck, with a serious injury having denied him the opportunity to top up his modest salary.

> Davie's point was a fair one: that injured players were getting a rough deal. He wasn't being unreasonable at all. I couldn't say anything at the time but, having been injured a fair bit myself, I agreed with him. The board wouldn't give any ground at all, though, and that was why he went out on strike with George later in the year. I thought that was the wrong way to go about things, but I could understand why they did it. What annoyed me later, especially after he left, was that Davie was made out to be greedy. There was a comment made that he and Louie had fancied the bright lights down in England, when it had nothing at all to do with that.
>
> It was Celtic who had been slow to move with the times and realise that these players were only looking for the money they were worth. The board could have afforded to give a bit of ground because, after all, these players had cost the club nothing. I'm not saying they should have matched what was being paid down south, but they could have at least narrowed the gap. That would have been enough for those players because both of them wanted to stay at Celtic.

The directors, though, were not the only barrier to achieving a resolution. Stein was unfailingly unsympathetic on the issue of wage disputes, to the extent that Ronnie Simpson remarked: "You would have thought it was his own money he was giving away." Hay, as a result, dealt directly with White, initially petitioning for a £35 rise to rebalance the salary-to-bonus ratio. But with no desire to leave, and having been brought no closer to a resolution by going on strike for five matches, he was ready to cut a deal. On one condition. "We (Hay and Connelly) got the chance to buy a lot of flats near the BBC studios," Hay explained in *Celtic's Lost Legend*. "They were to cost thirty grand – what they would be worth today you can only imagine. We went to Big Dessie [White] and thought 'we'll sign for £65 a week if we get the loan'. A lot of players were getting loans at the time for pubs and that. That was the club's way of compensating players for the contract issue. But we got totally kicked into touch."

Instead, White offered Hay £15,000, not as a loan, but as a gift. Again, there was just one catch: he had to leave. Chelsea had come in with a £250,000 offer and, despite Hay having excelled on his return from strike and later at the 1974 World Cup, White was eager to cash in. It would prove to be a disastrous transfer for Celtic, its impact as great – on the field, if not on the supporters' psyche – as Dalglish's departure a few years later. Danny McGrain, in his 1978 autobiography *Celtic: My Team*, wrote that, with the loss of Hay – whom he described as "one of our all-time greats" – "a special bit of character left the club and was never replaced".

Player by player, the Quality Street Gang was being dismantled. Celtic, it seemed, were embracing decline. Yet Bobby Lennox, the longest-serving player of that era, believes otherwise. He saw in the board not an acceptance that regression was inevitable, but a complacent conviction that standards would be maintained. "I think Celtic had been spoiled and started to take for granted that they'd be producing great players year in, year out," said Lennox. "They'd had one great team come through the ranks in the Lisbon Lions, then another straight afterwards, which allowed them to let some of the Lions leave without doing too much damage to the team. I think when they sold Hay, Macari and the rest of them, they felt they would be able to do the same again – just delve into the reserves and not notice a big difference." If Lennox's analysis is correct, Fallon had essentially become a victim of his own spectacular success.

> My aim was always to keep finding and producing players of the standard we had at that time. But that's easier said than done. You're talking about some of the best footballers Scotland has ever had – those kind of players don't just grow on trees. We were still bringing in good young players, but they should have time to learn from the senior players, as Davie, Kenny and the others had with the Lions. The problem was, once the club started selling the likes of Lou and Davie, it sent out a message to everyone. Players who'd been dreaming about becoming the next Lisbon Lions started thinking: 'Well, even if we do make it,

they'll only sell us.' And parents wondered if they were giving their boy in to become a Celtic player, or just as an asset we could use to earn a bit of money when it suited us. You couldn't blame them. The mentality had changed. Before, it had been about building a great side and entertaining the crowd. In those last few years, it was all about money.

Viewed through the prism of Celtic's current situation – unable to compete with the glamour and vast wealth of the English Premier League – the sales of Macari, Hay and, latterly, Dalglish might seem inevitable. The '70s, though, was an era untouched by the global sponsorship and TV rights deals responsible for the current disparity. Gate money remained all-important and, in that respect, Celtic had nothing to fear. Yet, still, White pleaded poverty.

The chairman was always saying how tight things were financially and neither Jock nor I could understand it. Celtic were getting great crowds in those days and it was a running joke that the figure reported was always a lot lower than the number actually inside the ground. It was frustrating for us because we had the most loyal support in Britain, yet Jock was never given the kind of money to spend that other managers had. When we sold a player for £250,000, Jock would get £20,000 to buy a replacement. That was just the way it worked. Even when we were winning the league every season and getting the best crowds in the country, Rangers were still spending more on wages and transfers than we were. We would speak to Desmond White about it but we never did get a good reason why.

White would have been unlikely to confess that Celtic's many assets – big crowds, world-class players, inspired management – were being squandered. Mismanagement at Celtic was already endemic and would continue until the arrival, nearly two decades later, of Fergus McCann. The popular image – of an amateurish, badly-run family business – is, according to Gerry McNee, rooted firmly in fact. "After Bob Kelly died, Celtic were in the unhealthy situation of having White as the chairman, secretary and treasurer," said McNee, who wrote an official history of the club in 1978. "He was running the club from a wee office in Bath Street and was accountable to no-one really. And there wasn't any great vision at all; Celtic just wanted to get by. Season ticket holders, for example, were seen as potential trouble-makers – people who could stamp their feet and demand change – so the club kept them to an absolute minimum."

Nor was suspicion restricted to the paying customers. Fallon and Stein quickly came to realise that the extent of their influence was regarded not with gratitude or respect, but with resentment.

Jock and myself didn't much care for most of the guys on that board and I know they didn't have much time for us either. Desmond, at least, was generally straight with you but you couldn't say that about all of them. It was obvious to us after a while that they felt we had too much say around the place and that they wanted to make their own mark on the club. Jock was untouchable at that stage, everyone knew he ran the place, and they didn't like that. Those directors wanted some of that control and limelight for themselves, and it became 'us and them', which had never been the case with Bob Kelly. We told the directors the things we weren't happy about and I'm sure that annoyed them. If they'd been able to get rid of Jock and myself sooner, I think they would have.

Yet it was at this time, with relations strained, that White found himself calling for Fallon's assistance in the most remarkable of circumstances.

I remember getting a call to his office and he was sitting there, panicking. It turned out that a letter had arrived at the park, claiming to be from the IRA, saying that the main stand was going to be blown up. I thought from the start that it sounded very unlikely but Desmond was taking it very seriously. He said, 'I know it's a lot to ask, Sean. But is there anyone in Ireland you could get in touch with who could help us sort this thing out?' Now, as you know, I was never political and I could never be bothered with any of the IRA stuff. I always felt that violence solved nothing and, like Jock, I got annoyed at all the IRA songs being sung at Celtic Park at that time. But I told Desmond that I would put in some calls over in Ireland to people who might be able to find out if there was anything to be worried about. Not long after, I got a call back saying that they could fix up a meeting. So there we were, myself and Desmond – Jock wanted no part of it – going over to Dublin for a meeting with, apparently, a couple of the IRA top men. I think I ended up doing all of the talking on our side. Desmond just sat there, white as a sheet. They had to tell him: 'Don't worry, Mr White, there are no guns here.' It was a strange situation to be in but I didn't feel threatened at any time; it never made sense to me that Celtic would be a target. The meeting didn't last long but these two IRA guys assured us that nothing would happen to Celtic Park and that it had all either been a misunderstanding or a hoax. So our minds were put at ease. That was quite a week though. Not one you forget in a hurry.

Nor was it the only threat of such potential gravity Celtic had to face down. In the early hours of April 24, 1974, Jimmy Johnstone awoke to the shrill ring of a telephone in his Madrid hotel room. The voice on the line announced simply, 'You're dead'. Stein would receive a similar message and while both men escaped the Spanish capital with their lives, this was an occasion when – unlike the IRA episode – the violence was very real. The first leg of this European Cup semi-final against Atletico Madrid is remembered with revulsion by those who were there, with Danny McGrain describing it as "the most disgusting display of football I have ever seen".

Atletico, like Racing Club before them, were not without ability. But the team that beat Celtic 2-0 in Madrid bore no resemblance to the side that, a fortnight earlier, had kicked, stamped and punched their way to an infamous goalless draw in Glasgow which included three red cards for the Spaniards. "Tonight, the effigy of football was burned," was how *The Times'* Geoffrey Green, in his inimitable style, reported on the match. "This was a shambles, a night when the stars threw down their spears and watered heaven with their tears." Photographs of Jimmy Johnstone, bruised and battered from the chest down, matched Green's words for vividness, and the brutality did not end at the final whistle. Johnstone was attacked once more as the players made their way from the field, sparking a punch-up in the tunnel in which players, police – even Celtic's affable assistant manager – found themselves embroiled. As Billy McNeill wrote in *Hail Cesar*: "Sean was at the heart of the battle, trading punches with the Spaniards and laying them out good style." Thirty-eight years on, he harboured no regrets.

As a player, I never raised my fists, and I was always proud of never losing my temper. But Atletico were a disgrace to football that night, and I wasn't going to watch while they kicked lumps out of our players in the tunnel after seeing what they had done on the pitch. What I remember most about that game, though, is how fantastic wee Jinky was. They called me the Iron Man but he deserved that name more than me because he never shirked anything, even when he was being kicked all over the place. How he didn't react to the punishment Atletico gave him, I'll never know. But both Jock and myself had never been prouder of him and we told him that. When he got that death threat in Madrid, though, we had a job convincing him to play. Jock told him: 'It's ok for you, wee man. I'm a sitting target in that dugout.' Jinky went out in the end but our fans had been told not to travel, and the hatred from their crowd was unbelievable. I've never experienced anything like it. If we had got through, I'm sure there would have been trouble.

As it was, Celtic were beaten comfortably, and would never again reach such an advanced stage of the European Cup. Indeed, amid the abhorrence of Atletico's cynicism, there was recognition that Stein's side were a much-diminished force. "The Lisbon Lions would have had Atletico for breakfast, no matter how hard or how often they kicked," wrote the *Daily Record's* Alex Cameron. "In the end Celtic lost on ability in Madrid, and no amount of moaning about the bad sportsmanship of Atletico will change this."

The manager himself acknowledged as much, saying: "I don't think Celtic would have been good enough to win the 1974 European Cup... It's no use tiptoeing through Europe kidding yourself on the team is capable of winning if it's not really up to it." The following season, Celtic would tiptoe only as far as the first round before being eliminated by Olympiakos. By then, Hay was gone, and George Connelly – having lost his one true friend in the Celtic squad – was on the road to premature retirement.

I remember being at a board meeting when they were talking about selling Davie Hay, and I told them then: 'If you sell Davie, you might as well sell George too'. And I didn't take any pleasure from being right on that one because George was a terrible loss to the team. The problem was, Davie was his only real pal at the time and, sure enough, once he left for Chelsea, that was it for George at Celtic. Jock and I spent a lot of time out at his house in Fife trying to reason with him and coax him back to the club, but it was no use. And what a waste it was because George Connelly could have been one of the best players in the world. He was someone who just couldn't handle the dressing room, unfortunately.

Some of the players didn't help us because they would deliberately tease and embarrass him. Maybe they saw it as just a laugh, but I used to get on to them about it because they knew as well as I did how shy and sensitive big George was. He used to go missing all the time, and either Jock or myself, or the two of us, would be out trying to bring him back. I could have driven that road to his house with my eyes shut. I just used to tell him that he had a gift, a God-given talent, and it was something to be enjoyed and shared. But I couldn't get through to him, and it has always been a big regret of mine.

The extent to which Fallon mourned this perceived failure was underlined by his youngest daughter, Sinead. She was born two years after Connelly quit Celtic for good in 1976, yet remembers her father, years later, choked with emotion as he heard about this favourite former pupil. She said: "Someone told dad that George hadn't been doing well and was now out digging roads and, knowing the talent that was being wasted, he was really upset by it. I remember him saying: 'What a tragedy. That boy should have been one of the greats.'"

The niggling doubt over whether he could have done something – anything – to prevent Connelly slipping into obscurity had, Fallon admitted, continued to haunt him. It was a question only the player could answer, and his verdict was unequivocal. "No way," said Connelly. "Sean did everything he possibly could for me; in fact, I'm amazed at how much he did, looking back. I knew that Sean genuinely cared about me and only wanted the best for me. Unfortunately, my problems at that time weren't the kind that anyone could fix. I was in a deep hole because my marriage was a mess, and I just wanted to be away from everything; to be invisible. I certainly didn't want to be a footballer. Maybe something more could have been done somewhere down the line, but not by Sean. He was like a father figure to all the boys in that great reserve team we had and he was particularly good with me. People might not realise but he made me captain of that team, and that gave me a real boost for a while – knowing that he believed in me that much."

At the start of the '70s, it seemed that everyone believed in Connelly, and in Celtic. But the trajectory of this flawed genius's career would, in the end, mirror his team's descent from greatness. Scovell's "soccer supremos" had, by 1975, become hobbled has-beens.

The nine-in-a-row era was at an end and so, too, unbeknown to him, was Fallon's time as assistant manager. Having perfected the role of quiet, influential deputy, he was about to find himself thrust into the spotlight. But this 'promotion' was no cause for celebration. Becoming Celtic manager, that old ambition, would be realised at the worst time, and in the worst circumstances.

Chapter 24
The Crash

July 5, 1975. A day that will change the Fallons' lives begins in blissful ignorance. If there are even the faintest flickers of sadness, they exist only because an idyllic summer holiday is coming to an imminent end. Soon, there will only be the memories of beautiful Rossnowlagh on the Donegal coast; of the songs, the family games and the fortnight of glorious, miraculous, uninterrupted sunshine.

But Sean, a glint in his eye, has a surprise in store.

"I'll always remember dad telling us that we didn't have to go home; that we could stay another week," said Sean's eldest daughter, Marie Therese. "It had been one of those fantastic holidays and no-one wanted it to end, so we couldn't have been happier. The hotel staff even made us baked Alaska with sparklers to celebrate. We were at the table, high as kites, when dad came back, completely ashen-faced."

While at the reception desk arranging the family's extended stay, Sean had been handed the telephone. "Call for you, Mr Fallon." It was over in seconds, and the information was so stunning that he struggled to comprehend what had just been said. But the bare, awful details – Jock; car crash; intensive care – were inescapable. "Everyone was so upset," recalled another of Sean's daughters, Siobhan. "I remember there was a priest at reception and the children all went over to ask could he please pray for our

Uncle Jock. Poor mum and dad were sick with worry. You have those times in your life when you just want to be home – you'd be beamed home if you could – and that's what they were like that day. We left straight away and I've never heard dad quieter than he was on that journey home. I think the only time he spoke was when we all said some prayers together that Jock would be ok."

The family's entreaties were answered, but it was a close call. Stein, who had been returning from Manchester Airport after a holiday in Menorca, had been involved in a high-speed, head-on collision, and suffered severe injuries to his head, chest and leg. A tracheotomy was performed at Dumfries Royal Infirmary to enable him to breathe, but the prognosis remained uncertain. "I remember speaking to poor Jean and she wasn't sure he would survive," said Sean's wife, Myra. "It was a terrible time."

Unable to speak, and sustained by various drips, tubes and pieces of medical apparatus, Stein was a sorry sight. Even when the immediate danger passed, it was clear that managing Celtic – for the foreseeable future at least – was out of the question. With the first pre-season matches just a couple of weeks away and the squad diminished by key departures, Fallon was a popular choice to fill the gaping void. "Sean was a great guy to have that season," said Bobby Lennox. "With him being there, I don't remember there being any great concern that the boss wouldn't be around to run things." Perhaps not from the players. Fallon, though, did have his misgivings.

> We knew we had a difficult season ahead but I expected they would ask me to step in until Jock had recovered, and I was happy to do that. He had had a small heart attack a couple of years before and missed a few games, and that was how it had worked then. I knew his way of working so well that I just kept things ticking over. But the club decided to announce that he would be taking a year off and that I'd be in charge for the whole season, which I wasn't sure about. I knew Jock would want to be back as soon as he was on his feet again, and that's exactly what happened. And I would have been happy to have him back earlier. We needed to be at our strongest that season because it was a bad time to be taking over.

'Bad' hardly does it justice. In the decade Stein and Fallon had spent as manager and assistant, Celtic had never been in a worse state. Bemusement still surrounded their capitulation the previous season, when a humbling 3-0 Ne'erday loss at Ibrox had sparked a spectacular collapse in the second half of their campaign. Won four, lost eight was Celtic's remarkable record during that run-in, and the prize on offer made it all the more baffling. Taking the run of successive titles into double figures had become an obsession, so much so that the board made an uncharacteristically lavish attempt to nudge the team towards the finishing line, offering a bonus of £1200 per player – equivalent to six months' salary – if the mythical 10 was reached.

It was to no avail. "We just came apart at the seams," reflected Dixie Deans in his autobiography. "Perhaps it was simply a case of some members of that team having run their course." That was certainly Stein's analysis. Billy McNeill was already retiring – "the right decision," his manager stated publicly – and Stein ensured that he was followed through the exit by a defensive stalwart, Jim Brogan, and the greatest Celtic player of them all. The news of a free transfer for Jimmy Johnstone, still just 30, stunned everyone, not least the player himself. "I virtually keeled over with shock," he recalled of the tearful meeting in which the devastating news was broken. Even Stein admitted that he was releasing a player "with a lot of football left in him", and his assertion that Jinky had "climbed too many mountains with us" did little to assuage an angry Celtic support. For Fallon, it was another occasion when his public stance had to conceal the gravest of private misgivings.

> I can't deny wee Jinky drove us both mad. Jock and myself used to often get calls at all hours to go and fetch him from this pub or that pub. We used every technique we had to keep him off the drink but there were always hangers-on with Jimmy – users – who took advantage of his good nature. I got fed up of hearing from him: 'Aye, you're right, Sean. I know you're right. I need to do something'. But I was still totally against the decision to give him a free transfer and I made that clear to Jock. I would have kept him on and tried to get him back to his old self, because he had shown at times he was still capable. I felt he deserved that chance, considering all he'd given to the club. But once Jock made up his mind about something, it was very difficult to change it.
>
> 'I've no more patience left, Sean,' he told me. It broke Jimmy's

heart, and the tragedy was that he kind of gave up after that. He went to a few other clubs but his heart was never in it. I missed him around the place and the team missed him too. The same went for Billy McNeill; in fact, I wanted Billy to come out of retirement. He started to regret hanging up his boots and I knew that he could still do a job with all the experience he had. But the club didn't think it was a good idea, and neither did Jock. That was hard to understand because Billy could have helped bring a bit of stability to the place. So many big personalities had gone that you had to worry about the way things were going to be.

Fallon's concern was well merited. The club had been shorn of its greatest-ever player, captain and manager, all in the space of one seismic summer. The effect on the dressing room was inevitable, with Deans describing Celtic Park as "feeling like a house with some of its favourite children having left home". Sir Alex Ferguson, then manager of St Mirren, watched the unfolding of events with interest and felt immediate sympathy for Celtic's caretaker boss. "He was very unlucky in his timing," said Ferguson. "I think Sean in his own right could have managed Celtic if he'd got the club at the right time. But by then, not only were expectations sky-high, there were also signs that Celtic were beginning to dip."

Danny McGrain was less diplomatic in his assessment of the squad Fallon inherited, writing in his 1978 autobiography that it included "enough passengers to fill a jumbo jet". "Too many individuals inside the club did not care enough for the jersey," he added. "It makes me angry when fans and critics blame Sean Fallon. Sean worked his heart out for the club that year... I honestly believe that even if the boss had been fit it would have made little difference... Celtic did not have enough good players on the park."

Stein himself later acknowledged that his assistant, in taking charge when he did, had been left with a thankless task. "Whether or not I was involved, season 1975-76 was going to be a difficult one for Celtic," he told the *Celtic View* in June 1976. "We were no longer the force that had taken the football world by storm in the late '60s and early '70s." Stein, in fact, was so convinced that an era had come to an end that he spent the summer of '75 debating whether to become Scotland manager. Another change of heart averted that outcome, but by the following January, he was again intimating his interest in the national job.

Others, too, saw that the glory days were over, and that the time to cut ties was nigh. Indeed, Fallon's first major task upon taking charge was to persuade the club's star player – his most famous signing – to withdraw a transfer request. It was also his first major victory, with Dalglish's determination to head south transformed into a willingness to sign a new two-year contract. In his autobiography, the player described that about-turn as an act of loyalty. "With Big Jock in hospital, I didn't want to leave Celtic and Sean in the lurch," he wrote in *Dalglish, My Story*. "If the circumstances had been different at the club, I would have walked out."

Yet, significant as his debt to Fallon undoubtedly was, it was not the only factor involved. Dalglish admitted after signing his new deal that there had been "a problem about conditions", and it was in this financial aspect of negotiations that Fallon proved particularly skilful. The Irishman had felt from the outset that an improved salary would be sufficient to sway his former protégé, but knew that securing funds would be difficult, particularly from a board only too willing to listen to offers. When the season began with debate over the fee Celtic would demand, Fallon made a point of stating his position bluntly, telling the *Daily Record*: "It's better to have the money on the park than in the bank." It was then, faced with a player keen to leave and a board ready to sell, that he found his solution.

> I was always sure Kenny would stay if we could get him a better deal and, more importantly, show him he was appreciated. Kenny didn't always feel that Celtic valued him as they might and I think he had a point. The two of us got on well and we spoke about the situation very honestly. I had one card I could play and it was the captaincy. With Jock still recuperating, it was up to me to decide who took over from Billy. So I said to Kenny, 'I want you to be my captain. You deserve it anyway because of your status in this team but, if you accept and stay at the club, I'm sure the fact you're captain will allow me to get a few extra quid out of the directors for you'. That was enough for Kenny. He wasn't a greedy lad – he just wanted to feel appreciated.

Thrilled though Fallon was, he knew only too well that solving one major problem did not diminish the scale of the others. Dalglish, after all, had been powerless to prevent Celtic's implosion the season before, and the side had since been weakened significantly. As well as doing without the departed trio of McNeill, Johnstone and Brogan, Fallon knew that injury would deny him the services of midfield linchpin Steve Murray and the hugely talented Brian McLaughlin. Yet August arrived without a single replacement having been recruited.

With the uncertainty over the manager's position having induced a state of near-paralysis at the club, it took until the day before Celtic's opening league fixture for the Irishman to make his first, and only, signing of 1975. Johannes Edvaldsson, the player in question, would prove to be something of a cult hero in his five years at the club, making almost 200 appearances. But the Icelander's early days in Scottish football were not entirely problem-free, and the player christened 'Shuggy' by the Celtic support recalled with amazement Fallon's efforts to smooth the transition.

He said: "Sean was my first real impression of Celtic, and what a fantastic impression he gave me. He would even take me up to his house to meet his wonderful family and have dinner with them, just so I would feel at home in Scotland. I remember being completely amazed, thinking: 'How does he have time to do all this?' He was trying to do the jobs of Celtic manager and assistant manager at the same time, yet he still managed to be like a baby-sitter to me. Sean was a true friend and, as a manager, I found him very impressive. The training was terrific and what I really liked about coming to work under him was that the football was so positive – it was all about attack."

For much of the season, it seemed this positivity would be rewarded. By October, Fallon had overseen 23 matches and emerged with 19 wins, two draws and two defeats. Celtic had scored 60, conceded just 14, and the nightmare of the previous season seemed to have been put behind them. With the team top of the table and assured of their place in the League Cup final, the consensus was that Fallon had steadied the ship. The Irishman had even got the team winning in Europe again, with a 9-0 aggregate victory over Edvaldsson's former club, Valur, the prelude to a memorable trip to Portugal in the last 16 of the Cup Winners' Cup.

Boavista, who were joint-top of the league, made for formidable opponents. Fallon, though, had done his homework, and the lessons learned were to serve Celtic well. Joao Alves, Boavista's influential playmaker, was assigned a man-marker in Jackie McNamara Snr and, with five minutes remaining, that plan had worked to perfection. Celtic, even without the injured Dalglish, were cruising to a well-deserved 0-0 draw, and Alves had cut a subdued and ineffectual figure. Even when Boavista were awarded a late penalty, Fallon didn't panic. He had watched Alves take, and score, a previous spot-kick, and had given Peter Latchford instructions on which way to dive. The penalty was duly saved and, for Celtic, the hard work had been done. A 3-1 home win would take them through to a well-earned quarter-final. Yet although the players involved remember the away leg in particular as a tactical triumph, Fallon himself had a less flattering story to tell.

> The thing I remember about that Boavista trip is taking the boys on a walk down to the beach. This was the night before the game and I thought, 'Ok, while we're here, I'll do a little tactics talk'. So I'm drawing out a pitch on the sand, setting out the players, trying to make it as detailed as possible. And then, just as I was about to start, this big wave came in and washed it all away. The bloody tide had come in and I hadn't noticed. Even at the time, all I could do was laugh. It didn't bode very well for our tactics the next night. But the players were tremendous and got the result they did by working exceptionally hard.

Those efforts seemed to impact on their performance three days later, when Rangers scored the only goal of a dire League Cup final blighted by brutal tackling. Yet by the time 1975 drew to a close, that was the only blot on the caretaker's copybook. "Fallon can look back on the year with quiet pride," wrote Alan Davidson of the *Evening Times*. Celtic, he pointed out, were top of the table and in the last eight of the Cup Winners' Cup with "a largely transient and relatively inexperienced squad", a fact which rendered their manager's performance "all the more praiseworthy".

Another area of success was in getting the best out of the team's star players. McGrain was outstanding throughout, while Dalglish finished the season as Scotland's top scorer for the only time in his Celtic career. Indeed, it was under Fallon that the Scotland star –

previously switched between midfield and attack – settled into the role in which he would earn worldwide renown. "I was just behind the strikers and coming through, that's what I really like best," he said in an interview at the end of the campaign, having scored 32 times in 51 appearances. "I'm used to roving, and I think that suits me."

While Dalglish dazzled, a new generation of Celtic stars also came to the fore. Tommy Burns was given his first start, and there were debuts for the 17-year-old duo of Roy Aitken and George McCluskey. Aitken remembers Fallon as "a tremendous influence", and all three teenagers rewarded his faith by impressing in Old Firm derbies before the season was out. Such was their impact that the board began to suggest that, perhaps, money did not need to be spent after all.

Fallon, though, was not fooled. He knew the squad was threadbare at best, and saw too that fine servants such as Deans, Harry Hood and Tommy Callaghan had seen better days. As Callaghan himself admitted: "The team needed a bit of work at that stage, but with the boss away I think Sean felt a bit restricted. He just concentrated on maintaining continuity and working on what we already had." It was mid-March before Fallon made his second signing of the season, when the club – and Stein – sanctioned a club record £90,000 bid for Ayr United's Johnny Doyle. The winger would become a firm fans' favourite in years to come but was of little help to the manager who signed him, lasting just 30 minutes of his debut before limping off with a season-ending injury. As Stein would observe at the end of the season: "Sean Fallon had a lot of the wrong kind of luck."

Yet the desire to strengthen had predated Doyle's arrival, with Fallon having set his sights on an emerging young defender at Partick Thistle a few months before. It was only 25 years later, when Alan Hansen released his autobiography, *A Matter of Opinion*, that this near miss – and the reasons behind it – came to light. "I still don't know why they didn't follow up their interest in me," he wrote of Celtic. "The only explanation I've had came from Davie McParland, who told me Jock Stein, who had just returned after his car accident, had disagreed with caretaker manager Sean Fallon's assessment of me." Celtic's loss was Liverpool's considerable gain. And while Fallon was never the 'told you so' type, Hansen's eight

English league titles and three European Cups would have offered him ample ammunition.

> I definitely wanted Hansen. I'd thought he was a good player with a bit of class about him and a big future in the game. But when it came to making an offer, Jock pulled the plug. That's the only problem with being an assistant: when there's a difference of opinion, it's never you who gets to make the final call.

This is the lament of every No.2, and yet surely Fallon was forgetting something. In 1975/76, he was an assistant no more. As manager for the season, and having signed Edvaldsson a few months before, surely the decision on Hansen was his to make?

> Earlier in the season and you'd have been right. But it all changed. Jock was back at the park quite soon after his accident and, although I was still officially in charge, you can imagine he wasn't keeping quiet about things. Even before then, he wanted to know everything that was going on. I'd be at the hospital every day and you should have seen him, strapped up to these tubes, asking, 'How's so-and-so getting on?' He'd go right through the team: 'Keep your eye on that one'; 'Watch out for him!' He couldn't let go.
>
> It was very hard for him to be in that situation, removed from it all, because Jock was a man who always wanted to be in control. That was his nature, and football was his life. Once he was on his feet and back at the park, he was involved in everything again. Sometimes I'd tell him: 'I wish you'd just go for a sleep and leave me alone.' But when it came down to it, whether I was caretaker or not, it was his team. I would never have shut him out after all the years we'd had together – and he would never have let me.

Stein had begun his break from the game with the best of intentions. A telegram wishing Sean and the players well before their first match of the season was the extent of his input, and he told the press: "I know everything is in good hands." But his wife, Jean, quickly saw that a year of rest and recuperation was a forlorn hope. "He was itching to get back," she said. "He couldn't be at peace." By August 25, less than eight weeks after his near-fatal accident, Stein was indeed back at Celtic Park, taking in a reserve match. A week-and-a-half later, he was given a standing ovation as he took his seat to watch the first team beat Dundee 4-0. Over time, these appearances became steadily more frequent, and his influence inevitably grew.

Fallon was still taking training, delivering the team talks and dealing with the press but, from December onwards, he was essentially manager in name only. And the players could sense it. "It was a strange situation, that one," said Bobby Lennox. "Sean was officially in charge but Big Jock always seemed to be in the background and would turn up at the ground and sit in on team talks. No-one was sure who was making the decisions but everyone knew that Jock would have his oar in. He wasn't the kind of man who could take a back seat." With the notional manager prevented from managing and the man in the background calling the shots, it must have seemed uncomfortably familiar to Fallon. The dysfunctional days of McGrory and Kelly had been recreated.

> I wasn't surprised Jock wanted back in and, for a while, it wasn't too bad. We had always been a team anyway and I didn't mind at all keeping him involved, talking things over. I appreciated his advice and, at first, he let me get on with it. Gradually, though, he wanted more of a say and, after a few months, he was starting to overrule me. It didn't happen often to be fair. Jock and myself were very much of the same mind on football, so we agreed on 99 per cent of things that were happening. He would sit in on my team talks and tell me later that he would have said exactly the same thing, word for word.
>
> But there were times when we disagreed: situations like Hansen, or whether to play a certain player. And if he was adamant, there was no way I could go against him – it was his team after all. But it was a frustrating time because I was being judged on decisions that, in a number of cases, I didn't agree with. And Jock, as everyone knows, wasn't himself after the accident. When we ended up losing the league, I got the blame for it. But what could I do? Go to the papers and say: 'It's not my fault.' No way. As far as I was concerned, that would have been disloyal to Jock and the club.

Suffering in silence might have been preferable to betraying his principles but, for Sean's family, the experience left a bitter taste. "It was hard, when things started going wrong, to hear Sean being criticised for things you knew fine well weren't his doing," said his wife, Myra. "And everything had been going quite well when Jock had just left him to it. But Sean's right: what could you do? Looking back, the only thing I wish he had done is say: 'Jock, if you're back, that's great. But come back officially in that case and everyone will know where they stand.'"

The question of why Stein did not simply announce his ahead-of-schedule return is not easily answered. Undermining Fallon might have been a concern, particularly as the season had been running smoothly. But a more convincing explanation is provided by Tom Campbell and David Potter in *Stein, the Celtic Years*. "Desmond White counselled Stein against an early return," they wrote, "concerned about the manager's health but also, as an accountant, pointing out a premature return to work would adversely affect the settlement with his insurance company."

Whatever his motives, Stein contented himself with silently pulling the strings, and left his assistant to learn the most salutary of lessons. His son, Sean Jnr said: "My dad would tell me: 'Son, if you're going to make mistakes in life, just make sure they're your own mistakes. That was what that season taught him. I seem to recall there was one game in particular when my dad wanted to play Roddie MacDonald at centre-half, and Jock insisted on someone else. Whoever Jock wanted ended up having a nightmare and my dad got lambasted for picking him. I think he regretted later not going his own way." No wonder. Fallon would have known that, in the eyes of many Celtic supporters, this would be the season for which he would be remembered. As Lennox said: "People put two and two together and blamed Sean. But the players knew he'd done a right good turn for the club and did well with a pretty weak team."

Even with a declining side robbed of its biggest personalities, Fallon still oversaw more wins – and goals scored – than the season before. Rangers, though, had raised their game, and raced to the treble on the back of a remarkable 26-match unbeaten run. Fallon took the brunt of terracing disgruntlement and, inevitably, the criticism took its toll. After a 3-2 defeat at Dundee United that effectively handed Rangers the title, Ian Archer of the *Glasgow Herald* wrote a revealing article entitled: 'Fallon too hard on himself.' "Sean Fallon looked a little shell-shocked yesterday. He had not slept well… He tortures himself in defeat, quite unnecessarily…

He has pushed the club well without enough good players."

The members of that 1975/76 squad were, to a man, supportive of Archer's version of events. Sadly, though, the subplots and subtleties tend to go unnoticed by most casual observers. The bare facts were that Fallon had led the club to its first trophyless season in over a decade and the great tragedy is that, for many, he is defined by that rather than his stunning successes as an assistant. The ultimate evidence of that came in stumbling across a fans' forum discussion in which a contributor asked: "Is it a widely held view that 10 in a row would have been achieved but for Jock's car crash?" I read on, anticipating an explanation that the accident had taken place after the tenth title had been surrendered. But no. "Undoubtedly," was the authoritative tone of the answer that followed. "Sean Fallon was an able No.2 but never up to the top job."

These were the kind of maddening misconceptions the 1975/76 season spewed. As much of Fallon's prior work had gone unseen and unheralded, this solitary season in the spotlight remained in the collective memory. Yet amid all the nonsense written about this cursed campaign, there was one worthwhile observation – simple and insightful – in Danny McGrain's 1978 autobiography. "Poor Sean. He never had a chance."

Chapter 25
Paradise Lost

As a wretched season reached it cheerless end, Celtic threw a party. Organised to belatedly mark the achievement of winning nine successive league titles, the event was a reminder of better days, but also of subsequent decline.

Stein delivered the keynote speech, and he kept it short and sweet. "There has been mention made by previous speakers of individual players," he said. "I don't intend to individualise at all. However, I will mention the backroom staff: Sean Fallon, Neil Mochan, Bob Rooney, Willie Fernie, and I must not forget Jim Steele. Anything that was achieved for Celtic was by a team effort."

Fallon would have appreciated those words, and the symbolism of the manager insisting on being joined by his assistant to take the audience's applause. Stein, for all that he had been a source of frustration during the closing months of the season, was still a friend and, together, they were still a team. Reprising that old partnership was something to look forward to.

Yet the directors who clapped Fallon on the back that night knew he would never get the chance. The board minutes would later show that, from early February – when Celtic were still top of the league – directors had been plotting to replace him as No.2. Pat Crerand had been the potential successor mentioned on that occasion but, two months later, they settled on another man:

Davie McParland. Fallon, it was decided, would head up the club's scouts.

Around eight weeks of the season remained in which to inform him of this decision and discuss his new role. Not a word was spoken. Fallon left for his usual family holiday to Ireland none the wiser, and returned to the news that his job now belonged to someone else. Not that it was portrayed as a snub. White applied the kind of verbose politician-speak in which he specialised, telling the media: "The time was ripe for an overhaul and reorientation of our strategy." Fallon's new role was presented as an exciting opportunity, and depicted as such in the *Daily Record*. "Celtic last night gave Sean Fallon the vital job of running an 'accelerated youth policy'," was how Alex Cameron reported the story. Fallon, though, saw through the spin.

I was being demoted. Of course I was; I realised that right away. And the 'accelerated youth policy' – that was all for the press. I never heard it mentioned once after that. I was chief scout, simple as that. It hurt and annoyed me at the time, and mainly because of the way it was all handled. They did it all without even speaking to me and let me go on holiday thinking I'd be coming back as Jock's assistant. I felt that, given all the years I had been there, I could have been shown more respect than that. But that was the Celtic board in those days. They didn't know how to treat people and, more importantly, they didn't know football. They made a point of how important this new job was and that the players I signed would be the basis for the team in years to come. I was hearing this, looking at all the players I'd signed, and thinking, 'What exactly do they think I've been doing?'

You feel that even if the general public doesn't always know that you've done this or signed a particular player, the people at the club will at least appreciate it. But it was obvious they didn't. I was annoyed for myself in that respect, but I was more annoyed because I felt it was the wrong decision for Celtic. With Jock coming back full-time, I felt I could have helped, knowing him so well, to ease him back into things. He wasn't himself after that accident, mentally and physically. Just from knowing him all those years and being able to cheer him up sometimes, I think I could have helped. But the board had made up their minds.

Few could understand the directors' thinking, and Fallon's

indignation certainly proved mild in comparison to the disgust felt in the dressing room. Danny McGrain wrote in his autobiography of having "hardly slept" the night he learned of his mentor's demotion and, 37 years on, his abhorrence of the board's actions remained intact. "It was disgusting," he said. "If it happened today, with the coverage football gets, there would be a scandal. It was an awful time for me. The players were all upset about it and we were never given a proper explanation as to why it had happened. Whatever their reasoning was, though, I wouldn't have agreed with it. Some decisions are just wrong, and that was one of them."

So shoddy was the club's treatment of this devoted servant, and baffling their motives, that even Fallon's erstwhile critics were united in condemnation. "There wasn't a single supporter who didn't view Sean Fallon's demotion with complete distaste," said fanzine writer Jimmy Payne. "A lot of people blamed Sean for the 75/76 season but there was still a recognition that he was a great assistant who had done tremendous things for Celtic. People couldn't understand it, and most of the blame at that time fell at the door of Jock Stein."

The assumption that the manager would have dictated this change in his assistant was understandable. But was it accurate? That question was answered in 1988 by Brian Wilson, who was granted access to board minutes for his club history, *Celtic, A Century with Honour.* "Stein was not consulted about the appointment of Davie McParland," wrote Wilson, "and was not particularly enthusiastic about it." That, according to Stein's son, George, was an understatement. "I've no doubt the reason the board didn't consult him was because they knew he wouldn't agree to it. The impression I got, though, was that it wasn't so much a reflection on Sean as an assistant, but a feeling that they needed to groom a successor. I think there was belief – or more likely a hope – that my dad wouldn't last much longer in the job, and they wanted someone younger in place to take over. But my dad was totally against them making that decision for him."

The idea of Stein, this managerial colossus, being so impotent on such a decision is difficult to comprehend. But even accepting that he did not arrange or agree to Fallon's demotion, he did not, as one might have expected, rail against it. Other managers, seemingly less formidable, have reacted to similar situations with a threat of: 'If he goes, I go.' Stein, though unhappy, acquiesced. "I do think he could have fought for my dad a bit more," admitted Sean Fallon Jnr. "Jock himself said the same, after he and my dad had both left Celtic. There was no big apology but he made it clear that he regretted not being stronger. I can appreciate though that the backdrop, with a board like that one, didn't make it easy."

There seems little doubt that, a few years earlier, the Celtic manager would not have proved so pliable. Sadly, the Stein of 1976 was not the manager, or the man, he had once been. "Jock's power inside the club had waned and his own personal powers had waned too," said Rodger Baillie, who ghostwrote the Celtic manager's newspaper column. "Desmond White was flexing his muscles and I think Jock just didn't have strength to fight at that point. There was always friction between Desmond and Jock over who would be the real power in the land, and Desmond wouldn't have liked the fact that Jock and Sean were still very much Bob Kelly's boys and had so much influence in running the club."

Myra Fallon, who was herself immersed in Celtic, saw her husband's sacking as a symptom of that particular power struggle. Sean, she believed, was demoted with the aim – at least in part – of undermining Stein. "The feeling at that time was that Jock had become too strong for the club and that White wanted rid of him," she said. "Demoting Sean and bringing in Davie McParland was part of moving away from the Lisbon era and isolating Jock. After they'd got rid of Sean, the next step was moving on Jock himself, which didn't take long. It was all very dirty."

If Machiavellian motives were indeed behind Fallon's redeployment, the outcome would have pleased the instigators. Indeed, perhaps the saddest aspect of this tawdry episode is that, for a time – though thankfully not permanently – it succeeded in dividing a seemingly indivisible duo.

> Jock and myself drifted apart a bit after I was moved to the scouting job. There was never any falling out; we just did our own things for a while. Whereas we'd always gone to games together, I started to watch my matches and he went to see his. We also stopped going out on the Saturday nights with our wives, all that kind of thing. I wasn't angry with him though. It's true to say that he could have fought for me more, and he realised that. But Jock had to look after

himself. It was a difficult situation for him at that stage because we both knew the club had changed and that neither of us was secure. I never held it against him because he had his own family to look after and they had to come first. He also had his eye on staying on as a director and he probably thought he couldn't rock the boat if he wanted that to happen.

Stein's actions, while not laudable, were certainly understandable. The same could even be said of the board's thinking, particularly if we accept the possibility that weakening the manager's powerbase was a factor. Appointing Davie McParland, however, remains difficult to fathom. There seems little doubt that Celtic saw the former Queen's Park manager as Stein's future successor, with the *Daily Record* reporting on the day of his appointment that he was considered "the heir apparent to one of the best, but most demanding jobs in football".

The question everyone wanted answered, though, was: what had he done to earn such a job? McParland's pedigree as a manager with Partick Thistle and Queen's Park amounted, in essence, to a solitary League Cup final win over Stein's side five years earlier. It had been an impressive victory, but he had done little since, and had no prior connection whatsoever to Celtic, which in that era was regarded as near-essential for any prospective manager. With Billy McNeill seeking a return to the game, John Clark coaching Celtic's reserves and Bertie Auld impressing as McParland's successor at Firhill, there were certainly more logical candidates to groom as future Celtic managers. Even Crerand, had the board pursued their initial idea, could have been understood. Instead, they opted for a man who, on day one, told the press that his first task would be to learn the players' names.

> Davie was pals with one of the directors, Jimmy Farrell, and I believe that's why he got the job. He wasn't a bad guy but, without being too critical, he was a yes man. Anything Jock said, he would agree with – and that was the last thing Jock needed. Not knowing Jock particularly well, it would have been difficult for him to come in and go straight into being brutally honest with him. I actually didn't even know they were looking at Pat Crerand but I could have seen the sense in that a bit more, especially if they were aiming at getting a younger man to succeed Jock. Pat

had personality, he knew the club and he knew Jock. Plus, he'd had experience in backroom jobs at Manchester United, so he was used to working at a big club. I'm not saying he would have been a great Celtic manager, but you could have at least pictured it.

For McParland, issues of pedigree and perception could, in time, have been overcome. Genuinely insurmountable, though, was the most significant barrier to acceptance: he wasn't Sean Fallon. "Looking back, I feel sorry for Davie because it must have been a hell of a burden on him to come in and replace a man like Sean," said Kenny Dalglish, who referred in his autobiography to a poor relationship with McParland. "He must have seen right away it would be very difficult."

From McGrain, too, there was retrospective sympathy. "I know the only reason I never took to Davie McParland was because he'd taken over from Sean. I felt sorry for him – not at the time, but later – because the way I felt about Sean leaving meant I didn't give Davie the kind of respect he merited. It was a shame because he had done nothing wrong. He just wasn't Sean. He wasn't the guy we'd known and respected for the best part of 10 years, and who'd brought us on from being boys to young men. And the chemistry between Mr Stein and McParland was never as good as it had been with Sean. How could it be? So he was up against it from day one."

McParland did, however, end his first season at Celtic Park with a championship medal. Stein succeeded in rejuvenating the squad with the signings of Joe Craig, Pat Stanton and Alfie Conn, with Stanton particularly important in solving the problems that had beset the club over previous years. But the revival was built on rickety foundations. With Stanton injured, Celtic finished fifth the following season and failed to qualify for Europe for the first time in 13 years. They also received a savaging from their captain. McGrain's *Celtic: My Team* remains an astonishing read and emphasises the depths to which the team had sunk. "By tradition when the chips are down then Celtic are at their most dangerous," wrote McGrain. "Too many players last season seemed to have never heard of that tradition… that made me sick… certain players were swanning around, smiling to friends, signing autographs and obviously not over-worried at pushing the club to its lowest ebb in 13 years."

The players might have been the chief culprits but the manager, too, had been decidedly below par. "Depressed and unable to lift himself or his players," is the candid description provided by Tom Campbell and David Potter in *Jock Stein, the Celtic Years*, and those who knew him best attributed this to the long-term impact of his car crash. "It seemed to take his enthusiasm away," said Billy McNeill. "It seemed to take his personality away to a degree." Fallon, while not the confidant and daily companion he had once been, felt there was an additional factor in Stein's slump.

> The situation with the board was draining too. It was a constant battle with them and he knew fine well that there were things going on behind his back. That's not a nice environment to work in.

Stein had also suffered a heavy psychological blow with the departure of Dalglish to Liverpool. Yet that transfer was seen by Fallon as an example of the Celtic manager's diminished powers, with the Irishman still adamant that keeping hold of King Kenny should not have proved impossible.

> Kenny came to our house in King's Park the day he left and he was breaking his heart. I still don't believe, deep down, he wanted to go. It proved the right decision for him in the end but I definitely think that, if things had been handled in the right way, we could have kept Kenny for a year or two more. But by that stage the board weren't even trying to keep him. They couldn't wait to sell, and Jock wasn't able to stop them.

Stein, in fact, performed admirably in preventing the directors from accepting the first bid that arrived for the club's star player. White and his cohorts would have allowed Dalglish to go to Anfield for £300,000, and began to panic when their manager insisted on turning down a further offer of £400,000. Ultimately, the final fee of £440,000 was still a small price to pay, and Fallon found himself agreeing with an old friend. "The most unbelievable thing I've known," was Bill Shankly's reaction to the deal. "I would rather have quit and got out of the game altogether than sold a player of his brilliance." Myra remembers a similar stunned reaction from her husband. "Sean was so disappointed," she said. "He kept saying over and over, 'They don't know what they're losing'. He just couldn't believe their attitude." Dalglish's departure was certainly an admission, were any still needed, that Celtic had given up any lingering pretence of challenging in Europe. Stein received less than a quarter of the money raised, and spent it on John Dowie, Joe Filippi and Frank Munro.

But while Celtic were in the process of offloading another all-time great, Fallon was busy replenishing their stocks. Having quickly overcome the unhappiness that followed his demotion, he pursued with typical diligence and enthusiasm the familiar responsibilities of scouting, and proved as successful as ever. The job came with its disappointments. Fallon remembered, for example, recommending Ronnie Whelan – then with Dublin side Home Farm – only for the board to balk at the £35,000 Liverpool proved only too willing to pay. Fortunately, there were successes too. One of the most notable came when he was tipped off about a youngster playing for Holy Cross High School in Hamilton. This player's brother was also said to be useful and, encouragingly, they descended from a long line of famous Celts. But the deal proved far from straightforward.

> Paul and Willie McStay were two of the last signings I made, and I was delighted to get them in. It looked for a while like we might lose Paul though. There were loads of clubs in for him and I remember Leeds United were the favourites. It was like the Eddie Gray situation – they were offering money we couldn't compete with. But what I did at that stage was to put everything into getting Willie to sign. Paul was a shy boy and I felt if he had his big brother around the place to make him feel more comfortable, it would make a difference in his decision. That's the way it worked out, although we had some competition for Willie too. Brian Clough was very keen on getting him down to Nottingham Forest I seem to remember. But he did a fine job for the club and Paul, as everyone knows, was a tremendous player – one of the best the club ever had.

At Fallon's 80th birthday celebrations, a special recorded message from Paul was broadcast, thanking the Irishman "for all the help and guidance you gave me". "If it wasn't for you bringing me to Celtic Park, I don't know what would have happened to me," he added. His elder brother also had cause to remember with great fondness the man who changed the direction of his career and, ultimately, his life. "I was all set to go to Forest," Willie recalled. "I didn't even know Celtic were interested. But I'll never forget the sight of Sean, who to me was Mr Celtic, walking up to my house in Larkhall. I was just blown away that Sean Fallon was trying to sign me. I'd have signed before he got through the front door if he'd let me."

Within a year, Fallon – Mr Celtic – would be gone. But it was not the last time Willie McStay would have cause to be grateful for his intervention. In 1993, it was a recommendation from Sean that won this intelligent aspiring coach, then just 31, the manager's job at Sligo Rovers. Even then, the Irishman's eye for talent had not deserted him; McStay duly led the Bit O'Red to an unprecedented treble.

The brothers represented a significant parting gift. When the fans voted for the greatest ever Celtic XI, returning a team packed full of Fallon signings, Paul – the outstanding player of the 1980s and early '90s – slotted in beside Bertie Auld and Bobby Murdoch in midfield. The last player brought to Celtic Park by Fallon was also a strong contender for that team. Ultimately, he lost out to Ronnie Simpson – himself, of course, a Fallon recruit – but Packie Bonner's performances over 600-plus appearances had nonetheless established him as one of the club's goalkeeping greats. And while he has been widely described as Stein's last signing, that was a myth he was glad to debunk.

"I was Sean's signing," said Bonner. "He'd spotted me at an Irish youth match in Dublin and arranged for me to come over on trial. When I arrived, Sean was even the man who would pick me up every day and take me into Celtic Park. I remember the first day I came in, he didn't bring me into the reserve dressing room; he took me straight in to meet the first team, so guys like Danny McGrain, Pat Stanton and Roy Aitken – big names. That was Sean wanting the club to make as big an impression on me as was possible – and he succeeded. It was the same in the car journeys too. He would spend the whole time telling me all these great stories about the old days, just bringing you into the club bit by bit. He was such a Celtic man and he wanted you to feel the same way. I didn't realise at the time how badly the club were treating him, but you would never have known. Whenever he would take me into the park, or later when he would have me over to dinner with the family, I never once heard him speak a bad word about Celtic. He was sacked quite soon after I arrived and I was very homesick in those days. But even after he left the club, Sean looked out for me and helped immensely in getting me over that. He was, by nature, a very caring man, and he was desperate for me to enjoy being at Celtic the way he had enjoyed it. I'm forever grateful to him for all that he did for me."

Bonner was a regular at Fallon family dinners when he first arrived, and it was a busy house, with Myra and Sean's sixth child, Sinead, having arrived on March 3, 1978. A few months before, mindful of this coming arrival, Fallon had sought a meeting with Desmond White. Though Celtic's directors seemed not to appreciate fully his talents, there were others who did and, since moving to the role of chief scout, job offers had kept coming. Among the most notable was the chance to become manager at Ayr United, then an established Premier League side, and an unexpected approach to take charge of the Greek giants Olympiakos. But Fallon, remarkable as it might seem, simply was not interested. Being a scout at Celtic, however undervalued, was considered preferable to becoming a manager elsewhere. But before turning down the latest of these offers, he was keen to establish if, with his family set to expand, his position at the club was secure.

> I appreciated that these clubs felt I could help them out, but I just couldn't see past Celtic. I would never have left if it was down to me. But I knew the board at that time were always up to something, so I spoke to Desmond White. He told me I had 'a job for life' and that was good enough for me. All I can say is that he obviously didn't see me living very long. Not long after, I was called into the office and just told that I wasn't being kept on. They'd also promised me a testimonial, originally as a joint thing with Jock – like they'd done with Jinky and Bobby Lennox – but that was forgotten about too. Jock got his testimonial and I got the sack. But what could you do? I could have kicked up a fuss about it, gone to the papers, but there was no way I was going to do that. Better to get out with your dignity.

Fallon was sacked on May 28, 1978, bringing to a cold and abrupt end almost three decades of unbroken service. Yet, incredibly,

Celtic had the audacity to make a public point of how fairly they had treated this old stalwart, feeding the press phrases such as "substantial golden handshake" and "generous financial settlement", both of which were dutifully relayed. Again, board minutes show that Fallon's fate – along with that of his successor, Davie McParland – had been sealed over a month before, at a board meeting on April 20 at the North British Hotel.

The day the news was finally broken is remembered vividly by his daughter, Louise. She said: "Dad always tried to keep things very positive and, even when the club got rid of him as assistant, the word 'demoted' was never mentioned. He just told us he'd got a new job and that everything was fine. But that day he was sacked, I remember coming back from school and he was sitting out in the back garden. He just said, 'I've left Celtic'. And I could see it in his face; I'll never forget how hurt he looked. It took him a long time to get over that."

The memory lingered, too, for the many players to whom Fallon meant so much. When, eight years later, Celtic approached Lou Macari about becoming Davie Hay's assistant, they were met with a flat refusal. "I'd have loved to have gone back but I'd have rocked the boat," he explained a couple of years later. "I didn't like what the people in charge had done to Sean Fallon." A quarter-of-a-century on, he felt as strongly as ever. "I lost my belief in Celtic, or what I thought Celtic stood for, when I heard about Sean being sacked," he said. "I honestly thought that the people running the club would realise, like the players realised, how important he was. It was staggering. If there was one person who should never been allowed to leave a football club, it was Sean."

These words might seem over-dramatic. Fallon was, by then, merely chief scout, and men in that position – removed from day-to-day contact with the players – are rarely mourned when they leave. But the Irishman, as Celtic's then captain explained, was a case apart. "It's when people disappear from the club that you realise how much you miss them and how intrinsic they were to everything that was being achieved," said McGrain. "Celtic lost something after Sean left. It was like the air being let out of the balloon; I certainly felt myself being deflated. I played on for another good few years at Celtic and had some great times. But you couldn't help but feel worse about the club, and certainly the board, after they'd done something like that."

The boy from Sligo who dreamed of playing for Celtic, and who lied about his age to make it happen, had enjoyed an association with the club spanning 28 years, two months, seven days and 30 major trophies. "Loved every minute of it too," he would say. But now it was over. Fallon was heartbroken, and yet those who knew both the club and the man insist that Celtic's loss was greater.

Macari once paid his old reserve coach the warmest of tributes by saying: "Every club in Britain should employ a man of his calibre." But last year, reflecting on his old mentor, he sought to qualify those words. "How many men of Sean's calibre are there out there? Very, very few," he explained. "Sean Fallon was one in a million. What a shame Celtic didn't realise it."

Chapter 26
Life After Celtic

"For God's sake, Sean, don't go to Dumbarton!"

The message rang out loud and clear. It always did when Jock Stein was dispensing the advice. And while Fallon would ignore his old friend on this occasion, the frankness of their conversation was a good sign. The coolness had gone; the distance disappeared. This great football duo had been reunited and reconciled, and it was all thanks to the Celtic board.

"It was after the club did the dirty on Jock that him and Sean became very close again," explained Myra. "I think it was the way they had both been treated that brought them together." But Stein had not joined his former assistant in the ranks of the unemployed. In September 1978, when the phone call warning Fallon not to take the Dumbarton job was made, Stein was already manager at Leeds United, and would return to Glasgow a month later to become Scotland boss. For a fellow victim, he was faring well.

A theory has, in fact, developed in the years since Stein's acrimonious departure that he engineered it all: took his £80,000 testimonial cheque, feigned outrage at Celtic's offer and headed south for a whopping pay-rise. "I felt Jock had a hidden agenda," said Billy McNeill. "He said he wanted to retire but I never, ever believed that. He never did anything ad hoc; never left anything to chance. I think the club handled it badly but I'm sure he knew he was going to Leeds." It is a theory for which Fallon had no tolerance whatsoever.

> I always felt, for as long as I knew him, that Jock was a step ahead of everyone. But the directors caught him out that time. He'd agreed to Billy coming in as manager on the understanding that he would become a director. I think he expected a kind of general manager role – almost like a director of football today. Instead, they gave him a job selling pools tickets, which they must have known he wouldn't be able to stomach. And it worked. As soon as he knew what he'd be doing, he left the club, took the Leeds job and was out of their hair. Jock felt they'd been very clever – getting rid of him without needing to sack him. And, like myself, he was very sad about it. I honestly believe if they had given him a decent directorship with some input into the football side, he would never have left Celtic. What they did was an insult. But that was just the way that board ran things.

Indeed, while Fallon and Stein moved on, a familiar Celtic drama soon began unfolding, with new actors playing out the same old script. By 1978, McNeill was back at Celtic as manager, and the sentiments he later expressed about Desmond White could so easily have been written by his predecessor. "Mr White was aloof and distant and I found him well-nigh impossible to get on with," was McNeill's verdict in *Hail Cesar*. "When it came to the chairman and the board, I had to put myself on a war footing... Managing Celtic seemed to be a constant struggle." Nor, it seemed, was White content for history to repeat itself merely in his relationship with the manager. By 1983, he was again pursuing his agenda through Celtic's assistant, demanding that John Clark be unseated as McNeill's deputy. "There were no grounds whatsoever for me to replace John," wrote McNeill. "My authority as manager was being undermined and this was yet another blatant attempt by the chairman to throw his weight about, irrespective of the consequences of his actions."

While Celtic continued to implode, Fallon and Stein could so easily have been cast as the wronged former employees, bitter about their shabby treatment. Yet Sir Alex Ferguson remembers his astonishment at finding both men to be entirely without rancour. Each, he recalled, was intent on sharing only the fondest memories of the club that had so callously cast them aside. He said: "I'd probe them about it because I couldn't believe, with the way they'd been treated, that they wouldn't have a few harsh things to say. But all that came across was how much they still loved Celtic. That's a tribute to Jock and Sean and says everything about their characters. And Celtic were the ones to lose out because they surely can't have realised how devoted these men were."

With Stein, the club that saved his career and rescued him from a return to the pits would always be more prominent than the version he encountered in those dismal final days. "Celtic have been wonderful to me," he told the *Evening Times* shortly before leaving the club. "You've heard of people coming back from the dead? Well it was Celtic that brought me back from the dead." Fallon, if anything, was even more starry-eyed. As Myra said: "If you'd come to see Sean the day after he was sacked, he'd have told you without blinking an eye that he still loved Celtic."

> Myra's right. I would have said that, and I would have meant it too. What happened hurt me a great deal and, mentally, I was lost for a while afterwards. But as far as I was concerned, that was individuals treating me badly, not Celtic. The club has always been bigger than any directors, any players and any manager. I know I always say it but my dream came true when I signed for the club, and to stay at Celtic Park for so long, well, it was just the icing on the cake. All I can think is that the man upstairs must have looked down and thought: 'Ah, he's alright, let's give him this one.' I'm always thankful for it and, when I look back, I only remember the good times. There's no way I would be comfortable bringing the club down. Even after I left, keeping up Celtic's honour and its traditions was always very important to me.

This principled stance faced an early test when he was approached by a *Sunday Mail* journalist offering £30,000 – an astronomical sum at the time – for a dirt-dishing exclusive. Fallon's refusal was immediate, emphatic and uncharacteristically ill-tempered. "That was Sean for you," said Ferguson. "All his life, he was a very strongly principled man; straight as a die. Everyone who's ever worked with him will testify to his loyalty, not only to all the players who worked under him, but also to friends like myself."

Ferguson gained a deeper appreciation of these qualities when Fallon, his friendship with Stein fully mended, began joining the Scotland management team during squad gatherings at the MacDonald Hotel. It was, the Irishman recalled, "just like the old days", with Stein – reluctant as ever to embrace sleep – talking long into the night about the game they both loved. This reprising of their former relationship even extended to the resumption of road trips, with Fallon soon criss-crossing the country as an unofficial SFA scout.

> Jock liked having me along on those trips. I think he enjoyed the company more than anything but he also respected my advice. Sometimes he'd even ask me to go out myself and check on a player he was thinking of, let him know what I thought. I remember Jim Leighton being one of those. Jock was trying to make his mind up but he never did like goalkeepers, and he wasn't sure about Leighton's kicking. So he asked what I thought. I told him I liked the player and felt he was well worth including and, sure enough, he was in the team next time they played. It was nice that we had that kind of relationship again because I had missed those days.

The old duo were on the road once more in September 1985, travelling to England to check on a player Stein was swithering over for the following week's fixture. It was a decision he had to get right, as Scotland's hopes of qualifying for the World Cup hinged on obtaining a positive result away to Wales, at Ninian Park, Cardiff. When they returned to Glasgow in the small hours of the following morning, and parted with Fallon wishing his friend luck for the big game, it seemed just like the last time; like every other time. Neither realised that there would be no next time.

> I'll never forget hearing on the radio that Jock had collapsed in the dugout. It's one of those moments that sticks in your memory. When they said he'd passed away, I nearly died myself. It was hard to believe for a while. Jock hadn't always kept well, but you felt he would always be around. It was very difficult getting used to him not being there. I felt I had no-one to talk to about football any more – not the way Jock and I used to talk about the game anyway. That's what I missed the most and what I still miss to this

day. He was a big figure in my life, so it's only natural I miss him occasionally. I spent almost every day with him for a long, long time, and we went through a lot together. When he died, I lost a great friend.

Fortunately, nothing was left unsaid between the pair. Any old grievances had been long since forgiven and forgotten, while mutual affection was taken as read. But Fallon did have one regret. "I should have bloody listened to him on Dumbarton," he said, smiling. In fact, while his comment might lead you to believe otherwise, Sean's spell at Boghead was far from disastrous. He succeeded not only in raising the club's profile, but in swelling its coffers thanks to some typically astute signings. But just as Davie McParland had suffered from not being Sean Fallon, so Dumbarton – through no fault of their own – found it impossible to compete with the Irishman's first love.

> I remember a few of the Lisbon Lions telling me that whichever club they went to after Celtic, they never felt the same buzz again. That was the way it was for me at Dumbarton. The chairman at that time was a guy called Robert Robertson and he was ambitious for the club to do well. But you could only do so much. I started off as a director and working as assistant to Davie Wilson, the old Rangers player. I liked Davie and I admired the enthusiasm he had for the job, but he struggled to make any headway, as anyone would. I had a season as manager myself after he left and managed to bring in some good young players. But it was never the same.
>
> The quality of the older players just wasn't there and the club had no money to bring in anyone else. Whenever we did produce anyone half-decent, they were sold. The players who were there gave me everything but you can't make a silk purse out of a sow's lug. Jock had warned me about that. He said I'd be mad to go; that I should wait for something better to come along. But it was a job and, as I told Jock: 'I need to have a wage coming in from somewhere.' And Dumbarton paid me more than Celtic, which tells you a bit about Celtic. But it wasn't great. I would be lying if I said to you that I really enjoyed my time there.

Fallon had, of course, already turned down more attractive offers, having been assured by White of his "job for life". And though none caused him sleepless nights, the most intriguing – and tempting – would have involved him managing a team he had once represented.

> Fran Fields was a great friend of mine and when he became FAI president, he spoke to me to see if I would be interested in taking over the national team. This would have been 1975 or thereabouts. It was a great offer, and I was very appreciative, but I felt I had to turn it down. I was tempted though, because it would have been a great honour to manage my country, just as it had been to play for them. But even though things weren't going well at Celtic at that time, I couldn't bring myself to leave.

The consequence of Fallon's decision was that, instead of World Cup qualifiers at Dalymount Park, he was left facing second-tier matches at the notoriously ramshackle Boghead. Joe Coyle, one of three brothers who played under the Irishman at Dumbarton, recalled that even the club's players were amazed when he accepted the post. He said: "I had known Sean from Celtic – he'd signed me there as a provisional in 1975 – and if you'd said to me then that he would end up at Dumbarton, I'd have told you where to go. I was delighted that the club were ambitious enough to go after him but I knew right from the start that Dumbarton wasn't fitting for a man like Sean Fallon. He should have been somewhere better and it must have been a massive come-down for him after Celtic. I must say, though, his attitude to the job was magnificent. I loved the guy. He was just a special man, and it was an absolute honour to work with him."

Fallon's career at Dumbarton proved to be wholly unspectacular, devoid both of stunning achievements and crushing disappointments. Yet Coyle is not the only former Sons player to speak of the Irishman in such effusive terms. His brother, Owen, who went on to enjoy top-flight success and international recognition, also retains the deepest admiration for the man who signed him as a short and skinny 12-year-old.

"I was playing with Glasgow schools at the time and I remember Sean would always be at those games," said the former Bolton Wanderers manager. "And what a tremendous reflection on his attitude and love of the game that was; that a man of his stature, having achieved all he had, was still willing to put in the hours watching schools matches on local parks. But it was no doubt that attitude that made Sean such a massive success in football. I had been fortunate enough at that time to be offered an S-form by Dundee United, but Sean still managed to convince everyone in my family, myself included, that Dumbarton would be the best place for me. He came to my house and, by the time he left, no-one was in any doubt that Dumbarton was where I was going. And I have to thank him for that because it was the best thing that ever happened to me."

Coyle would get his move to Tannadice eventually, but by that time he had earned an invaluable grounding under a man who stuck by him when others might not. As he explained: "I was 5ft 4in until I was 17 and very skinny, so if I had been at Dundee United, I'm sure they would have looked and thought I didn't have the physique to make it. But Sean was very wise in that respect and knew that physical development can come a bit later in some players if you're patient and trust they at least have the ability. And sure enough, he was proved right. I never got much bulkier but I took a stretch and that gave me the chance to push on. That was one of the reasons why I'd gone to Dumbarton in the first place: you knew you were going to be looked after by Sean. It wasn't a case of giving my family the chat to get me signed and then that's his job done. He always kept an eye on me and, more than that, he would always make a point of passing on little nuggets of wisdom that have stayed with me right through my career."

Nor was Coyle the only future international striker who thrived under Fallon's tutelage at Dumbarton. Everton legend Graeme Sharp, who would go on to win two English titles and 12 caps for Scotland, was another player spotted by the Irishman on Glasgow's public parks. And, like Coyle, he was convinced to turn his back on considerably more illustrious suitors. "I was playing for a team called Eastercraigs back then and there were a lot of teams watching me, including Celtic and Rangers," said Sharp. "But Sean managed to sell Dumbarton to my dad as the best place for me to be. My dad wasn't a big football man but he had so much time and respect for Sean as a person, and that was what swung it."

Fallon had, by this stage, taken on a directorial role at Boghead, and the deal to bring in Sharp brought him into conflict with the club's manager. "Sean had offered me £25-a-week and the gaffer at the club, Davie Wilson, was going mad," the striker recalled. "He wasn't happy that a fair chunk of his budget had gone on signing this young lad. But without saying anything too much about myself, Sean obviously knew a player. Dumbarton sold me to Everton a couple of years later for £125,000, so £25-a-week proved to be pretty good business. Sean was actually with me when we did the deal at Goodison and I always remember him saying: 'This is what you've always wanted. It's up to you now.'" The pair parted with a handshake – "with Sean, that nearly broke your fingers," Sharp recalled with a laugh – and the striker rose to the challenge. In the history of Everton, only one player – Fallon's old Sligo Rovers idol, Dixie Dean – has scored more.

Spotting and securing players such as Sharp and Owen Coyle proved that, if nothing else, Fallon's instincts were as sharp as ever. Yet his time at Dumbarton is remembered not for these inspired signings, but for a transfer that failed to materialise. On December 9, 1980, the day the world awoke to the news that John Lennon had been shot dead outside his New York apartment, the reports on the Scottish back pages were every bit as shocking. Morning coffees across the country would have been spat out at the mere headline: 'Sons in for Cruyff.'

It is a story that Gerry McNee remembers only too well. "I was with the *Express* at the time and I got a call in the evening, very close to the first edition deadline, from a contact I trusted. 'Dumbarton are trying to sign Cruyff', he told me. But when I got in touch with the *Express* to tell them to hold the back page, I had a hell of a job trying to convince them that it wasn't an April fool. I remember phoning Sean during a reserve match at Boghead to confirm the story with him and, typically of Sean, he was up front about it. 'Yes, we've spoken to the boy,' were his famous words. It was a massive story."

Massive, and almost too outlandish to believe. Johan Cruyff, a record three-time Ballon d'Or winner and the graceful, elegant personification of 'total football', had been *the* great player of the 1970s. Dumbarton were a club mired in mid-table mediocrity in Scotland's second tier. Why on earth would this superstar, at 33 and still with life in those legendary legs, consider playing his football at Boghead? Had Fallon, having worked for so long with a master in media manipulation, and remembering the coverage generated by Celtic's pursuit of Alfredo di Stefano, simply employed an old headline-grabbing trick?

> There was a bit of that involved. I knew it was always unlikely we would get Cruyff, but the way I saw it we couldn't lose. At worst, it got Dumbarton on the back pages for a few days and boosted the club's image and profile, which was very low at that time. At best, if we were really lucky, we might get a magnificent player. Cruyff was struggling a bit financially in those days because he'd lost all his money in a bad investment, so we felt offering him a few thousand pounds per game might tempt him. If you don't try, you'll never know. And he did agree to meet us. I went over with the chairman to Amsterdam and found him to be very polite and knowledgeable about the whole Scottish scene. But although I was normally quite good at talking players into signing, that one I couldn't manage. I set things buzzing though, didn't I? And I think I was closer to making it happen than some people think.

Confirmation of just how close arrived, remarkably enough, from Cruyff himself. While visiting Scotland for a pro-am golf tournament in 2012, the former Ajax and Barcelona star – though slightly taken aback by the question – well remembered Dumbarton's unexpected approach. "Was I tempted? Yes, of course," he said. "Playing in England, or Britain, was something I had always wanted to do. But I thought I was too old at that stage to go to Scotland, where you know the weather will be difficult. When you're old your muscles get stiff, and moving to a cold country is asking for problems."

So there we have it. If Dumbarton was only a little less dreich, Fallon would have pulled off the transfer of the century. As it was, Cruyff headed for Washington Diplomats in the star-studded NASL, while the spurned Sons boss – much to the disappointment of his players – resigned just four months later. "I was gutted," said Joe Coyle. "Anyone who was working with Sean Fallon and said they weren't sad when he left – they'd be a liar. But I think he'd realised by that point that Dumbarton had been the wrong club." There was, however, no attempt to find a new one. Fallon was in his managerial prime – not yet 58 – fit, healthy, and with a wealth of well-placed contacts. But he had reached a startling realisation.

I found that I didn't have much appetite for the game anymore. I had never thought I would say that but the enjoyment I used to take from going into training every day, and the excitement before a game on a Saturday, just wasn't there. To be totally honest, I never got it back after leaving Celtic. Maybe I picked the wrong club and would have enjoyed it more somewhere else, but my heart wasn't in it. Once I resigned at Dumbarton, I decided that was me: I was finished with football. That was the time I started going to the games with Jock a lot, and I think he was trying to fire me up again; get me back involved in some way. But I was happy just to call it a day.

It was, in hindsight, an appalling waste of talent. Fallon, still with so much to offer the game, restricted himself to helping Stein and passing on recommendations to Jimmy Dickie of Manchester United, an old friend and former scouting rival. Clyde succeeded in tempting him back in 1986 with the offer of a directorship but, again, he found genuine enthusiasm hard to muster. It was only during his visits to Neilly Mochan at Celtic Park that the old memories and sensations would come flooding back, and the blood would begin pumping.

> Neilly was in charge of the boot room in those days and I'd wait until everyone else at the park had gone home and go in and join him for a chat. There would be pots and pots of tea and we'd talk about the game and remember the great days we'd had together. It was lovely to do that with him, especially after Jock died. We were the ones who'd been there and done it with him, and Neilly was another very good friend to me. A great man and a great Celt.

A place had been found for Mochan after the 1978 cull, and 'Smiler' would remain a much-loved member of the backroom team until shortly before his death in 1994. Yet the scandal of the intervening period was that, for much of it, Fallon felt compelled to steal in unnoticed to visit this old comrade. Not content with breaking their promises and breaking his heart, the old guard of Celtic directors continued to make this magnificent servant feel distinctly unwelcome for years after his dismissal.

Even at the time, it was baffling. Indeed, former players remember wondering not only why the doors were not thrown open for this favourite son, but why a place was not found for him on the club's payroll. As Packie Bonner said: "I have never understood why the club didn't find a position for Sean in the '80s and '90s, when he could have really helped the club during some difficult times. Maybe they were fearful of his stature, but Sean was never the type of personality who would have gone in and told managers to be doing this and doing that. It was a waste of his abilities and a loss to Celtic. You talk about mentors for young managers these days; could you imagine a better mentor than Sean Fallon?"

Even more recently, with Fallon's health intact and his passion undimmed, others wondered why no attempt was made to harness his infectious love of all things Celtic. "Sean would have been the most wonderful ambassador the club ever had," said Danny McGrain. "I could never understand why people in authority didn't utilise that. Think about it: you couldn't have had a better person to be the face of Celtic. Imagine people coming for a tour of Celtic Park and bumping into Sean. They'd leave absolutely in love with Celtic – fans for life – just from having met him. I remember when Fergus McCann came in and revolutionised everything, I thought: 'This is great, but you could really do with a Sean Fallon at the club right now. Just someone to give the place a bit of soul.' Sean was never bitter about it though. He just got on with his life, kept on supporting Celtic and had plenty to keep him busy with that huge clan of his."

A new chapter in Fallon's life had indeed begun, and he embraced it with the same passion and enthusiasm that had shaped his career. Ask him about 1988, and he would remember it not as Celtic's centenary, but as the year in which his first grandchild was born. For the final quarter-century of his life, he was no longer the Iron Man, nor Stein's No.2. Fallon had a new title – 'Papa' – and found it to be his best yet.

Epilogue

"The man up there has been very good to me, son. I really couldn't have asked for any more."

This was one of the last things Sean Fallon ever told me. I realise now that I should have listened. He passed away the following week and, soon after, the process of detailing his remarkable life began in earnest. It was a task that, at first, came accompanied by a cause. For although I knew that Sean had died happy, proud and fulfilled, I simply did not agree that he could not have asked for more.

What about the accolades never received, but so richly deserved? The achievements that others were given credit for? The popular portrayal that invariably sold him short? The people who ask 'Sean who?'

The conviction that he had been undervalued became a fixation. In the process of "putting something down for the grandkids", as Sean had asked me to do, putting a few things right became almost as important. And I found that others shared this desire. "Sean deserves a lot more appreciation," said Danny McGrain. "You'll see people at Celtic Park looking at a picture of the Lisbon Lions and the staff, and saying: 'Who's that guy there?' And you're thinking to yourself: 'That's Sean Fallon. How can you not know?' It's a scandal really that he's not better known, given all he did for the club."

Sean's great friend, Norrie Innes, felt that he had a measure of the Irishman's rightful standing. He said: "I'm proud to say that I played against the Lions and the 7-1 team, and I've seen all the greats who have come and gone since. But Sean to me is the greatest Celt of all time." Innes, unbeknown to Fallon, had written to Celtic a decade before suggesting the club's hall of fame be named after a man who, as he pointed out, signed so many of its members. "He would have been annoyed and embarrassed if he'd known I'd done that, but I felt I had to do it. The fact Sean was never given a testimonial still rankles with me and he's long overdue some proper recognition."

Innes would have found a kindred spirit in Joe Coyle, one of many who expressed the hope that this book "would give Sean his proper place". "I really hope that happens because the status he has is nowhere near what he deserves," Coyle added. "Sean should be a god at Celtic. There should be a statue of him up there, I honestly believe that."

Like me, these men were well meaning; motivated by affection, admiration and a genuine belief that Fallon merited greater recognition. But I see now that we were missing the point. The first clues came during chats with Sean, Myra and their six children, when I realised that no-one in the family shared this fervent desire to see his image redressed. Yet, still, I felt I knew better. Inexcusably, I even found myself becoming frustrated by Sean's humility and the unfailing good grace with which he reflected on snubs, slights and the snatching away of credit. Fallon, I concluded, was his own worst enemy. The reason people did not know half of the players he had signed, or the many great things he achieved, was because he simply had not told them.

"It's the same in most professions," his eldest daughter, Marie Therese, told me at the time. "You'd like to think that just doing your job well will be enough, but people's memories are short. It's easy to become forgotten or undervalued if you are humble. It's the people who shout loudest and who make everyone aware of their achievements who tend to be recognised." 'Exactly,' I thought. 'If only your dad had shouted a little louder.'

I think it was then, realising what I was wishing for, that the penny dropped. In my obsession with gaining him a little more appreciation, I had wished away an aspect of Fallon's character that helped make him worth appreciating. I should, of course, have been celebrating Sean's steadfast refusal to embroil himself in this vacuous, credit-grabbing, self-promoting culture. He was simply a good, kind and honest man who loved what he did, cared about the people he worked with and allowed his deeds to speak for themselves. If those deeds went unnoticed or unappreciated, well, so be it. What he and his family realised a long time before I did was that recognition is not worth chasing.

"Maybe it cost me in the end, staying in the background," Sean admitted in one of our interviews. "But if I had my time again, I wouldn't change the way I did things. I was there for the good of Celtic – not the good of Sean Fallon. The way I saw it, my job was to help the club and to help Jock and the players, and I tried to do that as best I could. If people think I did it well, that's nice to hear. But I've always believed the most successful football clubs are the ones where the people involved care more about the club than they do about themselves. When Celtic were at our most successful, that was definitely the case. I never think: 'Ah, I'm annoyed I didn't get credit for this or for that.' Not at all. I just look back on what the club achieved and feel lucky to have been a part of it." Pressed on one occasion for the highlight of his remarkable career, Sean paused, looked skywards, sorting through the memories of Lisbon, 7-1 and the rest. Then came his firm and unequivocal answer. "Just being a Celt."

When you have realised a dream, as Fallon so often told me he had, kudos and column inches seem trifling in comparison. He was, after all, a man who won the European Cup with the club he had loved since he was a boy. Greedily grasping for more never interested him, and I saw in time that it should not concern me. It was liberating. No longer a man on a mission, I found myself taking even greater enjoyment in Sean's wonderful stories, and in the memories of his family, friends and former colleagues. I realised too, in speaking to them, that I had been wrong all along. By the people who knew him best – those he loved and respected – he was never undervalued.

In declaring his departure from front-line football in 1981 to be a waste, I was also a little hasty. For the game, it was; Fallon had much to offer and decades in which he could have contributed. But Sean, whose glass was always half-full, had seen the opportunities a clean break presented. Time not spent travelling between stadiums and training grounds was time he owed to Myra and his children, the youngest of whom, Sinead, had not yet turned four. What followed, he said, were not squandered years, but golden years. "Do you know, son, it has been great to spend more time with the family," he said. "The kids, the grandkids, are never away from the house and I love that. How do you think I've made it to the age I am? They keep me going. I spent too much of my time away from the house when I was at Celtic, although I always knew I had the best woman in the world bringing up the kids when I wasn't there. But I'm glad I'm not missing out on anything with the family now."

For all Fallon's weighty workload, his children remember a

blissfully happy upbringing. "Dad would always make time for us," said his daughter, Colette. "Every Sunday, he'd take us down to Wishaw swimming baths and, if he needed to work, he'd take us to Celtic Park, run the big baths in the dressing room and let us swim in there. Then he'd let us run up and down the stairs to the press box. We loved all that." At Christmas, Celtic's assistant manager would dress up as Santa for the staff and players' family party, handing out presents amid much hilarity. "You'll notice in the pictures that the children all look confused," said Myra, "wondering why Santa has a broad Irish accent." More recently, Sean could be found back at the public pitches that were once his favourite hunting ground, only this time in the role of supporter, cheering on his football-playing grandchildren.

"Sean was always the same," said Bertie Auld. "He had two great loves in his life: his family and Celtic. If he wasn't talking about one, he'd be telling you about the other." That is the Sean I remember. I will certainly never forget his genuine delight when I told him, over a sandwich and a cup of Myra's tea, that my wife was expecting our first child. "Ah, son, it's the best thing you'll ever do," he said, clapping me on the back. "Some things come and go but family is what's always there, and it's the most important thing of all. You have happy days ahead of you." A few months later, it was me who was doing the congratulating after hearing the news that grandchild number 20 was on the way.

Sadly, just as I never had the chance to introduce my daughter to this great man, who died just ten days before she arrived, so he missed out on meeting his newest grandson. Sean Anthony, born on May 4 – Sean and Myra's wedding anniversary – will nonetheless be brought up hearing fantastic tales about the man in whose honour he was named. He will also, in time, share the pride of his siblings and cousins, and hear of the delight that his late, great Papa took in their successes. "They're all so clever – much more so than I ever was," Sean would marvel. He fretted about them too, wincing as he watched one of his younger granddaughters turning on her rollerblades, and anxiously seeking news of her older cousins working in charity projects abroad. Occasionally, pride and concern would make for a potent emotional cocktail. "I remember meeting Sean at the reception at Celtic Park well into my career, and Marie, his eldest, had just qualified as a doctor," recalled Packie Bonner. "He was proud as punch but he went on to mention that she was going away to Peru to work and how he was so worried about her. By the time he finished talking, the tears were streaming down his face. I remember thinking what a lovely thing that was, especially from this tough old footballer."

Sean, in truth, loved a good cry. He might have been the hardest player in Scottish football at one stage but, away from football, an Iron Man he was not. "He's always been very emotional," said his daughter, Sinead. "'The Quiet Man' was his favourite film and he'd never finish watching it without bawling. And that was just at the fight scene. I would *YouTube* it for him in later years and the tears would be flooding down his face. Never mind that – he used to cry at 'Home and Away' and 'Neighbours'. Even when the children gave him something, a picture or present, the tears would be flowing."

A group of Fallon's older grandchildren told a similar story, remembering a Saturday night spent watching 'X Factor' together, rolling their eyes at the false, formulaic sob stories trotted out to earn votes. It was only when they turned round that they noticed their Papa sobbing uncontrollably in the corner of the room. "But she's had such a hard life," he protested. Fallon would readily laugh at himself in this respect. "The Iron Man? I'm as soft as they come," was his admission.

Yet he was a man who had known and lived with genuine grief, caused by the loss of parents, siblings and dear friends such as Stein, Bertie Peacock and John McAlindon. The deaths of former players also hit him hard. "I thought of those boys like sons," he said, again choked with emotion. But though his most recent get-togethers with the Lisbon Lions took place without Jimmy Johnstone, Bobby Murdoch and Ronnie Simpson, they remained the tightest-knit of football families. And Sean was the favourite uncle. "Any time we got together, as soon as Sean would walk in, everyone would be round him looking for a chat and a cuddle," said Bobby Lennox. "He was loved by that group of players."

There was a demonstration of that fondness just a few months before he died, when the Lions threw a 90th birthday party in his honour at Celtic Park. "I was glad we got the chance to do that," said John Clark, one of the organisers. "As a present, we framed a big photograph of all the players who were there at the time Celtic were so successful. You've the Lions in there, the Quality Street Gang – just an amazing collection of players. And there's Sean, right at the forefront. And that, really, was the message we were trying to put across – that he was at the forefront of things for us."

It was a thoughtful gesture, greatly appreciated, and this party was one of several occasions on which Fallon was thanked and acclaimed before he died. "That was a lovely aspect of the way things worked out," said his daughter, Siobhan. "It's so often the case that lovely things are only said and done after someone passes away. But we were so lucky that, prior to losing dad, we had things like his 90th birthday, raising the flag and, going back further, his 80th celebrations in Sligo."

That 2002 tribute weekend, organised by Sean Cunningham and Paddy Doherty, was remembered by Fallon as one of the great highlights of his latter years. Celtic stars past and present were joined by the then Lord Provost of Glasgow and Sir Alex Ferguson, who delayed flying out for Manchester United's pre-season tour to spend the weekend socialising and celebrating with a dear old friend. "I always remember we were playing golf together at Rosses Point and Sean started to get a bit breathless," Sir Alex recalled. "So we stopped, sat him down on the buggy and said, 'Right, let's go back, Sean'. 'No chance,' he said. 'We're one down!' That was the kind of man you were dealing with. And he made me promise not to tell Myra."

The long-distance love affair between Fallon and Sligo comfortably survived a 63-year exile. His eyes would light up at the mere mention of his hometown, and he never missed an opportunity to impress its attractions on the uninitiated. "A one-man marketing industry for Sligo," was the apt description applied by the town's former mayor, Tommy Cummins, during those 80th birthday celebrations. The final year of his life, as his health began to fail, was the first in which Fallon did not manage a trip to Ireland's Atlantic coast, though he was jubilant at news of Sligo Rovers' first top-flight title in 35 years. The club, like the town, has not forgotten its favourite son, and October 2013 saw the opening of the Sean Fallon Centre, a football hub aimed, in the words of Rovers trustee Tommie Gorman, at "keeping his name alive in the town for decades and centuries to come". It is an honour that would have thrilled the man himself. Few events gave

Fallon greater satisfaction than being made a freeman of Sligo during those 2002 festivities, and the honour was augmented by the opening of a footbridge over the Garavogue named in honour of his father. "I myself have had many honours," Sean said at the time, "but this is the best I've ever received because it's on behalf of my father."

Neil Lennon flew over from Leicester to take his place among the guests that weekend, and he remained fond of a man he considered to be "a kindred spirit". He said: "The first time I met Sean, a few weeks after I arrived as a player, he hit me with his shoulder on the way past and told me: 'You couldn't have been much of a Gaelic player with reactions like that, son.' He always had that bit of fun about him and a great sense of humour. I had great admiration for the man and I loved the fact he always remained so grounded and humble despite achieving so many incredible things. I was absolutely delighted when I heard the club had asked him to unfurl the league flag because it's people like Sean we should be holding up to the current players and saying: 'That's the standard you're aspiring to.'"

'Flag day', as it became known, was special indeed. It had taken him until the age of 90, but having spent close to three decades in the shadow of Stein and his more eye-catching team-mates, Fallon had his moment in the sun. And he relished it, basking in the fans' acclaim with arms spread open in acknowledgement. Yet, almost overwhelmed, he struggled to take it all in. "A few days later, I showed him a video of the fans signing, 'Happy birthday dear Sean'," said Sinead. "He couldn't believe it. He kept asking: 'Was that for me?' He was just bowled over." As Sean said: "More than anything, it was just nice to know I was remembered; that they still thought about me. My deeds for Celtic were a long time ago and it was nice to see that they still matter to the people at the club today. No matter what anyone says, it's always nice to be appreciated."

Yet the greatest thrill belonged not to Fallon himself, but to his grandkids, none of whom was born when he was still involved in football. For some of the younger children in particular, the sight of their Papa being mobbed by well-wishers and autograph-hunters was revelatory. "They had no idea that their Papa was so famous," said Sinead. "I remember [my daughter] Clodagh getting out of the car, seeing people flock towards dad, and saying to me: 'Mum, Papa's like Justin Bieber here!' Then to see him out there on the pitch, saluting the fans, his name being sung – that wasn't the Papa they knew. But they do now, and that's something special that day gave us."

It was a product of an attitude towards Fallon at Celtic Park that, thankfully, has undergone a radical transformation since the days when ingratitude and incivility reigned. The club encountered by the Fallon family before and after Sean's death was, in all respects, a model of generosity, kindness and sincerity. Lennon personified those attributes, inviting Sean's entire clan – "I bit off more than I could chew there," he said, laughing – to squeeze into his cramped office on flag day. Similarly exemplary was Peter Lawwell, who drove out with Lennon to visit Myra after Sean's death and spent the entire day with the family, listening to stories and pledging any practical assistance the club could offer. Fallon would have approved. Indeed, the highest tribute I can think to pay both men is that they conducted themselves in a manner befitting of the man they came to mourn.

It was clear, too, that they acted not simply out of duty, but of genuine appreciation. "As far as I'm concerned," said Lawwell, "Sean embodied all that is good about Celtic: its values; its roots in Ireland; its pride in Scotland; its competitiveness; its sense of fair play; its decency; its leadership... you could go on and on. You look at Sean as a player, a coach and an assistant manager, and he was someone who would always make you feel proud of the club and proud to be a Celtic fan." When Hearts visited Celtic Park the weekend after Fallon's passing, Lennon made him the focal point of his team talk. "I told the boys, 'Look, we have lost a great Celtic man and we should put on a performance that is worthy of him'." An emphatic 4-1 win followed.

The club was also well represented at Fallon's funeral on January 23, with chief executive and manager arriving accompanied by a posse of players, coaching and office staff. Sean had died five days earlier, surrounded by his children and grandchildren, who prayed and sang hymns with Father Hugh O'Donnell as their beloved father and Papa slipped away. The family, like Celtic, did Fallon proud in the days and weeks that followed. The funeral in his former parish of Christ the King was packed to the rafters and memorable for beautiful music and moving tributes from the grandchildren, Sean Jnr, Father Des Keegan and, of course, Sir Alex Ferguson.

Father Keegan even seemed tempted to take up my former crusade, comparing Fallon to St Joseph and St Barnabas. "Both," he explained, "were understated, arguably underrated, but men of great honour." Yet arguably the most poignant moment of all, as it had been at the rosary two nights before, was when 'The Isle of Innisfree' – Sean's favourite song – rang out through the church. "Dad would have loved the whole thing," said Siobhan. "We actually were laughing about it afterwards, saying, 'If anyone would have loved dad's funeral – the music, the lovely things being said – it was dad'. We feel exactly the same about your book; that he would have loved nothing more than reading it himself, remembering all the stories and seeing what people have said about him. I'm so sorry he won't be around to see it. But I know when we all sit down, open the pages and start reading, he'll be looking down on us as we do it."

With Fallon not around to give these pages a once-over, my only hope is that, in "putting something down for the grandkids", I have done justice to their wonderful Papa. All I am sure of is that the final word in this, Sean's story, should belong to him.

"I'm a happy man, son. I've had a great life and talking to you for this book has given me a chance to think back on all the great days I had. I'm losing a few of my memories now – more than I'd like – but I still remember enough to know how lucky I've been. I have a great wife and family that I couldn't be more proud of and, at this old age, people still put up with me and want to hear my stories. I never planned on doing a book but I'm glad I've done it because I'm sure you'll give the grandkids something that will be nice for them to read when I'm not around. They'll hopefully see that I tried to live my life the right way, and that I was happy; that I had a dream and I lived that dream. Not many people can say that, but I've been one of the lucky ones. The man up there has been good to me, son. I really couldn't have asked for any more."

Author's acknowledgements

I will be forever grateful to Sean, Myra and their wonderful family for entrusting me with such a precious and sought-after story. Their kindness, support and friendship throughout the research and writing process ensured that working on this book was not only a great privilege, but an immense pleasure.

A debt of gratitude is also owed to all those who readily gave their time to be interviewed. Not all are quoted directly but their insights were invaluable in building a fuller picture of Sean and an era I had not experienced first-hand. The overwhelming goodwill of the online Celtic community, typified by Chris McGuigan of the Lost Bhoys, spoke for the esteem and affection in which Sean was held. Individual supporters also submitted their own stories, and I was particularly grateful for the contributions made by Jimmy Payne, Gordon Cowan, Arthur Mitchell and John Donnelly.

Sean's great-nephew, Graham Bray, took time to scan and send photographs from Sligo, and my visit to the Iron Man's hometown was made all the more productive and enjoyable by Sean and Trish Cunningham's superb hospitality. While in Ireland, it was a pleasure to meet Oliver Fallon of the Connaught Rangers Association, who provided information and records on John Fallon that were not only useful for the book but of huge interest to Sean himself.

Pat Woods, the outstanding Celtic historian and author, was always ready to provide advice, as were the staff of the Sligo Central Library and Glasgow's invaluable Mitchell Library. Martin O'Boyle, my lead editor at FIFA.com, was accommodating throughout, and friends and former colleagues at Celtic were consistently willing to lend a hand.

I would never have written a book, far less contacted the Fallons about Sean's story, had it not been for BackPage Press approaching me. Martin and Neil's continued faith and patience has been greatly appreciated, as has the guidance and encouragement offered by Hugh MacDonald.

I should conclude with some well-earned words of thanks for my wife, Suzanne. It was she who steered us through a house-move and the birth of our daughter, Chloe, while carrying a passenger preoccupied by all things Sean Fallon. Her understanding, hard work and reassurance were priceless and I'm delighted to report that, though not a football fan, she ended this book having fallen in love with its subject.